# MARY CARRIES ON

## Reflections on Some Favourite Girls' Stories

by

## MARY CADOGAN

Girls Gone By Publishers

Published by

Girls Gone By Publishers
4 Rock Terrace
Coleford
Bath
Somerset
BA3 5NF

First Edition
Published by Girls Gone By Publishers 2008
Text © Mary Cadogan 2008
Design and Layout © Girls Gone By Publishers 2008
Cover illustration © Girls Gone By Publishers 2008

The sources used for verifying titles, dates of publication and authors mentioned in this book
were *The Encyclopaedia of Girls' School Stories* by Sue Sims and Hilary Clare; *Twentieth
Century Children's Writers* second edition, edited by D L Kirkpatrick, and *The Oxford
Companion to Children's Literature* edited by Humphrey Carpenter and Mari Pritchard.

Edited by Tig Thomas

Typeset in England by AJF
Printed in England by Antony Rowe Limited

ISBN 978-1-84745-040-1

# Mrs STRANG'S ANNUAL for GIRLS

Mary S. Reeve.

# SCHOOL FRIEND

## Annual
## 1938

*Mary Carries On* is dedicated to
Clarissa Cridland and
Ann Mackie-Hunter,
with affection and gratitude.

# Contents

# PART FIVE
## MISCELLANEOUS GIRLS' FICTION

# INTRODUCTION

This is my eightieth birthday book! I shall be celebrating that very special anniversary on the day that *Mary Carries On* is launched. Its title therefore seems extremely appropriate because I have been around for a long time, and also because I have now been an avid reader of children's fiction for about seventy-five years, and have written about it for over three decades. (I fervently hope that the carrying-on process will long continue!)

This book provides a post-*You're a Brick, Angela!* overview of the girls' story. I cannot claim that it is a fully comprehensive or an impartial critical assessment. Rather it conveys my personal responses to much of the fiction that has retained its appeal for me over many decades.

It is a great pleasure to have the opportunity of sharing these reflections with Girls Gone By's readers, who will, I hope, enjoy reading this book as much as I have relished the writing of it. I hope, too, that it will evoke happy memories for everyone who delves into it.

I am often asked what led me to become a writer—or a 'literary historian' (a term incidentally that I'd never use for myself, but which has sometimes been foisted upon me). There were several paths to this. First came my interest in how the children's books which appealed to my daughter differed from—or tallied with—those which I had enjoyed when I was young. Then, after serendipitously rediscovering the *Magnet*—the boys' weekly which both my brother and I had devoured in childhood—I made contact with an organisation that has a daunting name but a membership of delightful people: the Old Boys' Book Club. Their main interest was, and is, boys' books and papers; but after attending just two meetings, I was asked to speak about some girls' books of the 1920s and 30s. I did so, largely from memory (stupidly having long ago given away all my childhood books), and one visit to the British Library to refresh my recollections of the Cliff House and Morcove School weekly papers.

All this, and increasing contact with other book enthusiasts, nudged me when in my forties to begin writing. However, I can now see that, for me, the main stimulus for writing and talking about children's stories and popular culture was the sheer love of reading. This has been with me all my life—or at least for as long as I can remember.

I can't recall ever *learning* to read—although 'Pat sat on a log/He had a dog' from early elementary-school days stands out as the text which first opened the door for me to the magical worlds of literature! However, growing up in a home where books were few, I used to seize on everything readable, even the labels on jam and paste jars; and my understanding parents, intrigued by this, soon began to make sure that plenty of reading matter was available to me.

At first this was the *Rainbow*, a weekly comic paper which featured the exuberant antics of the animal characters Tiger Tim and Co. I adored it, reading every word and relishing the cosy, colourful pictures. Without knowing it, I was in excellent company, because the publishers had received, and hung proudly in their offices, a letter of appreciation of the *Rainbow* from the two 'little princesses'—Elizabeth and Margaret Rose—who were virtually contemporaneous with me. I soon moved on, through the public library services, to fairy-tales, then to so much else—including, of course, schoolgirls' stories.

Reading has always been a joy; so too has been writing, talking and broadcasting. It has all happened because, like so many other people, I just love books. *Mary Carries On* is my tribute to the many writers who have enriched my childhood and subsequent years. It is not an academic treatise but—I hope—a sharing of pleasures with Girls Gone By's readers.

I must express my warm thanks to Clarissa Cridland and Ann Mackie-Hunter, not only for giving me the chance to produce *Mary Carries On* but for all the wonderful books which Girls Gone By have made available to enthusiasts. I must also thank my editor, Tig Thomas, for many helpful suggestions about the contents and organisation of the book, and for several delightful chats about our shared interest in girls' stories. My thanks are also due to Adrianne Fitzpatrick for designing the book, and to Ruth Jolly for proofreading it.

So please, now read on—and enjoy!

Mary Cadogan
2008

# PART ONE

# VICTORIAN AND EDWARDIAN FICTION

# LITTLE WOMEN AND WOMEN'S LIB!

It is an intriguing fact that, despite the influence of Charlotte M Yonge and other 'home-grown' Victorian authors of domestic tales, the greatest stimulus for truly readable—indeed, addictive—early British girls' fiction came from two writers on the other side of the Atlantic: Louisa May Alcott and Sarah Chauncey Woolsey, who wrote as Susan Coolidge.

At first sight it seems strange that their stories, redolent in many ways of the slightly rustic America of patchwork quilts and pumpkin pie, should have such an effect on fiction designed for girls living in increasingly urbanised nineteenth- and twentieth-century Britain. The vitally influential factors, of course, were the zest and directness of their writing and characterisations plus their perceptiveness in portraying female friendships and relationships between sisters.

Also, in the expansive atmosphere of Louisa Alcott's and Susan Coolidge's stories, some of the main teenage protagonists, in their explorations of educational opportunities and the possibilities of careers outside domestic confines, can be seen as epitomising the desire of many real-life girls for participation in intellectual life. There are plenty of feminist touches which are embryonic precursors of the later women's liberation movement.

Louisa Alcott's *Little Women* (1868) quickly sold a million copies in America and was soon almost as popular in Britain. Susan Coolidge's *What Katy Did* (1872) also rapidly achieved success in both countries, apparently selling even better in Britain than in America. *Little Women* preceded *What Katy Did* by four years, and it is possible that Susan was influenced by Louisa's book in her writing.

Louisa May Alcott

However, there is no doubt that each of these authors was very much 'her own woman'.

Born within three years of each other in the 1830s, both authors as young women were to have challenging experiences of work outside the home, particularly when they were involved in the nursing services during the American Civil War. Louisa, whose transcendentalist philosopher father, Bronson Alcott, offered his wife and four daughters spiritual succour but few material advantages, realised early in life that she would have to become the main breadwinner for her family. She began writing for publication in her teens, and also worked outside the home by turns as a needlewoman, domestic help and teacher. (Some of her efforts to find satisfying employment are reflected in *Work*, her colourful 1872 account of Christie Devon's adventures as servant, actress, governess, companion and seamstress. Also, her nursing experiences are the well-spring of her 1863 *Hospital Sketches*. Both these books were originally intended for adult readers although the success of her March family sagas has brought them into the domain of girls' fiction.)

Both Louisa and Susan appreciated the importance of education for girls. Louisa, educated at home by her father, also received instruction and inspiration from Bronson's illustrious friends and neighbours in Concord, Massachusetts: the naturalist Henry David Thoreau, and the philosopher Ralph Waldo Emerson. Susan was educated at private schools, and her time at Mrs Hubbard's 'select boarding-school' in Hanover, New Hampshire, apparently provided some of the iconoclastic insights which eventually irradiated her most seminal book, *What Katy Did at School* (1873).

Louisa and Susan tackled fairly wide-ranging literary subjects; however, for each of them, abiding success was in what we now consider to be the girls' story genre. Neither author married, nor did either of them have children. Their insights into young people's lives were enriched by their involvement in real-life families. Louisa as one of four sisters had instant role-models for Meg, Jo, Beth and Amy March, and also for their mother, 'Marmee', and the somewhat shadowy father figure of Mr March. Susan also drew on memories of her childhood experiences in her 'Katy' books.

Let us look in detail first at Louisa's achievements, then at Susan's. There is no doubt that Louisa benefited a great deal from the Alcott family's friendship with Emerson and Thoreau. Emerson, the philosopher, essayist and poet of self-reliance and transcendentalism, was, like Bronson, quick to recognise Louisa's budding love of literature, and helped to infuse her with an appreciation of the works of Shakespeare, Dickens and Goethe. Her closeness to Emerson is illustrated by the fact that her early book *Flower Fables* (1854) consists of stories which she originally made up to tell to his daughter, Ellen. Her relationship with Thoreau, whose 'back-to-nature' books had become celebrated, fired her love of the outdoors, which found greater expression in her short stories, particularly, for example, *Will's Wonder Book* (1870), than in her domestic novels. In fact, her very first published work was inspired by her feelings for the natural scene. In 1851, when she was eighteen and writing as Flora Fairfield, her poem *Sunlight* was published in *Petersen's Magazine*. Her *Morning-Glories, and Other Stories* (1867) was an engaging selection of her nature tales. Louisa never forgot her childhood experiences of boating, gathering berries and making wild-life discoveries with Thoreau who, apparently, added magical touches to nature-lore (pointing out, for instance, that a cobweb was a handkerchief dropped by a fairy!).

It is interesting that Louisa, when first asked in 1867 to edit *Merry's Museum*, a magazine for the young, and to write a girls' story for it, protested that she would 'try', although she 'never liked girls or knew many' except her sisters! Her main literary interests at that time seem to have been her nature fairy-tales or fables and her sharply contrasting, pseudonymously written, bloody and thunderous gothic stories. Later, when she had acquired celebrity and been dubbed 'The Children's Friend', she remonstrated that she was tired of producing 'pap for the young'.

In spite of these somewhat daunting comments about her work, what seems to come

'Marmee' and the March sisters

across overwhelmingly in the warmly emotional *Little Women* saga and her other domestic stories is sincerity. Louisa brilliantly conveys so many aspects of family life, and especially the affection and antagonisms between sisters. Like other authors of tremendous talent, when writing about a very specific (and well known to her) social milieu, she managed to achieve a timeless appeal. This is because—to echo what Mr March says in *Good Wives* about one of Jo's stories—'There is truth in it …'

Louisa's real-life sisters, Anna, Lizzie and May, were the stimulus for Meg, Beth and Amy, and the author said categorically that *she* was Jo. Her mother provided the direct inspiration for the understanding but sharply discerning mother figure, while Bronson Alcott inspired Mr March.

With Jo's parents we appear to see two markedly different influences. Marmee embodies all the maternal values while managing also to impress upon her daughters the importance of independence in intellectual and practical matters. There is a feminist streak in her. Mr March, however, represents the wise but authoritative Victorian father stereotype, somewhat softened by liberal and unorthodox views, but still the controller.

For example, Marmee wants to see all her daughters safely and happily married, but nevertheless gives them the advice 'better be happy old maids than unhappy wives'. Jo, of course, (like Louisa in real life), particularly appreciates this admonition. As she says when she rejects Laurie, her childhood friend and first suitor: 'I don't believe I shall ever marry. I'm happy as I am, and love my liberty too well to be in a hurry to give it up for any mortal man.'

In contrast to the ever-present and concerned Marmee, Mr March on the surface plays only a small part in the books. However, he exerts influence on his womenfolk from behind the scenes with powerful effect. From the very first page of *Little Women* he looms off-stage but large. He is away, serving in the Civil War, but a letter from him, read aloud by Marmee, is not only overflowing with affection but with instructions to his daughters. It is, in fact, Mr March who in this letter gives the book its name, as he expresses the hope that when he comes back to his girls he will 'be fonder and prouder than ever' of his 'little women'. (And, of course, to become a 'little woman' is a very special challenge to tomboy Jo.)

In actuality, Bronson's wife and daughters had been involuntary subjects for the application of his liberal, but sometimes strange, educational and domestic theories. Because these stressed the values of plain living, temperance, simple clothing and cold baths, Louisa's childhood could be seen as rather austere. It was associated with a diet mainly consisting of apples, potatoes and unleavened bread, and with constant poverty, which resulted in the family having frequently to be uprooted by moving in search of affordable accommodation. However, in spite of what modern readers might see as Bronson Alcott's paternal inadequacies, Louisa's enormous respect for him was maintained throughout her life (father and daughter died within a day or two of each other in 1888), and she adopted his pro-suffrage and anti-slavery ideals. She unfailingly invests Mr March, in the fictional father-role, with nobility: 'I think it was so splendid in Father to go as a chaplain when he was too old to be drafted and not strong enough for a soldier.' (In real life, of course, it was Louisa and not Bronson who served near the front line. In his words, he 'had sent his only son to war'.)

It is possible that Louisa's great regard for Bronson helped to bring about a significant flaw in the second of the March family books, *Good Wives* (1869). Countless readers have never forgiven her for separating the enchanters, Jo and Laurie, and allowing her lively, endearing heroine eventually to settle for the middle-aged, prosaic, untidy and ungainly Professor Bhaer. This character's exasperating unworldliness seems to have been inspired by Bronson, and his learning by Emerson. Touches of Goethe's influence are thrown in to provide his 'poetic' German-ness! Despite the narrative view that Jo's and Laurie's strong wills and quick tempers would make a match between them inadvisable, Friedrich Bhaer, or 'Fritz' as Jo often calls him, with his ghastly fractured English and fussy manner, seems a poor substitute for Laurie as husband material.

He does, however, provide Jo with two sons. Fritz and Jo together, in *Little Men* (1871), create a residential school for orphaned and underprivileged boys, and some affluent parents' problem offspring. Here are practised Bronson's educational theories that self-knowledge and self-control are more important than academic learning. In this book and in *Jo's Boys* (1886), Louisa often opens out her canvas from home into a celebration of the New England countryside, as the boys have adventures in places reminiscent of the Walden woods, which the young Louisa had explored with Thoreau.

However, Jo's transition from teenage tomboy to great earth-mother is disappointing. Throughout *Little Men* and *Jo's Boys*, we find only pale reflections of the earlier fiery, whole-hearted and passionate Jo who is contemptuous of any kind of affectation. In *Little Women* she is shown as the archetypal—and surely the most loved—tomboy of girls' fiction.

She goes well beyond the naughty, mischievous, 'little pickle' type of character that sometimes adorned Victorian children's stories.

From *Little Women*

With Jo, Louisa established the tomboy pattern from which dozens of exuberant and challenging characters, created by a variety of British and American authors, were to follow.

We remember Jo in so many colourful vignettes: 'scribbling' in her attic retreat, reading till her eyes give out, or selling her abundant chestnut hair to provide money for Marmee's visit to her husband when he is in hospital after being wounded in the Civil War. In *Little Women* and *Good Wives*, Jo rails against acceptance of the classic Victorian passive female role. She is essentially always a 'do-er', but, despite her dominant tomboy personality, she still is shown convincingly to embody many feminine hopes and aspirations. At times the contrasts in her nature cause conflict and we see her feminism fighting with conventional values.

The tender side of Jo is expressed most compellingly in her relationship with her younger sister Beth, who, kind, gentle and physically delicate, is in many ways Jo's complete opposite.

When we read *Little Women* we sympathise with Jo's eldest sister, Meg, who, elegant and beautiful but starved of luxuries, is sometimes preoccupied with fripperies, and we are amused by the spirited vanities of spoiled Amy, the youngest and most artistic member of the family.

It is Jo and Beth, however, who command our deep affection. Like Louisa's real-life sister Lizzie, who inspired her creation, Beth dies young. Early deaths, of course, were regular ingredients of Victorian fiction, but none is more moving than Beth's. Oscar Wilde, irreverently commenting on Charles Dickens's most celebrated deathbed scene, said, 'No man of feeling can read the death of Little Nell without laughing.' I would adapt this to say, 'No woman of feeling can read the passing of Beth without crying.' Thousands of readers over several generations have wept and suffered with uncomplaining Beth as '… on the bosom where she had drawn her first breath, she quietly drew her last, with no farewell but one loving look, one little sigh'. (I've read *Good Wives* frequently and the tears come every time, both in the run-up to the death, when the love between Jo and Beth has its most perfect flowering, and in the actual deathbed scene. And whenever I give a talk on Louisa Alcott there is always an awful moment when I sense that the blubbing is coming on!)

Having established Jo and Beth as completely contrasting characters, Louisa deftly manages, as the story develops, to show not only how they bring out the best in each other, but how, at the end of Beth's short but lambent life, there is almost a merging of the two sisters. Jo, although grieving deeply, feels that Beth will always be a vital part of her life—in fact, virtually a part of herself. Is there any stronger female relationship in fiction than this?

The success of the four March family books inspired several further novels in the cosily domestic vein. The most memorable of these is *An Old-Fashioned Girl* (1870), in which Polly, the likeable and unpretentious heroine, draws attention to the absurdities of the fashionable follies of the Shaw home, and lets in the sunshine of commonsense. Louisa's crusade for liberal education and healthy, simple living continues in *Eight Cousins; or The Aunt-Hill* (1875) and its sequel *Rose in Bloom* (1876); also in *Under the Lilacs* (1877). *Jack and Jill* (1880) is in similar mood but features an entire village rather than a single family, and provides a colourful, atmospheric picture of New England life in Louisa's time, spotlighting skating excursions, school festivals, the local fairground and annual apple-picking events.

Like Louisa, Susan Coolidge reflected aspects of her own childhood in her stories. Born in Cleveland, Ohio, in 1835, she and her siblings lived near orchards, fields and woodlands which provided ideal settings for their explorations and imaginative games. Memories of these produced the Carr family's home background in *What Katy Did*, especially the 'Paradise' in which the six children played and lazed and spent idyllic hours. There are many similarities between Louisa's March family novels and the 'Katy' books. Both sagas overflow with warmth, and are perceptive about female friendships, sisterly relationships and the ups and downs of family life. In the 'Katy' series, however, we get a sense of the nineteenth-century domestic interiors opening out into the American countryside. This is because Susan provides us with many compelling descriptions of the natural scene as the Carr sisters' adventures in childhood and young adult life unfold.

Susan's literary career began after her family moved to New Haven, Connecticut, in 1855, and she met the author Helen Hunt, who encouraged her to write. They formed a close friendship, which lasted until Helen died in 1885, and in 1862 they volunteered together for hospital service during the Civil War. Helen's two marriages involved moves to Rhode Island and later to Colorado, and Susan maintained the close connection between them by taking up residence in Rhode Island, and then by visiting Helen in Colorado.

She instantly succumbed to the fascination of its rugged terrain of mountains, canyons, gorges and waterfalls, which she used as the main setting for the last two books about the Carr family, *Clover* (1888) and *In the High Valley* (1890). Susan's extensive travels, on her own or in Helen's company, when, daringly for the period, they sometimes camped out, showed something of the American covered-wagons-to-the-west pioneer spirit. We see reflections of this too in the character of Katy's younger sister, Clover, who becomes the heroine of the last two stories when Katy, the original star of the series, fades into marriage and domesticity in the third book, *What Katy Did Next* (1886).

But it was the first two 'Katy' novels which instantly captured the imaginations of readers, and made the title *What Katy Did* virtually part of the language. It is, in fact, more deeply embedded in the Victorian 'tales of hearth and home' than its sequel *What Katy Did at School* (1873), which, startlingly fresh and gently anarchic, can be seen as the first modern school story for girls, exerting its influence particularly in Britain.

In the first story Katy is a tall, rangy, self-willed twelve-year-old living with her widowed doctor father, three sisters and two brothers. 'Katy tore her dress every day, hated sewing and didn't care a button about being called good.' Her hoydenish nature has to be punished when, as the result of disobedience, she has an accident which prevents her from walking for several years. She is certainly made to suffer: confined to the house, and mainly to her own room, her life seems bleak and pointless until her saintly—and also severely disabled—Cousin Helen comes to visit, console and rally her. Subsequently, Katy, gaining psychological strength, becomes (rather like Louisa Alcott's Beth) the typical Victorian 'angel by the hearth' who, though physically confined, is the heart of the home. She is reminded by her father of her mother's dying wish that 'Katy must be a mamma to the little ones'.

From her wheelchair Katy begins to guide and generally look after her younger siblings. She also becomes the family housekeeper, holding 'the threads of the home firmly in her hands'. After four long years of disablement, she eventually

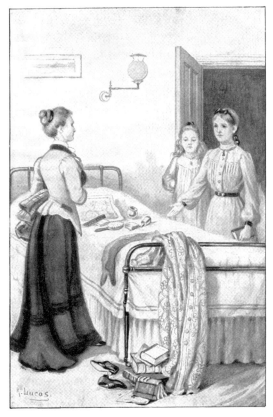

Katy and Clover in trouble with Miss Jane in *What Katy Did at School*

manages to stand up, then to walk and recover fully. There is a lot of talk about 'The School of Pain', and when Katy is well again she feels that there has been 'Love in the Pain'. Fortunately, it is only in the first book of the series that Susan Coolidge seems tied by Victorian ideas of punishment and retribution. *What Katy Did at School*, published only a year later, has a welcome exuberance and light-heartedness of style. In terms of the author's influence on nineteenth- and twentieth-century girls' fiction, it is by far her most important work.

Katy and Clover, then aged sixteen and fourteen respectively, go away to Hillsover boarding-school where one of their fellow pupils, Rosamond Redding ('Rose Red'), is the lively daughter of a senator. Many of their schoolmates are vacuous snobs, and Katy, Clover and Rose Red soon set about creating a more healthy atmosphere. Katy and Clover are unjustly punished by one of the teachers, the waspish Miss Jane, who is soured by her long and unfulfilling engagement to a missionary. Even when the incident is forgotten by most of the girls, Rose Red is determined to: 'Pay Miss Jane off.' It would be impossible to envisage a girl in one of Charlotte M Yonge's books of the same period being allowed to debunk a pompous adult in a position of authority, but Rose Red gets away with it. She sends Miss Jane a strange valentine, hardly in the best of taste. This purports to have come from a cannibal who has just eaten Mr Hardhack, Miss Jane's missionary fiancé, and who includes a testimonial that 'he turned out quite tender'. Rose Red's retributory enterprise typifies her independent, anarchic attitude.

She is not a tomboy but a 'madcap' who, engaging and always loyal to her friends, is constantly questioning authority, particularly when this is exercised by officious or hypocritical teachers. She is the inspiration for a long line of successors. This stretches from Mrs de Horne Vaizey's eponymous heroine in *Pixie O'Shaughnessy* (1902), through Angela Brazil's Gypsy Latimer in *The Leader of the Lower School* (1914). It continues, in the 1920s and 30s, through many other lively hardback characters, and also with Polly Linton in weekly-paper stories, to Enid Blyton's 1940 heroine, Elizabeth, in *The Naughtiest Girl in the School*.

*What Katy Did at School* contains the seeds of what were to become many other staple ingredients of schoolgirl fiction. Katy and her chums start what is probably the first ever schoolgirl secret society—The Society for the Suppression of Unladylike Conduct. The purpose of this is to deal iconoclastically with certain fashionable modes of behaviour, and particularly to discourage the silly flirting in which several of their schoolmates try to engage with the boys of the neighbouring college.

Other essential elements of schoolgirl fiction found in this book are: Katy and Clover having to learn when to go with the crowd and when to stand alone; how to respond to school traditions; and how to share a close friend's affection with others. For example, Katy has to overcome twinges of jealousy when it becomes obvious that Rose Red is especially fond of Clover, the 'little' sister whom Katy has until then regarded rather as her own property!

As in all good school stories, life at Hillsover can be seen as the world in microcosm, with Katy, Clover and Rose Red having always to be active in their own interests without parental protection. As well as enjoying the fulfilments of community life such as comradeship and shared endeavours, they have to learn to cope with situations of discomfort and occasional injustices. Another appealing and influential aspect of *What Katy Did at School* is Susan Coolidge's use of naturalistic and sparkling dialogue. There is a sense of spontaneity in the conversations which is a precursor of Angela Brazil's colourful and slang-interspersed schoolgirlish chat. There are jokes and schemes, too, and perhaps the only popular ingredients of girls' school stories to be missing are sports and games.

Of course, their schooldays bring about an even closer relationship between Katy and Clover than before, creating a strong bond that will never be broken even though their adult paths have to separate. Then it is Clover who becomes the more forceful and pioneering character.

It is curious that we can now look back over one and a half centuries and see that the quintessential elements of truly popular British girls' fiction had their roots in the American books of Louisa May Alcott and Susan Coolidge. As readable in the twenty-first century as they were in the nineteenth, the Jo March and Katy Carr stories have attained a timeless universality which was almost certainly undreamed of by their authors when they first wrote these classic tales of friendship and feminism.

'I'm going to be real good this term'

# ANNE SHIRLEY CENTENARY

It seems that 1908 was a landmark year for children's fiction. The feeling of expansiveness associated with the still fairly new twentieth century might well have influenced this, and it was surely no coincidence that Kenneth Grahame's *The Wind in the Willows* (for young children of both sexes), Frank Richards's *The Making of Harry Wharton*, his first story of Greyfriars School in the new weekly *Magnet* (intended for boy readers), and Lucy Maud Montgomery's *Anne of Green Gables* (for girls) were all published in 1908.

There had, of course, been many earlier popular tales for children on both sides of the Atlantic, but these three stories, very much empathising with the child, seemed to let the sunshine into the genre and open it up to the modern world.

*Anne of Green Gables* is truly a classic—timeless in the truth of its characters and concepts, and in the vitality of its writing. Like other classic heroines, Anne has not only been read about by many generations and by people from widely varied backgrounds but has been successfully transposed into film, stage and television presentations. It is, however, to the six books featuring her that we constantly return.

In these, Anne Shirley progresses from being a scrawny, wistful, wildly imaginative orphan to an outgoing and enquiring college student, a confident teacher and a happy and fulfilled wife and mother. There are gems in all the books; and it is interesting that L M Montgomery seems to have regarded them, after the first story, very much as books for adults as well as children. She said, in a letter to Lady Mary Wilson quoted in the foreword to the 1977 reprint of *Emily of New Moon*:

Anne Shirley

I am very glad my stories have given you pleasure. And I would be glad if you could recommend them to your friends when occasion offers, because so many people seem to be under the impression that my books are only for children!

When we come across *Anne of Green Gables* in childhood, we see events unfolding mainly through Anne's wide-open and wondering eyes. Re-reading it as adults, it is intriguing to see how often we are invited to respond to, and identify with, the grown-up characters' viewpoints of various situations and challenges. It is, for example, a delight to see how the quiet, inhibited Matthew Cuthbert warms instantly to Anne, the imaginative chattering child, and how the down-to-earth, cautious and sometimes caustic Marilla, through her initially reluctant relationship with Anne, finds amazing new depths of compassion and understanding in herself. It is easy to identify so much with Marilla that we could wish the author had focused on her more frequently as the series progressed.

The orphaned child had been a rather gloomy stereotype of Victorian fiction and a telling reflection of the high mortality rate in real-life society then. Life expectancy was considerably lower than now and, if fiction is any measure of fact, apparently a lot of youngish parents were struck down in their prime, leaving, of course, many sadly deprived orphaned offspring. L M Montgomery wrote other popular series with the background of Canada's Prince Edward Island, and interestingly she also chose to make Emily Starr, the heroine of three books, an orphan. (Actually, at the beginning of *Emily of New Moon*, her mother is dead but she still has her father. However, he dies early in the third chapter.) The three 'Emily' books—*Emily of New Moon*, *Emily Climbs* and *Emily's Quest*—were published respectively in 1923, 1925 and 1927, long after the first 'Anne' book appeared.

Emily, although about the same age as Anne, seems older and more mature in outlook. Perhaps this is because, although she is an orphan, her home background has been more stable than Anne's. The novels featuring her draw on Lucy Maud's own childhood memories more extensively than the 'Anne' stories: Emily becomes a writer and has mystical 'flashes' and moments of second sight which, apparently, her creator also experienced.

Like Anne, Emily has high-flown flights of fantasy which spring from a passion for natural beauty. LMM handles this theme compellingly, so that we really believe that Emily *can* slip away from mundane situations into 'eternity', and say with conviction, 'I washed my soul free from dust in the aerial bath of a spring twilight.' Perhaps her 'flashes' are believable because into most of our lives there come occasional hints of the numinous, particularly in response to the natural scene, even if these are fewer and less extravagantly expressed than Emily's. We are made aware of her mystical moments in the very first chapter of *Emily of New Moon*:

> It had always seemed …, ever since she could remember, that she was very, very near to a world of wonderful beauty. Between it and herself hung only a thin curtain; she could never draw the curtain aside—but sometimes, just for a moment, a wind fluttered it, and then it was as if she caught a glimpse of the enchanting realm beyond—only a glimpse—and heard a note of unearthly music.
>
> This moment came rarely—went swiftly, leaving her breathless with the inexpressible delight of it. She could never recall it—never summon it—never pretend it; but the wonder of it stayed with her for days. It never came twice with the same thing. To-night the dark boughs against that far-off sky had given it …

L M Montgomery

The 'Emily' series carries its heroine from childhood, through adolescence to adulthood. She is on the threshold of marriage at the end of *Emily's Quest* and will, we feel sure, not allow domesticity to dim her mystical flashes or her rapturous appreciation of the sun-steeped ferns in her Land of Uprightness. Similarly, Anne Shirley's saga makes clear that she will never allow the demands of her many offspring and busy doctor husband to eclipse her joy in the Lake of Shining Waters or the White Way of Delight.

In her 'Anne', 'Emily' and other books Lucy Maud handles the tricky transition from nature waif to wife and mother with great skill even though her pattern of young, developing love is predictable. After the heroine's original renunciation of romance ('I will not love—to love is to be a slave'), it creeps up from behind—and all around—like a game of Grandma's Footsteps. It then explodes in a burst of ecstasy and is consummated in happily married fecundity.

The author's other youthful heroines are Pat Gardiner in *Pat of Silver Bush* (1933) and *Mistress Pat* (1935), and Jane Stuart in *Jane of Lantern Hill* (1937). The books featuring them are, like all of L M Montgomery's, extremely readable, but Pat and Jane lack the spirit of Anne or the contemplativeness of Emily.

LMM is as adept in tackling the theme of late-flowering love as she is in writing of young romance. Her own experience might have influenced her in this: she did not marry until she was thirty-six, having devoted many years to caring for an elderly relative, and the rival claims of love and duty are frequently featured in her books. Her collections of short stories for adults, *Chronicles of Avonlea* (1912), *Further Chronicles of Avonlea* (1920), *The Road to Yesterday* (1974), and *The Doctor's Sweetheart* (1979) are sometimes tenuously linked to the *Green Gables* characters. These books are full of romantic misunderstandings and estrangements, jiltings and nostalgic longings for what might have been. There are also reconciliations, usually fairly late in the heroes' and heroines' lives, so that these resurrected romances seem pretty short on physical passion. Her adult stories also include touches of irony and realism, with descriptions of fine but fading ladies who hold out against the attentions of male admirers for one, or even two, decades, until they find their own 'air of distinction getting a little shopworn'.

The processes of courtship and consummation in LMM's tales are, as she says of the Canadian spring, 'long and ficklc and reluctant'. Romance for her older characters seems cosily domestic while for her younger heroines it is likely to be rapturous and spiritual. Because they generally inhabit a well-ordered world of new-pin neatness, where (to use one of LMM's own expressions) it must be a heinous sin to allow fluff rolls to build up on one's linoleum, bodily sex—a disorderly experience—cannot be allowed to disrupt the housewifely tidiness of the stories. Passion is sometimes folksy, sometimes fey, but rarely physical.

All this, of course, is in the tradition of Edwardian writing for girls and young women, but LMM brings much more to it. She is enormously perceptive about the conflicts and challenges of childhood and adolescence. Anne's and Emily's actions are governed not only by their emotional intensity and imaginative fancies but by their need to establish an independent identity. They have to learn to function in the—by turns—caring, unjust, confusing and gritty world established by the adults around them. Anne in particular embodies the vulnerability and power of childhood innocence and spontaneity in the face of adult certainty and prejudice. And in all Lucy Maud's stories inner struggles, fulfilments and joys are reflected in compelling evocations of changing Canadian landscapes.

Mark Twain suggested that Anne Shirley was 'the dearest and most lovable child in fiction since the immortal Alice'. In fact for many of us she is more appealing than Lewis Carroll's heroine; more rounded out, more realistic and—surely—considerably more imaginative. The 'Anne' books work at several levels, but it is essentially in the leading character that the author's literary skills are most evident. A full analysis of this resilient saga, and why we return to it with relish and affection, would fill a book in itself, so I now intend simply to point a few highlights from it.

Several of the most moving moments in *Anne of Green Gables* occur when LMM describes events from Marilla's viewpoint. In the beginning of the story Marilla has virtually made up her mind not to keep Anne. This is because she and Matthew had really wanted to adopt an orphan boy who could help with the farm work. However, she soon begins reluctantly to succumb to Anne's attractions. Anne instantly loves everything about Green Gables but, after just one night there, forlornly accepts that she may be sent back to the orphanage. She tells Marilla how she has named the geranium on the window-sill 'Bonny' and the cherry tree outside the window 'Snow Queen':

> 'I never in all my life saw or heard anything to equal her,' muttered Marilla, beating a retreat down cellar after potatoes. 'She is kind of interesting, as Matthew says. I can feel already that I'm wondering what on earth she'll say next. She'll be casting a spell over me, too. She's cast it over Matthew.'

Marilla then considers handing Anne over to Mrs Blewett, who wants 'a little girl to help her'. She realises, however, that this 'sharp-faced, sharp-eyed' lady intends to make Anne a child-minder and household drudge.

Marilla looked at Anne and softened at sight of the child's pale face with its look of mute misery—the misery of a helpless little creature who finds itself once more caught in the trap from which it had escaped. Marilla felt an uncomfortable conviction that, if she denied the appeal of that look, it would haunt her to her dying day. Moreover, she did not fancy Mrs Blewett. To hand a sensitive, 'high-strung' child over to such a woman! No, she could not take the responsibility of doing that!

Putting off an immediate decision, Marilla tells Mrs Blewett that she must talk the matter over again with Matthew, and from her tone it seems that it is likely, after all, that Anne *will* be allowed to stay at Green Gables:

'There's no scope for imagination in patchwork.'

During Marilla's speech a sunrise had been dawning on Anne's face. First the look of despair faded out; then came a faint flush of hope; her eyes grew deep and bright as morning stars. The child was quite transfigured; and, a moment later … she sprang up and flew across the room to Marilla.

'Oh, Miss Cuthbert, did you really say that perhaps you would let me stay at Green Gables?' she said in a breathless whisper, as if speaking aloud might shatter the glorious possibility. 'Did you really say it? Or did I only imagine that you did?'

'I think you'd better learn to control that imagination of yours, Anne, if you can't distinguish between what is real and what isn't,' said Marilla crossly.

There are many further instances of Marilla's compassionate appreciation of Anne, and of her inability to express this. Anne, at the end of her first year at Green Gables, says:

'I've been here for a year and I've been so happy. Of course, I've had my troubles, but one can live down troubles. Are you sorry you kept me, Marilla?'

'No, I can't say I'm sorry,' said Marilla, who sometimes wondered how she could have lived before Anne came to Green Gables, 'no, not exactly sorry.'

On another occasion, Marilla's feelings are less muted. Anne, playing with her 'bosom friend' Diana Barry and other girls at the Barry home, accepts a dare to walk the ridge-pole of the roof. She falls and breaks her ankle, and it is then that Marilla recognises the depth of her feelings for the child she has adopted:

> [Mr Barry] carried Anne, whose head lay limply against his shoulder.
>
> At that moment Marilla had a revelation. In the sudden stab of fear that pierced to her very heart she realized what Anne had come to mean to her. She would have admitted that she liked Anne—nay, that she was very fond of Anne. But now she knew as she hurried wildly down the slope that Anne was dearer to her than anything on earth.

Much later on, when Anne goes away for a year to Queen's Academy to work for her teacher's licence, Marilla bids her an 'untearful, practical' goodbye, but she then:

> … plunged fiercely into unnecessary work and kept at it all day long with the bitterest kind of heartache—the ache that burns and gnaws and cannot wash itself away in ready tears. But that night … she buried her face in her pillow and wept for her girl in a passion of sobs …

Anne's most dramatic exploits have a special edge because they occur against a background of stolid and conventional small-town relationships and events—all of which LMM has a flair for describing. Memorably vivid moments in Anne's early days at Green Gables include her (unintentionally) getting Diana well and truly drunk, the dyeing of her own red hair to a horrible green colour (instead of the raven hue which she had expected) and the cracking of her slate over Gilbert Blythe's head after he has called her 'Carrots'.

Of course, this last incident sets the pattern for her future relationship with Gilbert, a tall, good-looking boy with 'curly brown hair' and 'roguish hazel eyes' who is much admired by the other girls at Avonlea School. Anne—whose only real character flaw is 'an unpraiseworthy tenacity for holding grudges'—refuses to accept Gilbert's apology and his overtures of friendship, then or later on. She embarks on a course of trying always to beat him academically in class while, as far as possible, never publicly acknowledging his existence.

'You mean, hateful boy!' she exclaimed passionately.

Most readers of girls' fiction recognise that this kind of long-drawn-out battle between the sexes is likely to be the prelude to eventual, and romantic, reconciliation. It is not

# How We Went to the Wedding

### By L. M. MONTGOMERY

*A Long Complete Story by the Author of*

*" Anne of Green Gables "*

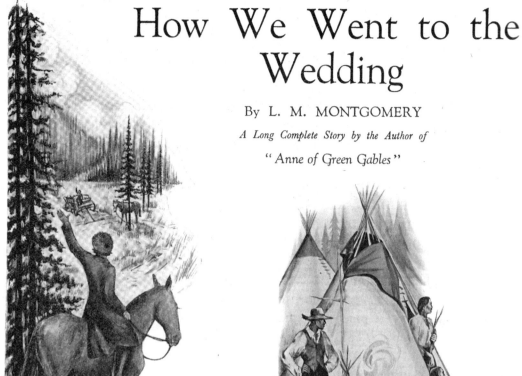

In the 1930s and early 40s
L M Montgomery wrote numerous stories
for girls' magazines.

# The Garden of Spices

### By L. M. MONTGOMERY

*Author of " Anne of Green Gables," etc., etc*

until the very end of the first book, when Anne and Gilbert are both sixteen, that she responds to his friendliness. After the sudden death of Matthew, Anne has decided to sacrifice her Redmond scholarship; instead of going away for a degree course she will stay at Green Gables with Marilla, who is in danger of losing her sight if she overdoes things. Without Anne's presence, Marilla knows that she will be unable to manage, and will have to move from, and sell, Green Gables.

To help Anne and Marilla, Gilbert self-sacrificingly renounces the position he's been given as teacher in charge of the local school, and suggests that the trustees appoint Anne in his place, which they do. When Anne expresses her gratitude for this, and the reconciliation between them at last takes place, Gilbert is very much the big-hearted and all-tolerant male. He jubilantly informs Anne that they were born to be the best of friends, and that she has 'thwarted destiny' for long enough.

This, however, is to be only the beginning of yet another frustrating phase in their relationship. Lucy Maud is of the school of writers whose attitude to her readers is: 'Let them laugh, let them cry, let them *wait!*' Throughout the second book, *Anne of Avonlea* (1909), when it becomes clear that Gilbert now sees Anne as very much the girl of his dreams, she is still unawakened to romance (at least for herself—although she can be an ardent matchmaker for others!); and Gilbert has to settle for friendship or nothing.

In *Anne of the Island* (1915) Anne and Gilbert are eighteen. In the first chapter they are out together at dusk, and in a warmly reminiscent mood. Gilbert breaks the spell by putting his hand on hers; Anne realises what he is feeling and, although nothing is said, she reflects, 'Our friendship will be spoiled if he goes on with this nonsense …' Here, of course, she is behaving in the tradition of so many popular teenage fictional heroines when confronted by declarations or even hints of passion from a male friend. (Slightly later examples are Dorita Fairlie Bruce's Dimsie, in *Dimsie Grows Up*, written in 1924, whose response to Dr Gilmour's proposal of marriage is: 'Oh Peter! … How can you say anything so horrible!'; and Elsie Oxenham's Jen, in *Queen of the Abbey Girls*, written in 1926, who, when Ken Marchwood shows romantic interest in her, confides to Mary-Dorothy: 'I don't want him to be an idiot and think of silly things … Mary, you don't think he's going to be daft, do you?')

When, much later in the book, Gilbert proposes to Anne, is rejected and desperately hurt, we begin to have a horrible suspicion that, like Louisa Alcott with Jo and Laurie in *Good Wives*, LMM is going to separate the enchanters for ever. But happily this is not to be. Despite misunderstandings and jealousies, and Anne's receiving proposals from three other young men, she comes to her senses when Gilbert—overworking in his efforts to qualify as a doctor—almost dies of typhoid. She has to live through bitter 'hours of storm and darkness' when she fears that her realisation of having always loved him has come too late; but, as soon as he recovers, he proposes again, and her acceptance is ecstatic. Lucy Maud, when the final romantic climax arrives, does not pull her punches! She manages convincingly to describe Anne 'shining with all the love-rapture of countless generations' and the pair of them walking 'together in the dusk, crowned king and queen in the bridal realm of love, along winding paths fringed with the sweetest flowers that ever bloomed …'

From then on, through the next books in the saga, *Anne's House of Dreams* (1917), *Anne of Windy Willows* (1936), and *Anne of Ingleside* (1939), every vicissitude can be coped with in the strength of their mutual love. Anne and Gilbert have five strong and healthy children, although very sadly their first-born child, a daughter, survived for only one day.

In the closing pages of the last book Anne reflects on what the future might hold for the young lives in her and Gilbert's care—'youth tip-toe … expectant … astir with its sweet, wild dreams …' The saga ends more or less where it began, in the world of Anne's gleaming imagination. This, with her delighted response to nature, runs like a warm thread through all the books in the series. It is hard to write about her without using adjectives like 'shining' or 'glowing': as Gilbert was to feel about her in *Anne of Avonlea*, she 'was one of the children of light by birthright'. This lambent quality, in Anne's character and in L M Montgomery's writing, ensures the lasting appeal of the stories. Fashions in literature, in heroines and in romance may have changed since *Anne of Green Gables* first came into being; but the book has remained resiliently in print for a hundred years, and will almost certainly reach out to many new generations of readers as the twenty-first century progresses.

# PART TWO

# HARDBACK SCHOOL STORIES

# LARKY AND LIBERATED

Angela Brazil, the founding mother of the twentieth-century schoolgirls' story, once remarked effusively but erroneously that 'schoolgirls—dear things' were 'the same the world over'. In fact her 'rosy, racy, healthy, hearty' pubescent heroines (chest-expanders, hockey-sticks and all) were peculiarly British. They and their descendants—ever since the 1907 publication of Brazil's *The Fortunes of Philippa*—have gamely defied fluctuations in literary fashion to remain potent symbols of youthful larkiness and liberation.

Their resilience is particularly surprising in view of the multi-faceted nature of girls' fiction. During the nineteenth century, this ranged from moral tales set 'in hearth and home' to Bessie Marchant's sagas of high adventure in the outposts of Empire. Early twentieth century themes varied from the charms and challenges of Guiding to career fantasies about girl aviators, racing-drivers, detectives, deep-sea divers, lumberjacks and lion-tamers. Social realism stamped itself relentlessly on the genre during the 1950s, and the point has now been reached when no subject is regarded as out-of-bounds for girl readers. Recent books, for example, have featured snobbery, racist bullying, inner-city violence, delinquent parents, dyslexia, sexual difficulties, bed-wetting, wife-and-child-battering, and the political situation in Chile.

To hold its own against these and other excitements, the gymslip genre has had to reflect certain social changes. Angela Brazil caught and glamorised the turn-of-the-century expansiveness of girls who were at last getting away from social restraints by going to lively boarding- or day-schools. She swept away the sentimentality of earlier school and college stories, and chronicled—as if from the inside—the average girl's interest in games and sport, education and careers. She also created an appropriately girlish jargon—'Miss Jones is a stunt, as jinky as you like'—for conveying the 'flaming intensities' of relationships within the single-sex school.

She reigned, however, only briefly as the undisputed queen of the genre. During the 1920s and 1930s, Elsie Jeanette Oxenham, Dorita Fairlie Bruce, Elinor M Brent-Dyer, Winifred Darch, Ethel Talbot and others skilfully took up the themes which she had popularised, and embellished the school structure with fictionalised accounts of girls' involvement in real-life movements like Campfire and country dance, Guiding and the Girls' Guildry. Their stories seemed to strike a more progressive note than Brazil's, and certainly to convey a surer sense of pace and drama. And a further exuberant crop of schoolgirl heroines was to grow from a different root.

Soon after books about 'gilt-edged bricks' and 'bosom chums' had become addictive, the school story was vigorously tackled by Lord Northcliffe's girls' weeklies. Here—surprisingly—it was developed almost exclusively by male authors, editors and illustrators (in accordance with Northcliffe's theory that women writers were over-protective of their girl characters while men would make them more adventurous). Mabel St John (Henry St John Cooper) kicked off in the *Girls' Friend* with the long-running and iconoclastic schooldays of Pollie Green and her black chum Coosha. Frank Richards (Charles Hamilton) then introduced into his boys' *Magnet* tales the girls of Cliff House School who, a decade later, were given their own paper, the *School Friend*. (This was established partly to reflect the wider horizons demanded by women and girls as a result of the social upheavals of the First World War.) Sister papers like the *Schoolgirls' Own, Schoolgirls' Weekly* and *Girls' Crystal* were set up to complement the immensely successful *School Friend*, through which male authors continued to project their exhilarating anima fantasies until these weeklies folded in the paper shortages of the Second World War.

In real life, the post-war period saw the decline of Empire, with fewer parents working abroad and sending their offspring back to England to boarding-school. It seemed that the single-sex girls' school story might become defunct, although Enid Blyton's 'Malory Towers', 'St Clare's' and 'Naughtiest Girl' series remained popular, and so too did Antonia Forest's 'Marlows' novels.

However, a new clutch of writers emerged who were able to produce memorable and addictive stories which combined the traditional ingredients of friendships and rivalries, sport and *esprit de corps* with a new liveliness and style. Nancy Breary in particular showed a playfulness bordering on irony in her plots, which gave full rein to both high jinks and dramatic effects, but her great theme was schoolgirl friendships. These were frequently cross-generational relationships between a senior and a junior girl.

The workmanlike and more serious Phyllis Matthewman adeptly portrayed individuals who swam against the tide, and she is best known for her 'Daneswood' and 'Priory' series. The New Zealand author Clare Mallory wrote urbanely and engagingly. One of her best books, *Juliet Overseas*, inventively used the well-worn theme of an 'outsider' from abroad tackling slackness in an English school. There are intriguing twists as she has to learn about British irony and understatement.

The 'Melling School' stories by Margaret Biggs have a satisfying warmth and realism. Unusually for the genre, Melling is a weekly boarding-school and thus, perhaps, able to appeal not only to readers who like boarding-school tales but to girls who prefer day-school and weekend adventures.

More recently, notable girl characters have emerged in well realised mixed-sex school situations, in feminist slanted stories by Gene Kemp (*The Turbulent Term of Tyke Tiler*, 1977), Jan Mark (*Hairs in the Palm of the Hand,* 1981) and Gillian Cross (*Save our School,* 1981), etc. The Grange Hill Comprehensive exploits proved to be amongst the most addictive school stories of the 1980s. Featuring girls and boys in fairly equal measure, these started as spin-offs from the 1970s television series. The success of the books was due in part to the keen ear of the various authors, particularly Robert Leeson, for the rhythms and resonances of school and playground dialogue, and their knack of communicating the robustness of working-class humour.

Grange Hill's popularity was superseded in the 1990s when the Harry Potter phenomenon burst upon us! There is no doubt that this has revitalised interest in the

boarding-school setting, even though the glamour of Hogwarts has more to do with magic than with traditional elements of the genre. The appeal of the saga also lies in its conveyance of juvenile empowerment—which of course has been a constantly reiterated theme in school stories since the first decade of the twentieth century.

In spite of the popularity of Harry Potter and other girls-and-boys-together adventures, the heroine of the single-sex school still survives. Just over a hundred years on from the launching of Angela Brazil's *The Fortunes of Philippa*, Anne Digby's 'Trebizon School' stories are to be reprinted by Fidra Books. This fourteen-book series was originally published between 1978 and 1994. Although it harks back atmospherically to the pre-Second World War *School Friend*, it includes some interesting concessions to social change. For example, girls are no longer packed off to boarding-school because their parents work in far-flung reaches of the British Empire, but because they are employed by the Saudis.

Girls Gone By Publishers have recently and successfully republished school stories by Elinor Brent-Dyer, Elsie Oxenham, Dorita Fairlie Bruce, Margaret Biggs, Clare Mallory and others. Angela Brazil's Edwardian 'frolicsome bricks' have now also been revived in their 'Fun in the Fourth' series, in which they are republishing stories by various authors whose characters generally appeared in single rather than series books. All these reprints, of course, are relished by nostalgic adults but—satisfyingly—they also pull in child and teenage readers.

# ANGELA BRAZIL—A HUNDRED YEARS ON

Not exactly a hundred years, in fact. Angela Brazil's first stories and plays with fairy themes were published rather more than a century ago, but her first boarding-school story, *The Fortunes of Philippa*—which was inspired by her mother's schooldays—actually appeared in 1907. Interestingly, when I first read her books as a child in the mid-1930s they seemed to me slightly old-fashioned, though nevertheless appealing. *Re*-reading them as an adult I'm often surprised how 'up to date' they seem in some respects, and how much in advance of her time Angela could be.

She was born at the end of the 1860s, and did not begin to write professionally until she reached her early thirties. (Previously she had considered a career as an artist and studied at Heatherley Studio in London, where one of her fellow pupils was Baroness Orczy, who also switched from art to authorship, and became the creator of the Scarlet Pimpernel saga.) Angela's first full-length book, *A Terrible Tomboy*, was published in 1904. It featured a *day*-school heroine, but it was only when she began to use boarding-school settings that she found her true *métier*, and became skilled in describing girls' ideas and ambitions as if 'from the inside'. There had, of course, been earlier school tales from other authors (notably L T Meade in England and Susan Coolidge in the USA), but it was Angela who put her stamp upon the ever-intriguing and resilient twentieth-century schoolgirl story genre.

From 1906 until she died in 1947 this indefatigable author created a succession of Winonas, Phoebes, Aldreds, Alwyns and others who were, in her own words, by turns 'frolicsome', 'earnest' and 'intent', and who (her words again) 'with sterling grit and grind' flung themselves into passionate friendships, educational experiments, progressive leagues and sporting endeavours.

As well as being an author, she was an inveterate committee woman with a great appetite for social functions. She organised *soirées,* lectures, musical entertainments, moonlight picnics and coffee-evenings—and also large children's parties, which were said by the guests to be 'out of this world'. She provided an autobiographical book, *My Own Schooldays*, in 1925, which, although informative, is probably somewhat romanticised.

Angela Brazil

Although Angela never stopped writing, it is evident that the books which she produced in the decade before her death in March 1947 lacked the vitality and appealing atmosphere of those created by her between 1906 and the mid 1930s. Her 'Works'—as she called them—had become so synonymous with the fictional British schoolgirl that even people who had never read any of her books were immediately stirred by mention of her name to burble about spiffing school stories, jolly hockey-sticks, dormitory feasts and bosom friendships. It is because she *was* such a potent symbol that when Patricia Craig and I were seeking a title for our first book, thirty years ago, we settled on *You're a Brick, Angela!* We actually covered in this far more than the school story, but Angela's name was then still sufficiently resonant to suggest not only the world of school but of girls' fiction in general.

Strangely, although the genre had been largely ignored for decades by mainstream publishers, *You're a Brick, Angela!* was followed two or three months later by another book which focused on Angela: Gillian Freeman's *The Schoolgirl Ethic*. So there was in 1976—and there still is—plenty to say and write about her as the pioneer of the twentieth-century girls' school tale.

It is particularly appropriate that Girls Gone By chose to feature Angela as the first author in their new 'Fun in the Fourth' series. Of her forty-nine or so novels, *A Fourth Form Friendship* is a fine choice for this; it is, in style and content, vintage Brazil at her best. Originally published in 1912, as its title suggests it deals tellingly with one of the author's favourite themes: that of schoolgirl friendships. She constantly explored these in their varied forms, fads and fashions, and *A Fourth Form Friendship* shows how perceptively she could convey an intense relationship between two girls of very different capacities and from very different backgrounds. We shall come back to this story a little later on, but first let us take a detailed look at its creator.

Angela was born in Preston, Lancashire, on 30 November 1869. She had two brothers and one sister, and was the youngest child of Clarence Brazil, a cotton-mill manager, and his wife Angelica (McKinnel). She was educated at The Turrets, a small private school in Wallasey, then in Manchester at the High School and Ellerslie College. Her own schooldays were short on amateur dramatics, hockey and other sports, secret societies, picnics and dormitory feasts; so, perhaps as a compensation, she created these in abundance in her books. She never married, and lived in Coventry with her doctor brother, Walter, and sister Amy, who were also both single. The elder brother, Clarence, was the only sibling to marry.

For over three decades Angela was a leading light in Coventry's cultural and social life, in 1920 becoming Vice President, and in 1928 President, of the city's YWCA, and, for a period, Vice President of the Coventry Natural History and Scientific Society. She travelled extensively, and her experiences abroad became colourful grist to the mill of her writing.

Her life seemed to swing from cliché and contradictions to clarity; and from extreme traditionalism and conservatism to openness, enquiry, and a willingness to embrace new and challenging ideas (such as, for example, Theosophy, pupil-power and fairly rudimentary feminism). I think it says a great deal for Angela's strength of character that, although she and her sister Amy were frequently characterised by their father as his 'dear little silly billies', she was to become not only a several-million best-selling author but a leader of Coventry's cultural life. She also became a public benefactor, leaving land which she had purchased near her holiday cottage in Cornwall to the National Trust, and bequeathing the royalties from her books to two separate charities: The Royal United Kingdom Beneficent Association and The Women's Careers Foundation. Interestingly, the latter was a direct offshoot of *The Girl's Realm* magazine, to which Angela had occasionally contributed short stories.

I mentioned the clichés in her life. These began with her mother Angelica, who, of Scottish parentage, was not only born in Brazil but, of course, married into the name! However, although Angela grew up accepting the fact that she was a Bra*zil* (and in the 1930s we *always* used that pronunciation when referring to her), she decided, when in her early forties and a successful writer and local community VIP, that her surname was no longer to be pronounced 'like the nut'. She was 'Angela *Bra*zil to rhyme with dazzle' (not, we note, to rhyme with anything so earthy or mundane as 'razzle' or 'frazzle').

I did several broadcasts about girls' fiction with Arthur Marshall, and, in a 1976 programme to celebrate the publication of *You're a Brick, Angela!* and *The Schoolgirl Ethic*, he mentioned that Angela had once been employed as a governess to the children of one of his public-school teaching colleagues, and that she was then definitely calling herself Miss Bra*zil*. Incidentally, Angela makes very little reference in her autobiographical book *My Own Schooldays*, or elsewhere, to this governessing period. It seems that from her young days there was a self-censoring of any reminiscences which did not fit into the *grande-dame* image of herself which she was to build up and zealously maintain. Governessing did not exactly create the right image for this!

We do not know precisely what prompted Angela to change the way her name was pronounced, but we *do* know that, always fascinated by Celtic mythology, when she came across the legend of the magical island of Hy Brazil, she was thrilled by it. According to Irish legend, this Blessed Isle is a kind of appearing—and disappearing—Shangri-La, springing up occasionally off the coast of Donegal. Its people were said to be god-like and possessed of intense healing powers. Angela equated the word Brazil with Blessed from then onwards, and certainly by 1911, when she and Walter went to live in Coventry, they were rhyming their surname firmly with 'dazzle' and not the nut. (Gillian Freeman, in *The Schoolgirl Ethic*, suggests another Celtic derivation for Brazil—from 'bres'—which actually means 'strife' and has nothing to do with being blessed. So perhaps Angela was barking up the wrong tree—or rather sailing to the wrong island!)

We can find many contradictions in her life, and between some principles ardently promoted in her stories but flouted in her own relationships. For example, in her books

Angela Brazil's fictional heroines and some real life girls of the period

snobbery arises but is fairly strongly put down, and the uppity girls do *not* prosper. In *The Little Green School* (1931) Angela creates a Fair Play Union, and in *My Own Schooldays* she writes:

> One thing for which I always stood up was fair play and equality. School, in my opinion, was a commonwealth where all were entitled to equal chances, and any suspicion of favouritism, especially of awarding popularity to a girl on the basis of her father's wealth instead of her own claims, invariably aroused my strongest antagonism. What a girl was at home mattered nothing; it was the school aspect of her that counted, and at that valuation I insisted she should be taken.

So far, so impressive. However, we know that such egalitarian feelings went out of the window when her brother Clarence married a woman whom Angela felt to be the social inferior of the Brazil family. Florence (maiden name Snozwell) was the sister of a piano-manufacturer, and so embarrassed were Angela and Walter by this fact that, apparently, they always denied having any knowledge of Florence's connection with the firm. Worst of all, they felt that Clarence and Florence's only child, John Walter, who was always an invalid and who died young, was somehow tainted by Florence's low birth. Angela seems rather snidely to have produced an unsympathetic version of her sister-in-law, whom she portrayed as a barmaid, in *A Patriotic Schoolgirl* (1918). The barmaid's baby son, Jackie, is shown as an angelic child who adores only his aunt—ie Angela in a fictional guise. Here is the little boy talking to the three schoolgirls who have befriended him:

> 'No, I don't want to know your real names. I like make-up ones better. We always play fairies when Titania comes to see me.'
> 'Who's Titania?'
> 'She's my Auntie. She's the very loveliest person in all the world.'

But I'm glad to report that Florence had the last laugh. Ultimately, after the respective deaths of Angela, Walter and Amy, she inherited the family estate. There appears to have been no nonsense about Florence—or Clarence—neither of whom ever wanted to be known as *Braz*ils. They continued firmly to be Braz*ils*!

However, in fairness to Angela, she was probably only too aware of her own character limitations and contradictions, and she might well have applied to herself the reflections of one of her most engaging heroines, Winona Woodward, in *The Luckiest Girl in the School* (1916):

> 'How horribly we live right inside ourselves!' thought Winona 'How few people know just what we're feeling and thinking, and how hard it is to let them know! The "I" at the back of me is so different from the outside

of me … we all live in our own little world and only touch one another now and then.'

It is sometimes tempting to see Angela Brazil as the Enid Blyton of her day, and there are certainly many parallels in their lives. Both, of course, became best-selling children's writers, whose works were so addictive to young readers that librarians, teachers and sometimes parents frowned upon them. In recent years, bans on Blyton by some libraries and schools have become well known and notorious. In Angela's case the bans were less widespread. Nevertheless, in 1936 the Principal of St Paul's Girls' School in London told her pupils during morning prayers that she would like to collect all books written by Angela Brazil and burn them! A decade earlier, in *John O'London's Weekly*, an article by Rose Macaulay (then a novelist of fame and distinction) really had it in for Angela.

Under the heading 'What Do Girls Read?' she devotes about half of her column inches to sneering at Angela's stories. Despite her eloquence about their so-called superficiality, it soon becomes evident that Rose Macaulay has never studied—and possibly hardly read—them! She quotes correspondence she's had about Angela with St Paul's Girls' School and Cheltenham Ladies' College. The former apparently said: 'People about eight like her; after that she is not taken seriously', and that P G Wodehouse, Edgar Wallace, Sapper, and boys' school stories were popular with the girls. The Cheltenham correspondent, after consulting the school library registers, also wrote that the girls' favourite reading (from eleven to thirteen) was boys' school and adventure stories and Sherlock Holmes, with Kipling topping the list. She goes on to say that 'nearly every girl at the age of eleven or twelve raves over Angela Brazil's books and reads nothing else for two to six months. Then she suddenly grows tired of them and never reads them again.' (How often have we, in recent years, heard similar comments on Enid Blyton!)

Rose Macaulay's article highlights aspects of literary criticism during the 1920s which tended to favour boys' writers. In 1926 it would presumably have been too early for Elinor Brent-Dyer to be considered, but surely Elsie Jeanette Oxenham and Dorita Fairlie Bruce deserved a mention! Dorothea Moore is rather grudgingly touched upon as being 'perhaps, rather better' than Angela, while Susan Coolidge's *What Katy Did at School* is irritatingly dismissed as 'sloppy' and 'uninteresting'.

Fortunately both Brazil and Blyton ignored and rose above such critiques. Other similarities between these two writers were that they had both been Head Girls: Angela at Ellerslie in Manchester and Enid at St Christopher's in Beckenham. Angela subsequently bemoaned the fact that she was selected for this prestigious role solely by virtue of her academic work, and that the position 'carried no authority beyond the honour of it'. Nevertheless, it is obvious that both Angela and Enid made their marks sufficiently strongly in their teens to become the recognised leaders of their schools.

However, despite this seniority, and their subsequent achievements in adult life, it can be argued that both authors were, in a sense, archetypal schoolgirls who never quite grew up. In her thirteenth year Enid suffered the traumatic experience of her adored father suddenly walking out of the family home, for ever, and it seems that part of her always hankered for the happy childhood days she had known before this. Angela wrote explicitly in *Answers* magazine in 1923:

> To be able to write for young people depends, I consider, upon whether you are able to retain your early attitude of mind while acquiring a certain facility with your pen. It is a great mistake to grow up! I confess I am still an absolute schoolgirl in my sympathies.

Both Angela and Enid were determined seekers of, and writers about, children's jolly times, and what Angela called 'jinky stunts' and Enid termed 'japes'. They also loved to dwell in their stories on the glories of sweets and cakes and other wonderfully tasty goodies.

They were both attracted to the concept of pupil-power—in Angela's case, considerably in advance of her time. In *The Leader of the Lower School* in 1914, for example, Gypsy Latimer succeeds in establishing what she calls 'freeborn democratic standards' at Briarcroft Hall School. In particular she demands and gets greater autonomy and control for the juniors in the school's clubs and societies. There are echoes in Enid Blyton's 'Naughtiest Girl' books of Gypsy's endeavours. Enid's iconoclastic heroine, Elizabeth, began her adventures in 1940 at Whyteleafe School, which had its own pupil parliament.

One of the most striking parallels between Angela and Enid is their deep feeling for nature and conservation. This is a joyous thread running through their works. Angela, who kept a detailed nature diary almost throughout her life, is able to express it quite movingly at times. Her girls are truly excited by finding and studying mosses and wild flowers and leaves and seashells, and by the sheer beauty and power of the natural scene. Those glorious botany walks, which were such a feature of her books, were warmly appreciated by her heroines, and indeed by their teachers. One of my favourite Brazil quotations is from *A Popular Schoolgirl* (1920) when the girls of Grovebury School, led by one of the mistresses, Miss Strong, are on a botany ramble and savouring the new life and expansiveness of springtime:

*The Nicest Girl in the School*

The birds were carolling it still in the hedgerows, and the girls caught the joyous infection and danced along in defiance of Miss Strong's jog-trot guide walk. Even the mistress herself, so wise at the outset, finally flung prudence to the winds, and skirmished through the coppices with enthusiasm equal to that of her pupils, lured from the pathway by glimpses of kingcups, or the pursuit of a Peacock butterfly.

Some critics, even those within our own circles, suggest that Angela was a superficial author. I don't agree. Oh yes, she lacked the depth and true romanticism of Elsie Jeanette Oxenham; the innovatory freshness and colour of Elinor Brent-Dyer; and the utter naturalism that Dorita Fairlie Bruce was able to embody in her more-real-than-life schoolgirls. But she *did* expand the views and boundaries and general entertainment quality of the genre. She was also one of the first writers to give it humour (sometimes unconscious) and touches of charm and whimsy. And, as mentioned earlier, she was in advance of her time in writing about pupil-power and conservation. She also explored simple feminism and the means to achievement in this field—ie education, sporting endeavours and female relationships. In her young readers, particularly perhaps in those who never had the privileges of attending good schools, she whetted appetites for enquiry into aspects of history, literature, myth and tradition, and foreign travel.

Also, unlike many children's authors of her time, she seemed able to write from the schoolgirls' point of view, without preaching, condescension or 'writing down'. So just how did she get into schoolgirls' minds and hearts? As indicated previously, in a sense she never grew up. As she wrote in *My Own Schooldays*:

> I have always had the strong feeling that if I had added BA to my name, forced myself into a scholastic mould, and become a head-mistress, I should never, never, NEVER have written stories about schoolgirls, at any rate not from the schoolgirls' point of view, which is the attitude that has appealed to me most.

Above all, she appreciated friendship and the magical lift that this brings into our lives. She could convey so-called ordinary friendships (and rejections) when a lot is taken for granted; when one's chum (or oneself) is sometimes awkward, moody, even mean, though generally supportive. She could describe the genuine joy and passion which underpinned many schoolgirl friendships, notably in the 'crush' or 'pash'—'If there were a peach competition she'd win it at a canter' (*A Harum Scarum Schoolgirl*, 1919)—but also in those more equal relationships which, begun in schooldays, were often of a wonderfully lasting nature.

Angela certainly enjoyed one of these in real life. She met Leila Langdale when they were both about ten years old and they were plunged into an almost instant friendship which was sustained until Angela's death. Angela wrote in *My Own Schooldays*: 'If human beings have auras, hers and mine must have instantly mixed.'

As we know, the four leading girls' school story writers of the twentieth century—Angela Brazil, Elsie Jeanette Oxenham, Dorita Fairlie Bruce and Elinor Brent-Dyer—were all unmarried women to whom same-sex friendships must have been very important. As I have commented elsewhere, the mainstream of English literature has not always been rich in fiction which celebrated friendships between women, although male friendships have been prominent. The so-called schoolgirl writers, however, have redressed the balance, and for this we should be grateful.

We should remind ourselves that Angela really *did* listen to schoolgirls' conversations on buses and trains. She also regularly visited several local schools in Coventry and stood around the edges of hockey fields on cold, wet and windy days to observe the play and to listen to young spectators' comments.

She had her foibles and vanities, and thought that real-life schoolgirls would see her as she was in her own eyes—a gracious, elegant and romantic figure—in fact, like the Pre-Raphaelite-ish, almost magical mauve-clad poetess, Lesbia Carrington, the 'Lavender Lady' so admired and beloved by Avelyn Watson in *For the School Colours* (1918). Actually it seems that some of the schoolgirls she encountered were far from reverent, inventing over-the-top slang for her special benefit, and seeing her as over-dressed and generally old-fashioned. Gillian Freeman reports one pupil remembering from the 1920s Angela's 'fussy' ensemble with a 'ruff and ruched coat and cream lace on an ornate hat'. Another recalls the author's very long, mauve, chiffon or voile dresses, and the bows on her shoes and flowers on her hats. I received a letter from a woman who'd been a 1920s schoolgirl, who described meeting Angela when she and a party of her schoolmates were on a winter sports holiday in Switzerland:

> We were much intrigued, and agog to meet the famous lady—more so perhaps because her books had been banned from our own school library as 'trash'! We thought she was a funny little old lady, dressed in very old-fashioned clothes. We at once got together and decided to provide her with 'copy' for her next book, which we felt sure was her object in joining us. So we invented all the most ridiculous slang phrases and expressions we could think of … Angela Brazil wore ancient buttoned boots, which we found vastly amusing, although I remember wearing them myself until I was about eight or nine …

Whether or not Angela's famous slang was accurate, she *did* generally manage to give a sense of authenticity to schoolgirls' conversations in her books. Incidentally, one point of her style which has often intrigued me is her reluctance to use or repeat the word 'said' when reporting such dialogues. Take almost any page of her descriptions of girls' chat and you will find a remarkable range of words which she uses rather than 'said'. On the second page of *Leader of the Lower School*, for example, her schoolgirls remarked/wailed/suggested/yawned/asked/sighed and snapped their conversational contributions!

# The QUEER GIRL AT St QUENTIN'S

by ANGELA BRAZIL

Reverting for a moment to critiques of Angela's works, it is perhaps bizarre that one of her admirers was that by turns schoolmaster and female impersonator, Arthur Marshall. In different media he seriously and favourably reviewed her books, although he also enjoyed sending up aspects of them in radio broadcasts. As one of Arthur's friends, I rejoice in the fact that, in a very dark hour of our nation's history, he put to splendid use the powerful effect of Angela's stories. This was during the evacuation of the British Expeditionary Force from Dunkirk after the fall of France to the Germans in June 1940. In her book *Thank You, Nelson* Nancy Spain describes how she questioned some of the captains of the now celebrated 'little ships' which helped to rescue the soldiers. Of course, it had been hell-let-loose there, with men waiting for hours on the beaches or standing in the water until they could scramble into the boats, all the time being shelled or machine-gunned by enemy planes. The skipper of one of the boats told Nancy:

'There were the remains of a regiment there … and one of the chaps in charge of them … Captain he was, but he's really a schoolmaster … he's made any money he has from being a female impersonator. There were machine-gun bullets spraying the beach from some Messerschmitts. Those chaps had to cross that beach to get to us to be taken on board … and they weren't a bit keen. Don't blame them. Now this schoolmaster feller, he gets up and walks up among the machine-gun bullets. One hits him in the ankle, and makes him stagger, but he pays no attention … "Come on, girls," he calls—"who's on for the Botany Walk?" Follow him? I'll say they followed him. When they came aboard they were laughing.'

That schoolmaster-officer was, of course, Arthur Marshall. He was desperate to urge his exhausted, dispirited men on, to brave the gunfire and get into the boats—and Angela's bracingly idealistic and very English writing suddenly gave him the inspiration he needed.

I hope I have managed to suggest that there is much to consider in Angela Brazil's books. Their overall keynote is friendship, and in my view her conveyance of this in *A Fourth Form Friendship* is outstanding. The friendship between a so-called 'ordinary' girl, Aldred Laurence, and the privileged and charismatic Mabel Farrington, whose impeccable family connections include being related to a bishop and a lord of the realm, is deep and demanding. At times it is *too* demanding for Aldred, who suffers from Mabel's hero-worship of her. How Angela handles the twists and turns, developments and fulfilments of the relationship provides fascinating reading. It makes an appropriate start for Girls Gone By's 'Fun in the Fourth' series—not only for fourth form readers but also for us mature appreciators of the genre.

Perhaps I can end—predictably and sincerely—by saying 'You're a Brick, Angela!'

# ELSIE OXENHAM AND THE (ALMOST) PERFECT GIRLS' STORY

The first half of the twentieth century produced a tremendous range of authors who were adept at writing school stories for girls, and, as adults today, we are fortunate in still having access to many of these books. Dipping and delving into them over the years, I feel that one stands out as the near-perfect girls' story: this is *The Abbey Girls* (1920) by Elsie Jeanette Oxenham.

It has all the expected ingredients such as depth of characterisation and the general intensity of friendships and rivalries, but, over and above all this, EJO deftly combines several engaging elements. As well as finely drawn vignettes of country dancing and a romanticised sense of history focused on Gracedieu Abbey, there are lovingly described May Queen ceremonies. These, derived from the rituals instituted by John Ruskin in the 1880s at Whitelands College in south London, appeal to most girls' passion for dressing up as well as their response at deeper levels to colourful traditions and symbolism.

Arguably, there are moments when the floweriness of all this goes over the top, but EJO's ability to create pretty and colourful scenes helps to provide the overall atmosphere of warmth and well-being that has attracted several generations of readers. *The Abbey Girls* gives us accurate (and now irresistibly nostalgic) glimpses into the life of many British middle-class girls during the 1920s and 30s.

However, although the story is extremely evocative of England during that period, it also contains pockets of universality and timelessness. It is permeated by the author's feeling for the natural scene, which she puts across with charm but without sentimentality: there is splodgy mud as well as glowing sunshine in the beech woods through which the girls tramp! EJO successfully combines realism with romance, and indelibly impresses her characters, and the values which they embody, on the minds of her readers.

Even in synopsis the richness of the story stands out. Its two heroines are the attractive, look-alike, flame-haired fifteen-year-old cousins, Joan and Joy Shirley, who live in the ancient Cistercian Abbey of Gracedieu (fictionally set in Buckinghamshire but actually inspired by Cleeve Abbey in Somerset). Cicely Hobart and some of her friends from Miss Macey's nearby school arrive to tour the Abbey. They are members of the Hamlet Club which has been formed to stamp out a plague of snobbery at their school, and to celebrate aspects of country life.

Joan, who loves Gracedieu and has steeped herself in its myths and magic, shows

Cicely and Co around. Much impressed by her sensitivity and intelligence, they learn that although she is a natural student she is no longer at school because her widowed and rather frail mother cannot afford to keep her there. Cicely offers her a Hamlet Club scholarship to Miss Macey's school. However, Joan—who longs to accept this—feels that she has sufficient determination to continue her studies at home on her own. In contrast, the lively and musically gifted Joy cannot apply herself to work and spends most of her time wandering all over the countryside, so Joan generously arranges for the scholarship to be switched to her cousin, who accepts it, although at first she has a rather superficial appreciation of what Joan is giving up.

Once at Miss Macey's, Joy is plunged into a world of strong friendships and rivalries, and has to battle with herself as well as some of the meaner girls before she can discover her own true nature, develop her musical talents and generally live up to the spirit of Joan's sacrifice on her behalf. Although Joan has given up her chance to attend the school, she *does* join the Hamlet Club and so is able to participate in the dancing and the May Queen ceremonies, and to become a member of Cicely's 'chummery'. Eventually her dedication to the Abbey secures its own reward, and there is a 'fairy-tale' ending to each cousin's story.

So far, so satisfying! The book's only real flaw, for me, is that the sensitive and introverted Joan, whom I've always preferred to the outgoing Joy, plays a smaller part than her cousin. Joy is put firmly at the centre of events, while Joan, her wonderful supporter—and indeed a good friend to everyone—has to remain somewhat on the sidelines. But, of course, without the contrasting personalities of the cousins, and Joan's capacity for self-sacrifice, there would be little plot or drama. EJO, having embarked upon this sequel to *The Girls of the Hamlet Club* (1914), must have known exactly what she was doing. Certainly it provides a brilliant base for the long series which was to follow.

It could also be argued that one or two lesser characters are ciphers. Mrs Shirley, for example, the mother of Joan and the aunt and guardian of Joy, though battling with poverty to do her best for the two girls in her charge, has about her a touch of the classic complacent, over-domesticated, melting-into-the-background mother figure. And Cicely fits rather too neatly into the role of the all-knowing and socially well-placed older girl. (Her judgement *does* come unstuck, however, when she lands Joy and Joan at a railway station, after dark, not realising that they have no money for their train fare home and, of course, are too proud to mention this fact.) Another character slotted into a conventional mould is Sir Anthony Abinger. He owns the Abbey and employs Mrs Shirley to look after it, but although he is Joy's grandfather doesn't want her to know of the relationship. He *can* be seen as the crochety, embittered old man of fiction and fairy-tale who turns out trumps in the end, but only after first suffering unnecessary estrangement from almost everyone in his family.

We are plunged into potential drama on the first page, in fact in the very first sentence, of *The Abbey Girls* when Carry Carter, on an outing with the Hamlet Club, grumbles, 'I don't see why they need choose such an out-of-the-way place to ramble to!' It is made clear that the pretty, fair-haired and spoilt Carry wants to deflect the ramble's main purpose, which is to reach and see over the Abbey. Moreover, we soon sense that she is likely to be a fairly regular thorn in the side of girls like Cicely, Miriam Honor, and the Gilks sisters, Edna and Peggy, whose response to the uplifting ethos of the Hamlet Club is more wholehearted.

EJO also wastes no time in bringing into her narrative two prominent background themes against which the girls' aspirations, friendships and rivalries will be played out. These are the appreciation of Nature, and the spiritual and romantic symbolism of the Abbey. The Hamlet Club girls' first sight of Gracedieu is conveyed with pictorial eloquence:

> The Abbey stood buried in great beech-trees. A tiny gate gave entrance to a footpath, and a short beech-path, soft with ruddy leaves, led them through the wood, till they paused to gaze across a lawn at an ancient gray building with pointed roof, the walls upheld by massive stone buttresses. A magnificent beech-tree stood at one side, its great branches bending lovingly towards the old gray stone of the walls and the green and brown and gold of the moss-covered roof.

In fact EJO is particularly good at describing first sightings of a variety of places and characters. Another example of this is when, soon after reaching the Abbey, the girls meet Joan Shirley:

> She was a slim girl of fifteen, taller for her age than Edna or Carry. She wore a dark dress and over it a big blue pinafore. Her brown eyes were wide with interest in her visitors, and looked the schoolgirls over with as much curiosity as they felt in her. Her hair was long and thick, tied back loosely with a ribbon, and very light and wavy in texture, of a colour which made Edna, gazing admiringly, whisper to Peggy, 'I say! New pennies! What a ripping colour! Talk about red!'

(In passing, I wonder just exactly what *is* the colour of Joan's and Joy's hair? Here it is likened to new pennies; later it is described as 'vivid bronze' and 'like a lamp', while in another instance it is compared to 'liquid flame'! So perhaps we should just settle for red!)

From the beginning, Joan's love of the Abbey and understanding of its history are impressive. Her capacity to express all this intrigued not only Cicely and her friends, but readers who over many years have visited the real-life Cleeve Abbey to see the inspiration for Gracedieu. Throughout the book we are given mouthwatering snippets of Joan's knowledgeable descriptions of the Abbey, but it is only when Sir Antony Abinger visits it, *incognito*, that we are treated to really detailed descriptions. Sir Antony, who cannot at first believe that a fifteen-year-old guide could do justice to the place, quizzes Joan relentlessly as she takes him round. His questions and her competent, informative replies give readers a fleshed-out picture of the wonderful beauty of the ancient building, and all that it stands for.

Here again, the author's pictorial sense, added to her feeling for history, is used to excellent effect. *The Abbey Girls* is rich in colourful word pictures. On their first visit to the Abbey, Cicely and Co, sheltering at one point from the rain, decide to pass the time by performing a morris dance in the cloisters. Joan is much intrigued by this. Much later in the book, Joan and Joy are dancing together and, unknown to them, Sir Antony is watching their performance, and deeply moved by it. Again, we are given a vivid picture:

> ... the sunny cloister garth, the ruined arches all around, the fierce old man, ill-tempered and lonely, peering through the doorway of the tresaunt, and two bronze-haired girls dancing a graceful minuet in the sunshine.

Dancing, of course, is a strong thread binding the story, and EJO adeptly conveys the routines and settings, and the girls' exhilaration in participating in their dancing evenings:

> The big barn would have been dim and shadowy by daylight, but now the lanterns swinging from the rafters gave plenty of light. The huge beams showed dimly overhead ... The barn was full of girls, laughing and chattering, all wearing dancing frocks, with white collars of smooth linen or frilled muslin, white hoods or sun-bonnets, white stockings and low black shoes.

The Abbey and the dancing not only add atmosphere to the story but also influence events. Similarly the May Queen rituals, as well as having links with the past, have a 'present-day' effect on the lives of the girls at Miss Macey's school. Every year a new queen is chosen, and after her coronation she is expected to play an important part in solving misunderstandings and quarrels between the girls, in looking after new, shy or nervous pupils, in righting wrongs and generally infusing the school with a spirit of helpfulness and trust. A tall order for any girl, but particularly for Joy when queenship is thrust upon her from the start of her time at Miss Macey's. It seems highly unlikely that in a real-life school a new girl would be given this position of honour and responsibility, but EJO just manages to get away with this device for carrying the plot forward.

The May Queen coronations are vividly evoked. Each queen adds to the charm of her robes by choosing the colour of her train and the flowers with which it will be decorated. Joy, with her love of the open-air, chooses green with wild clematis flowers: 'the little creamy stars that come all over the hedges in the autumn'. Joan and Joy call this 'Traveller's Joy', which is also the nickname applied to the ever-roaming and rambling Joy. At Joy's coronation we see the three previous queens in their robes. Marguerite's train is strawberry pink, bordered by white daisies. Cicely's is 'old gold decorated with hand-painted autumn leaves' and Miriam's is 'white with a dainty border of forget-me-nots'. (Later, when Joan becomes the next queen, we learn that her train is deep violet with 'white violets round the edge'.)

However, it is not just EJO's skilful manipulation of the Abbey, dance and May Queen factors which makes *The Abbey Girls* so outstanding, but her handling of the interplay between the characters. In the older pupils—Cicely, Marguerite and Miriam— we see protectiveness towards younger members of the school and the Hamlet Club, and there is very real affection between the two cousins. However, at first it almost seems as if Joy's somewhat carefree acceptance of the scholarship and all that goes with it might create a barrier between them. Joan helps to overcome her doubts and disappointments by giving further assistance to Joy: she rather touchingly sorts and adapts clothes from her own very limited wardrobe to ensure that Joy starts at Miss Macey's as well equipped as possible. (Perhaps, on reflection, Joan *is* occasionally a little too good to be true!) To Joy's credit she soon *does* begin to understand that, for Joan, the scholarship would have been 'just everything', and she then almost refuses to accept it. Of course, Joan continues to insist that it is right for Joy to have this opportunity:

> 'I'm awfully glad about it, honestly, Joy. We were worried about your music. It seemed such a shame you shouldn't have a chance … Now you'll have all you need … I'm honestly glad it's all fixed up …'
>
> Joy said no more at the time, but her arm slipped round her cousin's waist, and her voice was unsteady …

In this and other exchanges we have indications of hidden depths in Joy's happy-go-lucky nature. She also shows unusual maturity and perceptiveness in choosing the maverick Carry Carter to be her Maid of Honour. (Every queen has one of these to support her train and generally assist in the May Queen revels and rituals.) Joy hopes that by choosing Carry she will heal a threatened breach between various factions of the school; and, initially, she handles the situation with insight and delicacy, and becomes a popular queen and member of the school community.

However, Joy's natural impulsiveness and independence soon surface and nearly bring about her undoing. Bombarded with advice from various girls about how to perform her queenly duties, Joy starts to make, strictly for her own use, a 'guide-book' in which she enters their suggestions and admonitions, and her own rather caustic comments on these. Joan is shown the entries and declares, 'You certainly mustn't lose this book! Carry will have you up for libel if she ever sees it!' But, of course, Carry *does* see, devour and copy some of the entries from the book when Joy mislays it.

Joan realises that not only Carry but some of the other girls, even those whom Joy numbers among her friends, will be hurt by the way they are written about in the guide-book. Carry has a field-day, threatening to expose Joy; the Hamlet Club seems as if it might well break up—and it is only when Joy takes Joan's advice and puts the matter before Cicely and Miriam that Joy's position in the school is restored. She then shows greatness of spirit by forgiving Carry and allowing her to continue to be her Maid of Honour, thus bringing harmony again to the Club and the school.

*The Abbey Girls* ends on a high note: Sir Antony dies and leaves his grand home, the Hall, to Joy, and the Abbey to Joan. He also leaves them well provided for financially so that Joan as well as Joy will be able to attend Miss Macey's school. This bright-looking future, and the glowing mood of Joan's coronation as the new May Queen, are the stuff of fairy-tale. It is a measure of EJO'S story-spinning skill that she is able to combine the romanticism of the Abbey, morris dancing and May Queen ceremonies with conventional school story elements to create what, for me at least, is the practically perfect girls' story.

# DORITA FAIRLIE BRUCE—FAVOURITE AUTHOR AND FRIEND

First of all I should amplify my title: Dorita Fairlie Bruce is my particular favourite, and in saying that I am not, of course, decrying the other giantesses of the genre, Angela Brazil, Elsie Jeanette Oxenham and Elinor Brent-Dyer. This chapter will explain some of the reasons why I like Dorita's books so much, and why I see her not only as a favourite author but as a friend who has at several levels influenced my childhood and my adult life.

Friendship is a quintessential element in schoolgirl fiction—indeed, I've often felt that, although there are many famous male literary friendships, female friendships have not had their due in classical or popular adult fiction; and it has been largely left to the so-called 'schoolgirl' authors to explore and celebrate these in detail and in essence. In parenthesis, I'm not forgetting here the friendships and warm sisterly relationships in Jane Austen and, occasionally, the Brontës, or more recently in the books of Vera Brittain, Winifred Holtby and other women writers whom I admire. However, their probing of such relationships has been less sustained than those of DFB and Co.

I'd like here to strike a personal note which may well be echoed in the experiences of many of you. Let me first of all go back seventy-two years to my childhood. When I was eight years old, I was allowed to borrow from the lending library at my elementary school. This consisted of one large, battered cardboard box containing equally battered and serendipitously collected children's books. The box was passed round each classroom on Friday afternoons, and the undoubted 'star' volumes were *Dimsie Goes to School* (published in 1921 as *The Senior Prefect*, and in 1925 as *Dimsie Goes to School*) and *Dimsie Moves Up* (1921), both of which I borrowed and devoured more than once. Around that time I also read a reprint of *That Boarding-School Girl* (1925). I realised that it was written by the same author as the 'Dimsies' and therefore expected to like it; in fact, I became totally entranced by it, loving everything from the story to the embossed cover and the R H Brock illustrations.

With hindsight, of course, one can see that in this particular book, DFB skilfully exploited her capacity for creating realistic friendships, and that the triangular one shared by Nancy, Desdemona and Angela was particularly lifelike and memorable. Looking back, it seems that dips into the expansive, almost magically appealing worlds of Nancy and Dimsie considerably enriched my childhood. Like many other girls of my generation I frequently would ask myself, in moments of challenge or crisis, how Nancy and Dimsie would have responded in similar circumstances. There is no doubt that DFB was a provider of standards and values, and I have often felt that through her books she was giving me, as a *friend*, extremely acceptable and helpful advice. Most important were the images—perhaps ideals—of friendship; these were strong, unsentimental and compelling. For me, it is significant that a four-cornered friendship which I embarked upon so long ago in elementary school still exists, and that we *all* read and discussed together DFB's books. She influenced me very practically in other areas; to give just one example, there is a reference to Daphne Maitland having no problem in learning a passage of Shakespeare which was set for preparation, because she so often read him for pure pleasure. Struck by this, at a tender age, I remember dipping into my father's volume of Shakespeare's plays and finding these intriguing.

To continue the friendship theme into later years, let me mention Dorita's own friendly kindness to me and my daughter during the 1960s. I was not then a book collector, but because Teresa, my eight-year-old daughter, was then enjoying some of the Armada 'Chalet School' books, I bought for her a Brockhampton Press reprint of *Nancy at St Bride's* (1933) which appeared in our local bookshop. She loved it, and so, of course, did I. Until then I had no knowledge of DFB's personal life, or what she looked like, but the dustjacket of the book carried an arresting photograph of the author. Her strong, dark-eyed looks suggested great character, and I felt the urge to write to her, partly to convey my appreciation of her books and partly in the hope that she might help Teresa to build up a collection of her out-of-print works. I shall never forget my daughter, with the supreme and uninformed confidence of an eight-year-old, saying, 'Let's collect absolutely *all*

Dorita Fairlie Bruce

of Dorita Fairlie Bruce's books.' I guessed then that this would not be an easy task— but I had no idea that, once I became avid about acquiring her books, it would take me a full twenty-five years to get them all. *Nancy in the Sixth* (1935) was particularly difficult to find, and *Mistress Mariner* (1932) eluded me until the very end of that quarter of a century.

My first letter to Dorita, dated 4 February 1966, ran:

> For thirty years your books have given me so much pleasure—I remember reading my first 'Dimsie' book when I was eight years old—and now I see that there is a new edition of *Nancy at St Bride's* by the Brockhampton Press.
>
> Now I have an eight-year-old daughter, who is also a keen reader, and I would dearly love to obtain for her a complete set of 'Nancy' and 'Dimsie' books. I still have one or two copies of my own from the old days, though I gave away several to nieces years ago. It seems dreadful to trouble you about this, but if you could help me in any way, with either new editions, or second-hand copies of your books, I should be really delighted. I managed recently to get the first two 'Dimsies' in the Spring Books series, but I don't know if the rest of the series is available from them.

Thank you for your fascinating and loveable schoolgirl characters; they are like real friends, even after all these years! One feels that you love writing your books.

I somehow imagine that your home must be in Scotland, but if ever you are in or near London, I wonder if you would let me have the privilege of meeting you and taking you to lunch? In hopes of a reply I enclose a stamped addressed envelope. All good wishes to you for happiness and good health, now and in the future.

Yours, etc MC

I sent my letter c/o her publishers and to my delight she replied quickly. Her letter of February said:

Dear Mrs Cadogan,

Thank you so much for your kind letter, which was forwarded to me yesterday, and for the appreciative things you say about my books. You don't know how warming it is to a retired author (over eighty!) to hear that her tales are still giving pleasure, and the characters are still alive for some readers, even though the books are almost all out of print and unobtainable.

For that reason, I fear I can't be of much help, as I can't get them myself! but I have one or two stray copies, and if you have not already got these, I should be delighted to let your little girl have them. They are:

*Dimsie, Head Girl* }
*Dimsie Goes Back* } Reprints
*Dimsie Moves Up Again*   2nd hand

As to 'Nancy', I know of none, except the new reprint, recently brought out by the Brockhampton Press, but hope, if that is a success, that they may bring out the rest of the series. Thank you very much, too, for your kind invitation, but I fear I shall not be in London again, much as I should enjoy meeting you; but I am too crippled with arthritis to face the long journey, and—as you see—you guessed right, and I do live in Scotland! [The address, embossed at the top of the notepaper was Triffeny, Skelmorlie, Ayrshire.] Perhaps you will come and see me, if you ever come North? You would be very welcome.

With the kindest regards,
Yours sincerely,
Dorita Fairlie Bruce

As you can imagine, receiving this friendly, handwritten letter was a great thrill for me. Basely, perhaps, the offer of some of her books prompted me to lose no time in replying! I wrote on 11 February saying that Teresa and I would love to have the books she mentioned, and asking if she would sign them for us. I also said that the process of creating fiction interested me very much: 'A mind that has produced vibrant characters like Dimsie, Nancy and their associates must be extremely alive and creative. I wonder, did you live with your characters, getting to know them day by day, as you were writing about them—or did they come into being, with all their attributes, in a flash?' In the same letter I mentioned having found Skelmorlie in our atlas, and expressed the hope that I would indeed travel to Scotland to see her in the near future.

She replied on 17 February, thanking me for the postage stamp which I had enclosed for postage of the books, saying firmly that I had sent too much and enclosing the change in stamps. She told me that the books had been sent off that morning.

She then wrote:

> It will be delightful if you can come and see me when you are up North … Skelmorlie adjoins Wemyss Bay, which is our station, for we have no railway of our own, thank goodness! My characters just materialise in the first instance and come alive of their own accord. And I go back to school with them, and trot behind taking notes! I never attempt to guide or control them, nor to interfere in any way! If I did, all the spontaneity would vanish, and they would become—just characters in a book.
>
> With many thanks for the nice things you say about them and hoping to meet you before long. And best wishes to Teresa.
>
> Yours sincerely,
> Dorita F. Bruce

Well, the books arrived, signed and personally inscribed; treasures of course. DFB and I continued our contact, mainly through the sending of Christmas cards carrying short notes. Then, sometime in 1970 (when I was seriously into the business of collecting children's books of many genres), my husband and I were planning a trip to Scotland. I was determined that I would visit DFB and I telephoned the Wemyss Bay number (3124) on her letterheading. When I got through, I asked to speak to Miss Dorita Fairlie Bruce, and the voice at the other end of the line said, 'Oh, I'm so sorry … Miss Bruce died some months ago.' This was indeed daunting, but for a moment, so great was my determination to meet her that I found myself beginning to say, 'If I send a letter, will you please forward it.' (Incidentally, when I mentioned this episode some years later to Dorita's great-niece, Mrs Vivien Northcote, she said that 'Aunt DB', as the family called her, would have loved the idea of my wanting to send her a letter after her death. Apparently, Dorita had a strong sense of the supernatural. Vivien Northcote remembers that once, when she sensed something unusual on the landing at Triffeny after her great-aunt's friend and companion, Mrs Morrison, had died, DFB had said, 'I feel Mrs Morrison about me all the time. She's always here. You mustn't worry …')

Another debt that I owe to Dorita is that my interest in her books virtually started me off as a collector, also—tenuously—as a writer, comparing what I read and liked in childhood with what my daughter enjoyed. I also looked then at how girls and women in different eras were conditioned by what they read into forming certain images of themselves and their place in society, or of what they could or should—or couldn't and shouldn't—do. Interestingly, Dimsie, with her forthrightness in breaking established social barriers, and with her 'new age' approach to healing through herbalism (though this is, of course, based on long-held traditional lore) was in the vanguard. Not a conventional feminist, but a real inspiration to the young girl reader to get to know herself and her true aspirations and to follow these, even if they seemed somewhat at odds with what was later to become known as 'the establishment'.

All this eventually and circuitously led to my writing *You're a Brick, Angela!* with Patricia Craig. This, as Eva Löfgren says in *Schoolmates of the long-ago*, seems to be considered a pioneering work in bringing schoolgirl fiction (hitherto relegated to patronising 'jolly hockey-sticks' dismissal) into the light of serious socio-literary criticism. I know that not everyone agrees with all our findings—some of which I have modified over the years—but we did, I am told, through *You're a Brick, Angela!* do much to make the schoolgirl genre a suitable case for academic treatment.

Touching again upon DFB's use of the theme of friendship, I am always impressed at the range of friendships in her stories. It is interesting that in her first published school story, 'The Rounders Match' (1909), she writes of a three-cornered friendship, and that such triangles recur throughout her works. Authors often concentrated on the two-best-chums or bosom-friends relationships—which offer obvious satisfactions to the reader and can generally be fairly neatly made to run smooth after challenges and vicissitudes. However, although DFB frequently tackles the best friend twosome, with equal flair she conveys the threesome and large groups or gangs, which are very true to real life for many readers: she also excels in describing cross-generational friendships and the special quality of relationship between teaching staff and girl pupils.

It is all there in the books. To study DFB on friendships comprehensively would be a lengthy business, but I would just like to mention a few examples which are, for me, outstanding. These are: the relationship between Dimsie, Rosamund and Pam—that over the years subtly changing threesome within the broader-based friendships of the Anti-Soppist group; then there is that very different triangular relationship of two close friends and the interloper—Meg, Primrose and Nita; also the compellingly conveyed friendship between Dimsie, when a senior, and Hilary, the younger girl. I have already, of course, mentioned the threesome between Nancy, Desda and Angela.

As well as her fine depictions of friendships, I'd like to speak of other aspects of DFB's writing which in my view put her at the forefront of the genre. One is her feeling for, and ability to describe, the natural scene. Another is her—again vividly accurate—capacity to show girls *pictorially* in their school settings. (I always felt that I was there with them—just like DFB herself, who tells us that she went back to school with her characters.) She does this frequently, and with great economy of words—never holding up the action of the plot. This moment from *The Senior Prefect* illustrates how comments on nature can be just a word or two:

1940s versions of Dimsie

'What dog?' asked Nancy good-naturedly, as they turned off across the short thymy turf, where (late autumn though it was) countless tiny wild flowers glimmered up at them from the grass.

'His name's Laird,' explained Dimsie …

And DFB often skilfully uses nature to echo or contrast with a situation, relationship or a girl's inner mood as in this extract from *Dimsie, Head Girl* (1925):

The gas was lit and the red curtains drawn in the Head-girl's study at the Jane Willard Foundation. Outside a tempestuous March wind was howling across wood and playing field, bare down and stormy Channel, but within all was cosiness and peace—except in the soul of Jean Gordon, senior prefect, who sat, chin in hand, staring disconsolately at the lesson books spread out before her on the ink-stained crimson cloth …

To make us feel that we are really there with our heroines, Dorita often describes two or more schoolgirls discussing an important topic of the day—with one of them perched on the schoolroom desk or the study table, or on the window sill while she idly plays with the tassel of a blind; or someone is simply shown pushing her chair back under the table as the girls get up from lunch.

In her stories the orderliness of school life comes across persuasively: the routines; the walks in crocodile; the changing of clothes for different occasions; the music practices; earnest confabs in classrooms, studies and bootholes; standing around for hours on boundaries fielding at cricket matches—and so on. Although DFB is more interested in friendships and character-conflicts than in pranks and mysteries, she is equally good at conveying these and all kinds of dangerous adventures in the face of elemental challenges. Like most memorable fictional schools, Jane's is well equipped with secret passages leading to smugglers' caves and cliffs—and also, of course, with dormitories, cubicles, studies, bootholes and music-rooms for less drastic exploits.

DFB harnesses every ingredient of the genre with panache, but the thread which so successfully binds these is the likeability and realism of her heroines, and the sheer charm of the stories. We appreciate too the humour of the books, which ranges from the straightforward to the whimsical. Some of it is unintended perhaps—but for every blissfully amusing Arthur Marshall-type quotation, there are many realistic and wonderfully atmospheric descriptions or passages of dialogue which encapsulate the authentic mood of girls' pursuits of friendship, recognition of leadership, respect for learning and careers, and their other aspirations. It was a sad day for many of us when DFB wrote to Regina Glick in 1949, 'I can't write another book about Jane's—having already done nine which should be plenty.'

I'd like to say something about Dorita's life, but before doing so, can't resist some random reflections about her possible empathy or identification with one or two of her characters. There is a gorgeous moment in *Dimsie, Head Girl* when Dimsie discovers Jean Gordon 'making up poetry indoors' on a lovely day, and says disapprovingly, 'Fancy frowsting indoors on a day like this. Why don't you come out and read in the wood like the rest of us?' (It must have been *hell* to want to be alone at Jane's.) I often wonder if Jean, with her preoccupation with poetry and writing, is based on aspects of DFB herself? Certainly Jean's dereliction of duty as Head Girl because of her literary dreaming gives us a dramatic and moving story, and it might well be that DFB's path to maturity included dealing with the conflicting demands of her writing and her other (school and, later, family) responsibilities.

Then I also wonder how much of the real-life Dorita went into the fictional Miss Yorke. Contemplating that rather intense, dark-eyed portrait of DFB on the 1960s Brockhampton Press dustjacket which I mentioned earlier, I can't help comparing it with Miss Yorke's very keen glance which the Jane Willard girls were 'beginning to dread' in *The Senior Prefect*, and with her 'kindly dark eyes which … were also very penetrating' in *Dimsie Moves Up Again* (1922). Certainly, Miss Yorke is often the mouthpiece of thoughts and commentaries which one feels might well have come from DFB personally. What do we really know about Dorita's life? Eva Löfgren's meticulous researches have been tremendously helpful in providing us with a strong sense of her background, relationships and work. Until she undertook this, DFB, although a great influence on our lives, was a shadowy figure for many of us. We know now that she was born on 20 May 1885 in Palos in Spain, the daughter of Alexander Fairlie Bruce, a civil engineer, whose family travelled wherever his work took him. At one time he worked in India; Scotland was always 'home', but the family settled for a long time in Ealing when Alexander was involved in the building of the Staines Reservoir.

DFB's birth certificate gives her names as 'Dorotea Morris Fairlie Bruce', but it seems that she was always supposed to be 'Dorita'. As a child she began to write, and won a prize for a poem at the age of six. She later became a boarding-school girl, attending Clarence House School in Roehampton, and, when grown up, appears to have pursued no other career than writing. Although much concerned with this and her Guildry work, she put the needs of her family first (like so many women writers, then and now). DFB looked after her invalid mother and later her ageing father. Scotland was always apparently her 'paradise lost', and after her father's death, she returned to it, settling at Skelmorlie, close to Loch Shee (the Loch of the Fairies of her stories)—near where Dimsie, Pamela and Erica were supposed to have lived after their respective marriages. She died on 21 September 1970 at the age of eighty-five.

We glean snippets of information about DFB's interests and relationships from studying the dedications to her books, but she modestly never seems to have put on record anything about her personal life. Eva quotes from 'The Interview' (1935), whose source is unknown:

'So long as it really is your best—
that's what matters most.'

> She is so shy that she cannot, even after years of writing, bear another to touch or read her work until it is in the hands of her publishers. She has often thought of getting someone to type her work, which she writes in notebooks, but she has always held back and continued to do her own correcting and typing herself.

(There are surely here shades of Jean Gordon, who couldn't at one time bear the other Anti-Soppists or anyone else to see her 'scribblings'.)

When authors are as retiring as DFB appears to have been, we are, of course, dependent on their families, friends and associates for biographical information and comment. I am very grateful to Vivien Northcote, who shared memories of her great-aunt at a meeting of the Children's Books History Society to mark Dorita's centenary in May 1985, at which Eva and I also spoke. Vivien said that DFB was 'like a third grandmother' to her. Dorita had in fact largely looked after Vivien's mother, Jean Hornby, when Jean's mother became a widow early in life and had to go out to work. In fact, some episodes in the books are drawn from Jean's schooldays. Apparently the cosmetics and corsets sections from *Dimsie Intervenes* derive from an adventure of Jean's which got her into some trouble at school, so Dorita was rather admonitory about this in the book.

Vivien stressed that her great-aunt always made her feel wanted and cared for. She had very deep religious faith, and a Scottish Presbyterian background. This informed everything she thought and wrote. Although she rarely wrote overtly about religion, deep Christian principles lay behind her assessments of all situations, and the relationships between characters in her stories. Vivien said, 'Aunt DB taught Christianity in that sense. Everything I know about loyalty and integrity comes from her. Sadly, although by today's standards many would say she was straitlaced, she stood for something that we've lost, not for something that we have been liberated from.' Vivien felt that DFB would be very upset about what is happening in some children's books and in life today, with falling standards and materialism everywhere. She stressed Dorita's love for animals and her warmth and sincerity. Apparently she had been a vast reader of Edwardian novels and a good

Nancy striking out

seamstress (Vivien still possesses a tapestry screen made by DFB). A very private person, she left no letters when she died, and, though having strong familial feelings, she never married. (Vivien thought there might have been a boyfriend who was lost in the First World War—but admits there is no hard evidence of this.)

Her sense of family cohesion and continuity is exemplified by the fact that 'when writing, Aunt DB always liked to wear her mother's engagement ring'. Her routine, when at Ealing and looking after her parents, was to supervise the housekeeping and go to the shops in the morning: then she would lunch with her family, and write throughout every afternoon (except on Sundays). She did her own typing, but had maids to help with the housework. Vivien said, 'I am most grateful of all to her for giving me faith in God—and in myself and my identity as part of this nature, which was very important to her.' Dorita's unashamed patriotism was not just for Scotland but for Britain as a whole. Nevertheless, I asked Vivien if DFB had a Scottish accent, and she said, 'Just a slight lilt; possibly slight because she spent so much of her childhood away from Scotland.'

Of all the writers in the genre, it is Dorita who celebrates the beauties of Scotland, and creates heroines of distinction from its terrains and traditions.

Happily these are also universally appealing, and it is good that the current Girls Gone By reprints are giving readers a chance to discover (or to re-savour) the wide range of Dorita's books.

# A LONG-LASTING LITERARY LOVE

I was asked to write about *That Boarding-School Girl* after I had, at a recent conference on girls' fiction, declared that it was my favourite book in the genre. I am more than glad to do so because this has plunged me into an avid re-reading of DFB's stories.

Before getting down to why I am so partial to this particular book, I should like to make one or two general comments. I have been privileged to write and broadcast about Dorita Fairlie Bruce on one or two occasions, although there were times when I despaired of any widespread interest in her work. For example, when she died in 1970, I could find no obituaries other than five or six not entirely accurate short lines in the *Glasgow Herald*.

I had written a feature on her for *Twentieth-Century Children's Writers* in 1979 and for the *Birmingham Post* in 1981, but few newspaper or magazine editors then wanted appraisals of her books and their influence on readers. During her centenary year (1985), I was able to choose one of her 'Dimsie' stories for BBC radio's 'Storytime', to speak about her for Radio Scotland and to contribute a longish illustrated feature on her to *The Scotsman*. Her centenary was also celebrated by a Children's Books History Society meeting at which Vivien Northcote, Eva Löfgren and I spoke, and the publication of the Goodchild volume of short stories, *Dimsie Takes Charge*.

Stella Waring, with *Serendipity* magazine, Sheila Ray, Monica Godfrey, and, of course, Eva Löfgren in her fascinating *Schoolmates of the long-ago*, have made valuable contributions to the canon of DFB appreciation and assessment. Three of her books, *The Bees of Drumwhinnie*, *The Debatable Mound*, and *The Serendipity Shop*, were broadcast on Scottish radio's Children's Hour, respectively in 1953, 1954 and 1955, but it seems impossible to find tape-recordings of them.

Now—at last—back to Nancy and *That Boarding-School Girl*. I first read it when I was eight, and an imaginative aunt by marriage (whom I had never actually met) sent it to me as a Christmas present. I had, of course, read many other school tales including one or two 'Dimsies' which I had liked very much, but the exploits of Nancy, Desda and Angela seemed especially real to me. I felt immediately that I was there with them: this was probably because of the book's day-school setting, for, like so many 1930s readers of school stories, I was a day-girl at a state school, even though I cherished fantasies of going away to boarding-school.

With adult hindsight I can see that *That Boarding-School Girl* is rather patchy (as indeed is the whole 'Nancy' series, which seems to have been written out of sequence, with several afterthoughts and 'prequels' on the author's part), but Nancy's spirited personality always compels and charms me. Unlike Dimsie, she is never too good to be true. Talented at music and sports, loyal, candid, independent, and extremely engaging, she can also be stubborn and headstrong (thereby ensuring my empathy!) and very much in need of the support and advice that Desda, 'the peacemaker', so often provides.

THAT BOARDING
SCHOOL GIRL
*By Dorita Fairlie Bruce*

LONDON·HUMPHREY MILFORD
OXFORD UNIVERSITY PRESS

Their friendship should surely be a model for real-life schoolgirl relationships. There is Nancy's no-nonsense appreciation of her chum: 'Of course you're an awful idiot in heaps of ways, Desda, but you're an extraordinarily decent idiot. Why are you always doing things for other people?' And, when things look dark indeed for Nancy, after news of her expulsion from St Bride's reaches Maudsley, Desda's response is a shining light of loyalty: 'No, don't. Don't tell me a thing! Do you suppose I need to be told it was all a mistake and somebody else's fault? If you were to talk till you were black in the face, Nancy, I'd never believe you'd done anything mean or sneaky!'

As well as celebrating schoolgirl friendship, *That Boarding-School Girl* catches the mood of schoolgirl rivalries in the long-running feud between Maudsley Grammar School and Larkiston House. Satisfyingly, Nancy and Desda have sufficient moral courage to go against the stream and to make a chum of Angela Stephens, who attends the hated rival school, and DFB skilfully handles the theme of enmity between the Mudlets and the Skylarks becoming too intense and getting out of hand, and of the positive influence of the Guildry on girls of both schools. (I was an escapist eight-year-old, preferring to spend my few weekly pennies on tap-dancing classes rather than invest them in the character-building activities of the organised youth movements. Nevertheless I enjoyed reading about these.)

The poised, enigmatic, and highly individualistic Charity Sheringham adds spice and fascination to the story, as do all the members of the Blackett family with their thespian background and colourful Shakespearean names. It is hard to analyse just what makes this book appeal so much to me. I have to come back again to DFB's flair for making the reader feel that she is really there with her heroines and not just an offstage bystander. A factor in this is the strong sense of continuity that flows from descriptions of Nancy and Desda conversing while changing their shoes in the cloakroom, slipping on their coats, going off to get their bikes, and then riding these home: 'Nancy cleared her throat abruptly and stared straight ahead over her handlebars … "You're a ripping pal to have, Des, though I'm not very good at saying so …"'

I'm afraid that my assessment of *That Boarding-School Girl* is, like its own text, rather patchy. But it firmly remains my favourite, and without any hesitation I can attest that it is a brilliant picture of a proud, rather self-concerned girl learning the true value of friendship and of team-spiritedness:

Nancy lay back on the short turf of the lawn, with her arms beneath her head, and gazed dreamily at the perfect blue sky above them.

'Yes, but it will be all for the school, of course,' she said. 'If you are at all decent … you don't care about winning honour and glory just for yourself—you want it for your school. And afterwards, when you've grown up and left school, you want it for your country.'

Two random thoughts triggered by re-reading *That Boarding-School Girl*: first, Nancy's father, Alex, is described as being 'abnormally proud' and irked that Nancy wasn't 'as much a success as he knew she could be'. Dorita Fairlie Bruce's father was called Alexander: is there an autobiographical hint here? Secondly, in her early days at Maudsley, Nancy puts her foot in things by condemning rounders, which is played there, as 'rather a kid's game'. Of course, her schoolmates are strong in its defence—rather in the spirit of Miss Yorke when she introduced the game to the Jane Willard. And one of DFB's earliest stories (possibly the first ever published—in the July 1909 *Girl's Realm*) was 'The Rounders Match'. Did she have a special partiality for this game? I may never know the answers to these two questions, but I do know that, even after all these years, I can always rely on *That Boarding-School Girl* for an entertaining and uplifting read.

# ELINOR AT HER VERY BEST

So much has been written about Elinor Brent-Dyer's Chalet School stories that perhaps there is little I can add in the way of commentary and appreciation. I am no expert in Chalet School lore, and the books—despite their excellence and appeal—were not my first childhood favourites among school stories.

Of course, I was intrigued by the glamour of the international trilingual school and the charm of its setting—those mist-swathed mountains and the lake 'alive with dancing shadows'! But possibly for me the gentians, marguerites and alpenroses had a slightly unreal, Technicolor quality. Also, the many dramatic happenings of the series seemed somewhat over the top to my young imagination, which, I realise, was more prosaic then than now. As a child from a very ordinary south east London home, I found it hard to empathise with girls falling into icy rivers or getting stranded on mountainsides, and with Jo Bettany saving so many lives.

For example, just to remind everyone, *The Princess of the Chalet School* (1927) provided two kidnapping attempts, and that outsize thunderstorm which breaks every window in the valley and manages to set the school's playing fields on fire. The school buildings are saved from total destruction only by an equally violent hailstorm which apparently covers everything with five inches of hailstones in as many minutes! All extremely exciting, but a touch unbelievable, making it difficult for me to identify with Elinor's schoolgirl characters—even though they were extremely engaging, *and* they wore brown tunics with flame-coloured ties, very like the uniform of the real-life school which I was attending! (Our blouses weren't shantung, though: only rather coarse white cotton.)

However, even when I read Elinor's books as a child, I sensed that with *The Chalet School in Exile* (1940) she could claim a long-lasting and very special place in juvenile literature. My adult re-readings and appraisal have confirmed this, but in this chapter I'm especially concerned to convey the book's impact on myself, and others like me, as young teenagers reading it during the Second World War, not long after it was written.

By many standards *Exile* is an unusual book. It was one of the first fictional studies to point out the horrors of Nazism and the disruptions which this pernicious regime would, indirectly as well as directly, inflict upon so many people's lives. Europe's boundaries were to be ridden over roughshod and cruelly dismantled; worse still, its long-established Christian and democratic values were threatened with extinction. All this, of course, was strong stuff for children's books in the early 1940s, but Elinor did not pull her punches. As early as 1933, in *The Exploits of the Chalet Girls*, she had already hinted at the incipient dangers of Nazi policies when she drew attention to the spirit of the arising 'Young Germany' from which the Chalet School's new pupil, Thekla von Stift, should be protected.

With her knowledge and love of Austria, Elinor must have viewed with great sadness and apprehension the growth there of Nazi influence between 1933, when Hitler came

THE
CHALET SCHOOL
IN EXILE

ELINOR MARY BRENT-DYER

to power in Germany, and the Anschluss in 1938 when Austria formally became (to use Elinor's own description) 'merely a province of the Greater [German] Reich'.

By the time *The Chalet School in Exile* was published Britain was at war with Germany. It was then, naturally, easier than in peacetime for an author to be outspoken about Hitler's racial policies, but, nevertheless, *Exile* achieved distinction for containing one of the first accounts of Nazi Jew-baiting to appear in children's literature. Actually the very first mention was possibly Richmal Crompton's *William and the Nasties*, published in the *Happy Mag* in July 1934 and later in the book *William the Detective* in 1935. William and his gang, the Outlaws, temporarily assume the roles of Fascists—the 'Nasties'—with William as their dictator-leader, *Him* Hitler. (He can't accept 'Herr' because it sounds feminine!) In Nazi style they decide to use force to eject Mr Isaacs, the Jewish sweet-shop owner, from his premises and to take over his stock. However, their plans go awry and they end up by preventing his shop from being burgled by another party. They become heroes in Mr Isaac's eyes and, needless to say, are rewarded with lavish presents of sweets. This was, for Richmal Crompton, a surprisingly tasteless incident, hardly comparable with the Jewish persecution episode in *Exile*.

Elinor's account was certainly hard-hitting. The persecution of the old Jewish jeweller, and in contrast, in the same book, the establishment of the life-affirming Chalet School Peace League, had so great an impact on me as a young reader that I have carried these images with me from 1940 to the present day.

Another absolutely indelible vignette from *Exile* is, of course, Miss Wilson's sudden and total change of hair colour after she and the girls were caught up in the Herr Goldmann episode:

> 'Miss Wilson! Your *hair*!' [Jo] gasped.
> 'My hair?' Miss Wilson lifted a strand of the curly mop still flowing about her, and now the other girls were all staring at her with the same expression of stupefaction. As she saw her hair, she ceased to wonder. It was snow-white!

This seemed entirely credible to me. Early in the war I had collapsed during a shopping expedition with the pain of what turned out to be acute appendicitis. Rushed off to hospital for immediate surgery, before regaining consciousness after the anaesthetic I apparently displayed symptoms of scarlet fever, which was then regarded as an extremely serious illness. I was removed to a different hospital where I had to be isolated for several weeks—no visitors were allowed because of the danger of infection. When eventually my mother came to take me home, I was astounded to see that what I remembered as her lovely black hair was then *very* heavily streaked with white. She attributed this to the shock of my illness, accentuated perhaps by general 'Home Front' wartime stress. So Miss Wilson's transformation of hair colouring, although dramatic, rang true for me.

In view of what I wrote at the beginning of this chapter about my inability to believe in many of the Chalet schoolgirls' exciting exploits, it is rather strange that the book in the series to strike the strongest chord in me should be *Exile*, which is, of course, a highly suspenseful drama with much emphasis on spies and spy-catching. Some readers now might consider this to be unrealistic. However, growing up in Britain in the early 1940s, schoolgirls—like all members of the civilian population—were tremendously aware that there might be enemy agents in our midst. On hoardings and in notices in newspapers and magazines, the slogan 'Walls Have Ears' constantly alerted us to the fact that spies might overhear our conversations with friends and family on buses and trains, in shops or the workplace. Even a humble schoolgirl might inadvertently, by the 'careless talk' we were so often warned against, provide scraps of information for the listening enemy about troop movements (brothers or fathers being posted overseas, etc), or targets which had been hit during air-raids, and so on. So when I read *Exile*, Frau and Hermann Eisen's trailing of Joey and Co, which Elinor uses to good effect, seemed only too believable.

To quote Charles Dickens, writing about a different period in *A Tale of Two Cities*, the years of the Second World War were 'the best of times [and] the worst of times'. That they were the worst needs little definition—people suffered bombing, bereavement, pain and endless anxiety, as well as shortages of food, fuel, clothes and so many everyday necessities. There was also, for the men and women in the services, terrible danger and often the need to endure conditions of great hardship. For many civilians, in factories and elsewhere, there were long hours of grindingly hard work.

But yes—it *was* the best of times too. We saw people from every sphere of life giving their best, working together and caring for each other. (There *were* 'spivs' and profiteers but they were comparatively few.) Despite recurring bad news from the fighting fronts, despite hideous uncertainties, despite tedium and restrictions, we lived in an overall atmosphere of hope and optimism. The press, the 'wireless' and many popular songs like 'It's a Lovely Day Tomorrow' expressed the belief that, out of this ghastly war, good would surely come.

One feels certain that Elinor must have been acutely sensitive to all this, and she conveys the essence of it in *The Chalet School in Exile*. Jo, on whom the vitality of so many of the stories rests, is frequently expressive of the overall mood. At the beginning of the book she is described as a tall 'wiry young person', already an established author but psychologically 'not so very far removed from the Head Girl' she had been in her last four terms as a Chalet School pupil. Her physical frailty has long gone, her impishness occasionally surfaces, but she is generally a rock-steady 'popular, wise' and understanding character. Her qualities, like those of Robin and others, are all to be put to the test as the narrative proceeds.

Although no longer a regular inmate, Jo's influence on the school remains strong; and because this book sees her married to Dr Jack Maynard and then becoming the mother of triplets, she is—even more than usually—a life-enhancing role-model.

The action of *Exile* begins before the Anschluss, but already rumours of a German take-over of Austria are rife. Jem Russell in particular is so disturbed that he urges Madge to agree to move the school up to the Sonnalpe as soon as possible, where the pupils and the female staff will have male protection should Gestapo agents—already very active in Austria—start to make trouble. Fortunately Jem has already bought a vacant hotel building. He had originally intended to use this for enlarging the Sanatorium, but now, of course, it can be adapted to house the school.

When Jo hears of the removal plan, she characteristically makes the best of it, even succumbing to the initial excitement which was often felt by children and young people who did not fully appreciate the long-reaching and horrific effects of war and political disruptions:

> Jo turned to leave the room … 'You know, this is the most thrilling event I've ever known. I'd no idea we were going to be mixed up in such a penny-dreadful, shilling-shocker thing as the secret police of *any* country! I ought to get a book out this!' She fled, laughing.

However, soon after the June 1938 Anschluss, Jo becomes aware of the seriousness of the situation, with pupils of various nationalities being withdrawn by anxious parents, and, more menacingly, Austrian and German pupils being forced to leave to attend 'Nazi schools'.

Because of these very sad happenings, the girls form the Chalet School Peace League, which Jo endorses, agreeing to write inviting some 'old girls' to join too. The League's main aim is 'to promote peace between all our countries'. Jo takes charge of the document recording the oath and statement of intent which all the girls have signed. Because many of them are Austrian or German it is, of course, essential to ensure that this document never falls into Nazi hands. The importance of the League, with its ideals of internationalism and tolerance, cannot be over-rated, and its concealment from the Gestapo, its temporary loss, and eventual retrieval form a symbolic thread of hope which runs through the book.

Jo becomes the mouthpiece for decency and tolerance when, soon after the foundation of the League, she offers reassurance to Gottfried Mensch. He, with Jack Maynard, is guiding Miss Wilson and the girls who were concerned in the Herr Goldmann incident over the mountains and out of Austria to safety. On the long, dreary trek Gottfried is deeply disturbed:

> … it went to his heart to see how white and weary they all looked. Most of them were only children, however plucky they might be. The young Austrian ground his teeth together as he thought how, in his proud, free land, things had come to such a pass that schoolgirls must be fleeing before the government.
>
> He said nothing of his thoughts, but Joey, with her queer gift of insight, guessed at them … she put her hand on his for a moment. 'Gottfried! It isn't *you*: it's the Nazis. We don't blame you; we don't even blame the German people for all this … We've lived in Tyrol too long for that!'

There are several further incidents in *Exile* of Chalet School staff and pupils making clear that the enemy is not ordinary Austrians or Germans but their Nazi leaders. Not surprisingly, this kind of understanding was not always prevalent in the real-life war, when because of Nazi ruthlessness men, women and children were suffering hardships and dangers. Nevertheless, there were many people in Britain who shared Jo's views. I remember vividly that, at my grammar school, our teachers went out of their way to suggest to us pupils that it was not the German people we were fighting but the terrible Nazi regime. To endorse this, they very deliberately exposed us to the beauties of German music and poetry. Again, Elinor had caught and expressed a significant attitude.

One of her greatest strengths as an author was her ability to write from the standpoint of adults, particularly the teachers, as well as to empathise with her young girl characters. There are several moments in *Exile* when we are particularly drawn to Madge Russell, the school's founding mother and constant friend. Fairly early in the story, when the staff and pupils have been moved up to the Sonnalpe, Madge—though deeply worried that her school may not survive—gives the girls an inspirational address:

> 'Now we are on the hills themselves, I tell you to keep your thoughts high … You, who are to be the mothers and teachers of a future generation, can do much by showing the children to come that divisions and false ambitions, cruelty and unfairness, must always make for misery.'

She ends by stressing the need for courage: 'So take this for your motto for the rest of this year: "Be brave!"'

Of course, a little later on after the girls have intervened to try to protect Herr Goldmann, it becomes evident that the school will have to uproot more drastically and leave the beloved Tyrol, because Gestapo agents, now alerted to the challenge of the school's liberalism, are on the warpath.

A representative from the British Consulate warns Madge and Jem that the school will almost certainly have to close. Madge tearfully protests:

'It's *my* School, Jem. I built it up from nothing, and though it's I who say it, it's a good School, and it's done good work. Must I finish it just because a set of men have gone quite mad?'

However, she has to accept the situation and with a reflowering of optimism decides to move the Chalet School to Guernsey.

When eventually it is resettled there, it is realised that war is looming and there is to be no island idyll. The headmistress, Miss Annersley, talks to the girls about the 'terrible forces of evil abroad in the world' and reminds them of the Chalet School Peace League: 'I want to make that League a living thing. Don't be carried away by bitter feeling. If war should come, remember that to many of those whom we must call the enemy it is as hateful as it is to us.'

The school has now been reduced from 211 to 52 girls. There is very real concern for the Austrian and German girls who have been forced to stay in their own countries and to conform to Nazi regimes, and Elinor does not fight shy of writing about the terrors of torture and concentration camps which some relatives of the Chalet School girls might well be facing.

The spy theme re-emerges when a new girl, Gertrude Beck, joins the Chalet School. She claims to be English, but Robin feels that her speech 'cadence' is distinctly unBritish. When Gertrude probes for information about Austrian and German former pupils, she is suspected of being a spy by Robin, Polly and Lorenz. Surprisingly, however, in view of the school's past history, Miss Annersley dismisses the girls' suspicions as 'the usual spy-fever we always get in wars'.

THE CHALET SCHOOL GOES TO IT

ELINOR M. BRENT-DYER

Gertrude Beck (real name Gertrud Becker) *does* of course turn out to be a Nazi spy. But she becomes more and more reluctant to carry out her beastly activities as she begins to succumb to the wholesome attitudes and influence of her fellow pupils. Elinor paints a strong picture of a girl in conflict and her eventual touching response to goodness and tolerance. This was moving as well as stirring stuff to English girl readers in the early part of the war.

I hope that I've managed to convey that for me, a schoolgirl in the 1940s, *The Chalet School in Exile* was astoundingly rich in haunting images. Nothing in my previous reading, for example, had quite the impact and immediacy of the descriptions of Herr Goldmann's persecution. There is the horror of the brutality of the rabble; then the truly touching picture of Robin, the delicate schoolgirl, rushing to his aid, followed by Jo and the other girls. This is perhaps another example of the best and worst of times. The stark ugliness and cruelty of the crowd represents the worst, while the courage of Robin, Joey and Co, 'Bill', and the priest, Vater Johann, who helps them at risk of his own life, represents the best. However, Elinor does not leave readers with a rose-tinted version of wartime death and loss. Despite the courageous rescue attempt by the girls and the priest, we learn that Herr Goldmann and his wife were subsequently killed, as was Vater Johann for his part in helping them escape.

On an emotional par with this episode is an encounter towards the end of the book. Joey visits Maria Marani, the school's current Head Girl, who is in the sanatorium having 'collapsed with something very like a nervous breakdown'. For a long time Maria's life has been overhung with sadness because her father is in the hands of the Nazis. She does not know what he might be suffering or whether he is alive or dead. (In fact, like Herr Goldmann, Herr Marani is not miraculously rescued. It is only his ashes that are recovered for his family. Very few children's authors of the time would have tackled so uncompromisingly the hideous realities of Nazi policies.) Maria's nervous collapse comes after she and some of the other Chalet girls have rescued two German flyers from the flaming wreck of their crashed plane. The shock of the burns she received then, the 'long-drawn agony of uncertainty about her father' and the knowledge that 'she dared not return to her own country as long as the present régime remained in power' completely overwhelm Maria.

Jo finds her in bed in a darkened room, rigid, bruised and bandaged, and hardly able to speak above a whisper. With touching sensitivity Jo decides not to try to converse with Maria but to sing for her. She does so—and, as the spell of her voice, 'sweet and full of tears', singing favourite hymns, floods over Maria, 'the awful rigidity' begins to pass and 'silent tears' roll down her cheeks. The healing process is beginning.

Soon afterwards there are several joyful happenings as the story reaches its ending. Jack, now in the army, returns on leave, and there are other happy reunions—not least the ecstatic return to Jo of her much-loved St Bernard dog, Rufus, whom she feared she had lost for ever.

Of course, almost everyone who has ever read *The Chalet School in Exile* has done so with the hindsight knowledge that the girls' stay in Guernsey was to be curtailed as the German army's advance through France relentlessly progressed and threatened the Channel Islands. This knowledge adds to the poignancy and power of the book which, in my opinion, is the finest and certainly the most memorable in the whole saga.

It is, in a sense, a goodbye to innocence for the inmates of the Chalet School—and, in the 1940s, for its young readers and admirers. It does, however, leave them with something else: a belief in the unquenchable spirit of people from all walks of life and in the power of decency and courage.

Elinor at her very best, indeed!

# ENID BLYTON AND THE WORLD OF SCHOOL

I was always an avid and omnivorous reader, but, surprisingly, Enid Blyton's wide-ranging stories seem to have had little influence on my childhood. Her books, like *Adventures of the Wishing Chair* (1937), *The Enchanted Wood* (1939), and *The Magic Faraway Tree* (1943), and her innumerable tales about dolls and teddies and gollies and other toys coming to life, as well as her chronicles of the exploits of fairies, brownies, elves and goblins, passed me by. So too did her nature, adventure, and detective series, and even her school stories, which began to appear from 1940. At that time I was twelve years old and, though still relishing certain books by DFB, EJO and EBD, I was reading adult novels and starting to feel that I had grown out of children's tales. (How astoundingly wrong that judgement proved later to be!) I *did* occasionally and covertly dip into issues of *Sunny Stories* on newsagents' shelves but felt quite guilty about being attracted to the kiddy-like atmosphere of these engaging and beautifully illustrated little magazines.

However, before now considering Enid's 'Whyteleafe', 'St Clare's' and 'Malory Towers' school series, I should explain that her work actually *had* impacted upon my childhood, although at the time I had not realised this. In fact she had made me a queen for a few days—and a fairy queen at that—when I had the immense fulfilment of acting this role in our infant school Christmas play. I can still recall the thrill I felt seventy-three years ago at being decked out completely in pink and silver. My mother had bought me silver shoes (a blissful dream come true) and made me a pink crepe-paper dress, a wand—painted silver—and tinsel-edged pink crepe-paper wings.

For me and my school friends the play was the high spot of the run-up to Christmas. Its magic stayed with me for years, indeed decades, afterwards and, as an adult, I would often wonder what it had been called and who wrote it. When my interest in old and new children's fiction developed, and I asked other enthusiasts if they knew anything about this play and its authorship, no-one could provide answers. However, I eventually came across Enid Blyton's *The Teacher's Treasury* (1926), and there, to my utter delight, I found *my* play. It is *The Christmas Fairies*, a three-act play with a simple plot which is for ever etched on my mind as wonderfully warm and glowing.

When, belatedly, I realised that I had Enid to thank for those memorable childhood moments, I was prompted to look seriously at her books, and I then discovered that, despite dismissal by some critics, librarians, and teachers, she was a writer of remarkable creativity as well as something of a pioneer in her tales of nature and conservation—and in her school stories.

Enid's own childhood is to an extent reflected in her writings. She says in *The Story of My Life* (1952), 'I loved school, every minute of it. I loved learning. Nothing was dull to me …' She was, we gather, 'top' at 'essay competition and story-writing', and there is no doubt that her capacity to hold an audience with a great tale was manifest very early. Throughout her schooldays she continued to produce stories and poems,

and in her mid-teens she won a national poetry competition and had the satisfaction of seeing her verses professionally published. As a child she read widely and voraciously, but the books she fondly remembers in her autobiographical account are largely classic stories. Schoolgirl fiction is not mentioned as an influence on her life and work, although she *does* reflect that in Louisa Alcott's *Little Women* 'the children were real children', and one wonders if tomboy Jo was an inspiration not only for Enid's tomboy character George in the 'Famous Five' series but possibly also for some of her liveliest schoolgirl heroines. Significantly, she couldn't bear Grimm's *Fairy Tales*, which she found 'cruel and frightening', commenting that 'ordinary children don't like cruel or too-sad tales'. This feeling, coupled with an emotional deprivation which occurred during her early teens, might well have influenced the deliberately light-hearted overall atmosphere of her school and other stories. These, as is well known, have been called bland and superficial by some critics. When Enid was thirteen her adored father, Thomas, without warning walked out of the family home and left his wife, daughter and two sons for good. He and Enid had always been tremendously close and he had vigorously encouraged her writing and musical studies. Together they had taken frequent nature walks through the woods and meadows around their home in Beckenham, which was then—in the first decade of the twentieth century—a very small town not much removed from a village. Enid was devastated by her father's sudden departure, even though he would still occasionally come and take her for walks or theatre visits.

Before and after Thomas's departure, Enid threw herself with gusto into games, lessons and other activities at St Christopher's, the Beckenham school which she attended from the age of ten. Her enthusiasm for school events seems similar to that shown by the heroines in her 'Whyteleafe', 'St Clare's' and 'Malory Towers' series, and, apparently, she based several fictional characters on St Christopher's girls and teachers. Also some events from her years there found expression in her stories.

She was a popular schoolgirl and at the age of sixteen became Head Girl, a position which she held for two years. Although she didn't use the name of St Christopher's for any of her main fictional schools, she sometimes mentioned it in the books (for example, when the St Clare's girls play a lacrosse match against a St Christopher's team). Interestingly, too, despite the fact that netball and hockey were by far the most popular winter games during Enid's schooldays and afterwards, the pupils at her three main fictional schools always played lacrosse—which was the regular game at St Christopher's. Incidentally, although she went on record as saying that she was not very good at games, she became the school's tennis champion and the captain of its lacrosse team.

Another aspect of her schooldays which influenced the books was her friendship with Mademoiselle Louise Bertraine, the St Christopher's French teacher who, when Enid was sixteen, took her on her first trip abroad to Annecy. Enid never forgot the excitements of the journey, and the light and colour of the lakes and mountains that she saw in France. Her friendship with Mademoiselle Bertraine continued for several years after her schooldays ended, and it seems that this mistress was the direct inspiration for 'Mam'zelle Abominable', the French teacher in the 'St Clare's' series, who inspired both awe and affection.

Other memories from Enid's own schooldays which provided stimulus for episodes

St Christopher's Lacrosse Team:
Enid is second from the right, top row.

in her books arose from her flair for practical jokes. She was the deviser of many exuberant tricks on her form-mates and teachers, using rubber- and tin-pointed pencils, artificial blots, and further trick-producing apparatus. In school story fashion, she and two close friends produced a magazine and created their own secret code in which they corresponded. All this, of course, was grist to the mill of Enid's eventual writing of school tales.

Decades after Enid left St Christopher's my daughter became a pupil there, and my husband did a spell as one of the school's governors. It was still, as in Enid's time, a very happy community with a strong Christian atmosphere, and emphasis on good relationships between staff and pupils, and between older and younger girls. There was a chair in the school hall which bore Enid's name (I've sat in it!). Let me hasten to add that her name was not carved into the chair amateurishly with a pen-nib; it was on a properly affixed and engraved plate. There was a St Christopher's custom that when a girl ended her years there she gave the school a leaving present. Apparently Enid donated a chair (possibly more than one). Like many other independent schools her *alma mater* was not always flush with money, so probably help with furnishings etc was sometimes appreciated. (Incidentally, after my daughter had left and gone to university, it was suggested to her that she might like to make a gift to the school of a copy of *You're a Brick, Angela!*, my first book. I was pleased about that, feeling that it very tenuously linked my writing with Enid's.)

When Enid's first full-length school story *The Naughtiest Girl in the School* was published in 1940, she was already a very well-established author, with teaching experience which seems to have helped her to develop great empathy with children. Her school adventures were written mainly in the 1940s and 50s. They appeared at a time when the boarding-school story generally was in decline, and it is to her credit that she was then able to infuse vitality into the genre. It can be argued that her school tales lack the depth provided in those of 'The Big Four' and other authors who first made their mark in the 1920s and 30s. However, Enid's style and zest made her books addictive to thousands of readers and now, some sixty years on, her school stories remain popular and still in print.

She knew always how to keep the action moving along briskly, but when, on the way, to linger temptingly on some of the much-loved trappings and treasures of the genre. For example, in a natural and straightforward way she conveyed the importance for her schoolgirl characters of food (especially of dormitory feasts), of animals (especially horses), and simple word-play, comic images and jokes. Slipped into all this is an unpretentious emphasis on moral values, although these pills are coated with the jam of lively and atmospheric exploits. With all this going for her stories, Enid helped to make her readers feel excited but safe and in control. She tried to give them the emotional stability and security which had eluded her after her father left home.

As well as her three main series, she wrote many short stories with school settings. Some featured boys, some focused on girls, and some had co-educational backgrounds. One of her best school tales for girls is 'The Cheat', a short story which originally appeared in *Enid Blyton's Treasury* in 1947, written after the 'Whyteleafe' and 'St Clare's' series had ended. This brilliantly shows how a schoolgirl, suffering badly from examination stress, is tempted to overcome her problems by cheating. Susan stumbles on the next day's examination papers in her form-mistress's study, and, in a long and restless night of inner conflict, tries to look up the answers. When morning comes her conscience has got the better of her: she is so appalled at having become a cheat that she is determined to answer the questions wrongly—even though this means she will fail to win the scholarship she yearns for. It turns out, however, that the exam papers of which she has had a preview are *not* those which are relevant to her form—so she is able, after all, to sit the examination and to do her very best. Of course this story has an extremely obvious moral, but it is so well written that from start to finish it grips the reader's attention. Several of Enid's other short school stories concentrate on heroines who are younger than those in her full-length books and whose adventures, therefore, are usually less compelling. The 'Whyteleafe' ('Naughtiest Girl') series from 1940 to 1945 was not only engaging but progressive. The school is co-educational—a forerunner, like her 1943 *Mischief at St Rollo's*, of the co-ed secondary schools which were to be established after the end of the Second World War.

Enid wrote *St Rollo's* as Mary Pollock, using the surname of her first husband. It is a short book, hardly even a novella, designed for younger children, and it doesn't fit into the mainstream school story genre. Michael and Janet, its leading brother and sister characters, are involved in exploits whose simplicity is akin to those experienced by the young heroes and heroines of some of Enid's adventure series. Girls at St Rollo's seem less active in their own interests than those at Whyteleafe, and the main initiators of events are boys, particularly Tom, the stereotypical iconoclastic 'worst boy in the school', and Michael. Whyteleafe is a much more mature co-educational establishment, with its own pupil parliament which plays an important role in setting and maintaining the school's customs, procedures and general ethos. This too presages 'pupil power' groups, which were features of several schools in the early 1950s.

Elizabeth Allen is a spoilt eleven-year-old when she first comes to Whyteleafe, and she makes up her mind to be so naughty that she'll soon be sent home. This emphasis on being 'naughty', of course, makes her appear much younger and far less responsible than the inmates of the Jane Willard, the Abbey or the Chalet School. Enid recognises this immaturity, and, throughout the three-book series, refers to Elizabeth as 'the little girl', which, I feel, is a distancing of the narrative view which might have been disconcerting to readers.

Elizabeth's first shock comes when she is interviewed by the two headmistresses, Miss Belle and Miss Best. (One wonders whether Enid introduced these two fictional characters as a tribute to those celebrated headmistresses of the 1850s, Miss Beale and Miss Buss!) Elizabeth tells them of her plan to behave so badly that she will be sent home, and is amazed when, instead of being angry with her, they both throw back their heads and laugh heartily. When she petulantly states that she doesn't care how they punish her they point out that they '… leave any naughty person to the rest of the children to deal with'.

Of course, Elizabeth finds that it's more fun to be a co-operative member of the community than to go against it, and she soon forms friendships, plays lacrosse for Whyteleafe with appropriate *esprit de corps*, and goes on to become a Monitor. The parliament, or School Meeting as it is called, strikes a responsible and progressive note throughout the series and adds considerably to its appeal.

Enid wrote the 'St Clare's' series in parallel with Elizabeth's adventures from 1941 to 1945. Its leading lights are the twin sisters, Pat and Isabel O'Sullivan, who have been 'top dogs' at their previous elitist school and who initially have difficulty settling into the robust and democratic St Clare's. However, it is not long before they are enjoying dormitory feasts, sports and games, and friendships and rivalries with the other girls. Memorable moments from the series are those in which the twins show compassion for girls less fortunate than themselves. When, for example, in *The Twins at St Clare's* (1941) they discover that their chronically hard-up form-mate Kathleen has been stealing, they go to the headmistress, Miss Theobald, to plead for her because they feel that '… Kathleen isn't an ordinary kind of thief—and if she gets branded as one, and sent away, she may really become one, and be spoilt for always'.

They are shown as always being on the side of the underdog. When sneaky Prudence denounces Carlotta, the dark, intense new girl, because she is 'a horrid, common, low-down little circus girl', the twins lead the other inmates in declaring that Carlotta's circus background—far from being something to look down on—is 'marvellous' and 'simply wonderful'.

Another episode which stands out is the twins' cousin Alison's 'crush' on the pretty but vain and flighty drama teacher, Miss Quentin. Enid perceptively conveys Alison's devastation when she discovers that her idol has feet of clay, and the way in which the girl manages to find new strength in herself to overcome her disillusionment.

Events in the Malory Towers saga (1946 to 1951) follow a similar pattern to the St Clare's stories, though possibly the friendships in it are explored in greater depth. The relationship between the arrogant Daphne and timid Mary-Lou is particularly moving, especially when it matures from a one-sided to a mutual friendship.

An amusing factor in both series is the ability of some of the teachers to turn the tables on their pupils by playing the kind of tricks which the girls normally inflict upon them! At Malory Towers Mam'zelle horrifies everyone with some absolutely ghastly trick teeth, while at St Clare's Miss Ellis leaves the classroom and shuts the girls in there after they have released a stink-ball.

The heroine who links the various exploits of the Malory Towers girls is the likeable and attractive Darrell Rivers. She moves up through the school and convincingly matures from a twelve-year-old to a responsible senior girl. She responds positively to the words of the headmistress, Miss Grayling, who, in *First Term at Malory Towers*, addresses the new girls and explains to them that success at Malory Towers means more than just academic achievements:

> 'One day you will leave school and go out into the world as young women. You should take with you eager minds, kind hearts, and a will to help. You should take with you a good understanding of many things, and a willingness to accept responsibility … I count as our successes those who learn to be good-hearted and kind, sensible and trustable, good, sound women the world can lean on …' The words were spoken so gravely and solemnly that Darrell hardly breathed. She immediately longed to be one of Malory Towers' successes.

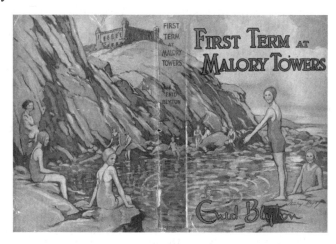

So—unlike the O'Sullivan twins—Darrell identifies with her school from the very start. There is in general a slightly more rounded-out feeling about the Malory Towers girls than the St Clare's inmates, possibly because Enid had honed her skills as a school story author with St Clare's and used these to greater effect in the 'Malory Towers' series.

However, in richness and depth of characterisation, and in descriptions of inside and outdoor settings, Malory Towers still falls short of the wonderfully developed worlds-in-microcosm which we find in the school sagas of EJO, DFB and several other writers who preceded Enid. The atmosphere at both Malory Towers and St Clare's is more bland: one feels that serious retribution for wrong-doing is less likely to be visited upon the girls there than on the pupils at Jane's and the Chalet and Abbey schools, who are expected to be seriously responsible for their actions. There *are* character reformations at all three of Enid's main schools, brought about by the influence of schoolmates and staff, and the girls are generally warm and kindly towards each other. But we do not find the same sustained intensity in the schoolgirl friendships, or the sense that these will be long-standing, surviving even beyond schooldays. Enid was not concerned with her characters growing up. Perhaps here we have hints of her fictionally recapitulating and clinging to the childhood innocence which she lost prematurely in real life when her father deserted his family.

She has to be credited for carrying the genre forward into the middle of the twentieth century and beyond. There was an indisputable modernity about her ideas, expressed at Whyteleafe through particular emphasis on the school parliament, and at St Clare's and Malory Towers in relaxed but effective disciplines. She tellingly used many stereotypical characters—swanky pupils like the American Zerelda at Malory Towers, who has to be cut down to size; those other non-conformist but appealingly mischievous foreign girls such as the French Claudine and her sister Antoinette at St Clare's; the bossy over-confident girl represented by Daphne at Malory Towers, and so on.

There is, however, about these and the more 'ordinary' characters a sense that they are not always fully fleshed out as individuals. Reading the books sequentially from start to finish one feels that virtually the same characters reappear in various years, just under different names. This, of course, is a weakness which probably irritates only critical adults and is unlikely to bother young readers who are caught up in the saga.

Another weakness is the lack of locational atmosphere, which is curious because in her adventure stories Enid had a flair for building this up, and also for establishing, when appropriate, a sense of *frisson* which we do not find in the school tales. She deliberately eschewed the most conventional trappings of excitement and suspense which earlier authors in the genre had harnessed: we don't, for example, stumble across secret passages and monkish treasure at her three schools, and even dramatic rescues from cliff-falls, drowning and other forms of death are rarely used.

Enid concentrates the action on and around friendships and rivalries, conformities and reformations—all well conveyed and convincing. The difference, for me, between her school stories and those of EJO, DFB, EBD, and the story-paper writers is that at Whyteleafe, St Clare's and Malory Towers we are *watching* events unfold and characters develop, while in stories by the best of the earlier authors we have that vital sense of *participating* in the action, the mischief, the drama and the friendships.

To end on a note of speculation—Darrell Rivers finishes her schooldays as Head Girl of Malory Towers, but although she makes it into the sixth form, the O'Sullivan twins' school life is cut off prematurely. In *Fifth Formers at St Clare's* (1945) it is announced that, in the following term when they'll go into the sixth, Pat and Isabel will be joint Head Girls. But, mysteriously, Enid did not complete the saga. The twins never came into their crowning Head Girl glory. One wonders why. It was not because their author had become tired of writing school stories, because in the year after the last 'St Clare's' book appeared, she had started the 'Malory Towers' series. We just have to be grateful that, even without this, we can savour the wealth of school stories which have flowed from Enid Blyton's vivid and colourful imagination and added sparkle to the lives of so many schoolgirl readers.

# THE SUPPORTING CAST

In the galaxy of twentieth-century girls' fiction writers there are the great stars (EJO, DFB, EBD and so on) who constantly receive our attention and affection. But, of course, they are not the only authors who enriched our childhoods: there were very many others whose books and short stories about school life we devoured with relish. I'd like to draw attention to four of these writers, whose works particularly appealed to me in between my bouts of reading about the Jane Willard and Maudsley, the Chalet School and the Abbey. None of these members of the supporting cast created series—had they done so their lights might have shone more brightly for readers.

## DOROTHEA MOORE

Like Bessie Marchant, Angela Brazil, and others who were writing at the start of the twentieth century, Dorothea Moore endeavoured to produce a more robust type of fiction than the unexciting domestic stories that had hitherto been staple reading matter for girls. Her books were popular for almost four decades and her range was wide. She contributed poems, plays, and well-structured short stories to several children's magazines, including *Little Folks* and the *Girl's Own Paper*, and to *Blackie's*, the *Oxford* and *British Girls'* annuals. The liveliness of her short stories, however, was not always conveyed in her novels, which, particularly after the 1920s, sometimes lacked style and inventiveness.

Some of her school stories feature rebellious characters, like the heroine of *Tenth at Trinder's*, who initially resist discipline and conformity but are nudged by staunch chums, admired prefects, and fearfully understanding headmistresses into acceptance of team-spiritedness and loyalty to the school. Dorothea Moore makes strong use of the customary alarms and accidents of the genre (girls rescuing schoolmates from burning, drowning, or literal cliff-hanging, etc). But she is at her best when describing lower-key aspects of school life, in a series of persuasive images of girls cycling to school in broad-brimmed felt hats and well-brushed blue serge gymslips, or changing into white frocks for 'exuberantly cooked' suppers, and dutifully awaiting their turns on bathroom rotas, and so on. These vignettes convey not only the rhythms of school routines but also a greater sense of period (the 1920s) than the author managed to achieve in her historical stories. *The Luck of Ledge Point* (1909), *Cecily's Highwayman* (1914), *In the Reign of the Red Cap* (1924), and several other of her historical novels lack this integral feeling for period, although with plenty of peripheral excitement and atmosphere they succeed at the romance level.

A Girl Guide Commissioner, Dorothea Moore made her most significant contribution to girls' fiction with *Terry the Girl Guide* in 1912. This was the first full-length Guiding novel to be published, and its authentic re-creation of the pioneering mood set a pattern that other authors were to follow for some thirty years. She produced colourful variations on the theme in several stories of teenage princesses from vaguely Ruritanian backgrounds, who were redeemed—either physically or psychologically—by contact with the idealism, resourcefulness, and grit of the typical British Girl Guide (*A Young Pretender* in 1924, *Brenda of Beech House* in 1927, etc). By 1930, however, she seemed at last to have exhausted Guiding as a story writing stimulus, and *Judy, Patrol Leader* (1930) is no more than a disappointing rehash of the ingredients that made her vigorous early books on the theme so memorable.

Many of her heroines experience engaging flashes of wry self-awareness, but the main characteristic of her stories is that they have an overall charm that has ensured their long-lasting appeal to girls—and to women who now read them nostalgically. In 2007 Girls Gone By republished her 1923 book *The Only Day-Girl* in their 'Fun in the Fourth' series.

## May Wynne

May Wynne's output for children was prodigious, and her style altered noticeably after the first decade of the twentieth century, when the more extroverted girls' school story had largely supplanted the domestic tale. Her first stories were more appropriate in mood and setting for mid-Victorian readers. In *Life's Object; or, Some Thoughts for Young Girls* (1899) she reprovingly insists on the girl's place being firmly in the home, and deplores the influence of sport which she considers destructive of 'the tender womanly woman': in *Mollie's Adventures* (1903) some of her child characters are engaged in making matchboxes in a London basement, in conditions of employment that were grisly even for Edwardian times. She was then writing moral tales in which pace and characterisation were sacrificed to narrative sermonising and admonition. Yet soon afterwards, in a spate of lively stories, she was plunging her adolescent heroines into hectic adventures on school hockey fields, and in Girl Guide camps in remote and surprisingly hazardous areas of the English countryside.

She carried into her stories for girls many of the elements which also proved successful in her adult romantic novels (kidnappings, strange encounters with gypsies, ancient houses, crumbling clock towers, abundances of secret passages, and so on). In complete contrast to her turgid early stories, pace became all important in her books during the 1920s and 30s. Many of her heroines went abroad, to get the better of Balkan brigands or jungle 'savages'. Her foreign adventures followed the tradition set by Bessie Marchant, in which no corner of the globe seemed too remote or dangerous to attract the British schoolgirl. And also like Bessie Marchant, May Wynne was especially partial to Canadian settings (*A Cousin from Canada, Comrades from Canada*, etc).

In addition to her numerous full-length books, she wrote short stories for periodicals like the *Girl's Own Paper* and *Little Folks*, and for several annuals.

## Ethel Talbot

For most of the 1920s and 30s Ethel Talbot was remarkably prolific as a writer of juvenile poetry and prose. She covered a wide range of themes and skilfully adapted her style for different age groups. As E Talbot she wrote several school and adventure stories for boys in *Chums*, *Little Folks*, and the *Boy's Own Paper*, but she is best known for her full-length school and Girl Guide novels for girls.

Her achievements are somewhat overshadowed by more celebrated writers of the period (Brazil, Bruce, etc) and she never succeeded in creating characters who became as popular as theirs. Nevertheless, she wrote with similar zest and, at times, rather more imagination. Many of her stories are spiced with touches of magic and fantasy that are associated with symbolic places or objectives, like the old, protective tower in *Carol's Second Term* (1928) and the shepherdess tapestry that dominates the school hall in *Patricia, Prefect* (1925). She is possibly the only 'schoolgirl' author who managed successfully to combine the disparate themes of down-to-earth school routines and elusive woodland magic ('The Girl Who Found the Fairies' in *Little Folks*, 1919).

In keeping with the traditions of the genre, her heroines are usually 'blade straight', 'gamesey', 'comradey', and passionately concerned with *esprit de corps* and the honour of their schools. (The greatest compliment one girl can 'gulp' out to another in her more emotional moments is 'You're Chads!' or 'You're Cyprians!') However, she also considers the problems of the talented, artistic individualist forced by the confines of school life into prolonged uncongenial associations with ordinary or 'philistine' girls. With more frankness than other school story writers, too, in *Patricia, Prefect* she explores in depth the even trickier subject of a really intense relationship between a senior and a junior girl.

Her Girl Guide stories contain the expected excitements and demonstrations of adolescent pluck—spy-spotting while picking sphagnum moss on the moors during the First World War, for example, in 'Luck' (*British Girls' Annual*, 1919). But as well as conveying the expansive spirit of the early days of the movement, she produced some entertaining vignettes of over-enthusiastic tenderfoots, whose approach to the business of Guiding was bizarrely removed from that of Baden-Powell.

Despite her versatility and occasionally challenging approach, Ethel Talbot is now remembered mainly for her conventional school stories about energetic chums who enjoy experiencing 'the extreme joy of aching muscles after a topping afternoon's hockey', and who wholesomely follow this up by dancing foxtrots and Charlestons to gramophone accompaniments in the gym!

CHRISTINE CHAUNDLER

Christine Chaundler was a colourful writer who, for several decades, contributed stories on school, Girl Guide, and fairy themes to many children's magazines and annuals, as well as producing full-length books. She was an editor of *Little Folks* from 1914 to 1917, and some of her most memorable works (*Meggy Makes Her Mark*, published in book form in 1928, *Jill of the Guides* in 1932, etc) were first published in that periodical. Her fairy poems and stories for younger children were refreshingly unsentimental, and as Peter Martin she also wrote stories for boys. She was best known during the 1920s and 30s, however, for her school stories. These were variations on classic themes of the genre established by Angela Brazil and developed by Dorita Fairlie Bruce. But

BRENDA OF BEECH HOUSE

*Dorothea Moore*

THE HONOUR OF THE SCHOOL

JAN AT ISLAND SCHOOL

BY ETHEL TALBOT

TRIUMPH SERIES

BUNTY OF THE BLACKBIRDS

*CHRISTINE CHAUNDLER*

Christine Chaundler failed to achieve a comparable degree of recognition—possibly because her characterisations were less acute, and because she never extended the adventures of any of her heroines beyond a single novel into a series.

She managed to inject a strong sense of realism into her books, even when exploiting vivid and dramatic situations. One of the most distinctive elements of her writing was the capacity to deal with the girl who finds herself suddenly against the tide of popular standards and opinion. She first used this theme persuasively in *Pat's Third Term* (1920) with a junior who refused to make the expected gestures of homage to the generally idolised Head Girl; she developed and refined it in *A Disgrace to the Fourth* (1923) and *Jill the Outsider* (1924), and, with considerable wit and style, in *The Chivalrous Fifth* (1927). This was an attack on the type of snobbery that was so often associated with traditional, elitist boarding-schools: a new girl, Jane, is tolerated rather than accepted because she has told her form-mates that her mother keeps a second-hand shop, but this turns out to be a Bond Street antique gallery, and Jane's mother is a Viscountess!

She wrote numerous stories that catered for the enormous enthusiasm that surrounded the early days of the Girl Guide movement. Here again, however, she was careful to steer clear of high-flown sentiment; her Girl Guides were not always the epitome of efficiency and preparedness that they were in stories by many other Guiding writers. In *Bunty of the Blackbirds* (1925), for example, one girl is shown as unable to light a campfire without setting the common alight, ripping her skirt from hem to waist, and burning a hole in her knickers. Similar uninflated realism was the keynote of her excellent 1919 series of *Little Folks* short stories, 'How We Won the War', in which the over-ambitious patriotic efforts of a family of children repeatedly and entertainingly misfire.

Christine Chaundler continued to produce inventive fiction well into the 1930s. Later, in the 1950s and 1960s, she concentrated on writing a series of informative, religious non-fiction books, and 're-tellings' for younger children. One of her earliest and most lively school stories, *The Right St John's* (1920), has recently been reprinted in the Girls Gone By 'Fun in the Fourth' series.

# PART THREE

# SCHOOL AND ADVENTURE STORIES IN MAGAZINES AND STORY-PAPERS

# THE HEYDAY OF THE *GIRL'S OWN PAPER*

The *Girl's Own Paper* is certainly one of the best-known periodicals of its kind and had a large following from the late nineteenth century through to its eventual demise in 1948. In its early years the GOP became known as *Woman's Magazine and Girl's Own Paper*, and many of its features were addressed to housewives and mothers. With volume 52 in 1931, the monthly magazine entitled *Girl's Own Paper* finally became a periodical for young girls rather than women, and adult female readers were diverted to *Woman's Magazine*. So the paper of the 1920s was successfully split into two independent publications.

The new *Girl's Own Paper* was a very attractive and vital affair, featuring many excellent illustrators and some of the most popular writers for girls of its period. Among the famous names who contributed stories and articles were Angela Brazil, Elsie Jeanette Oxenham, L M Montgomery, Baroness Orczy and Elinor Brent-Dyer. As well as items from these 'giants' of the girls' story genre, there were splendid short stories and serials from lesser known but addictive authors like Frances Cowen (who covered a wide range of fiction), Wallace Carr (a writer of historical tales), Sybil Haddock (who produced humorous episodes) and Dorothy Carter (whose forte was girls' flying stories).

*By Baroness Orczy*

The publishers, who no longer produced the paper as the Religious Tract Society but as the Lutterworth Press, gave girls good value for the sixpence (in old money) per month that the paper cost. As well as the fifty or so large pages that made up the basic paper, each issue contained twenty pages of GOP Club news, fashion and career chat, and colourful advertisements. The most striking and appealing feature every month was the full colour cover, which specialised in glowingly healthy outdoor girls engaged in brisk country walks, strolls with a wide variety of dogs (from dalmatians to dachshunds), or in skating, sledging, hockey, lacrosse, boating, tennis, cricket and almost any other sport one could think of. There were occasional double numbers, priced at one shilling, to celebrate Christmas.

Apart from its fictional content, the GOP ran many factual articles and photographs, which provide a wonderfully comprehensive commentary on what it was like to be an adolescent girl in the run-up to the Second World War, and actually during the period of hostilities. This is social history of the most immediate and effective kind, rarely to be found in the less ephemeral publications that are generally available to students in schools and universities today.

During the 1930s, the physical culture movements that were then in vogue cropped up constantly in the pages of the GOP. Youth Hostelling and hiking are favourite subjects,

By Elsie Jeanette Oxenham

Author of "Peggy and the Brotherhood," "Rosamund's Tuck-Shop," "Maidlin Bears the Torch," etc., etc.

by NOEL STREATFEILD

By DOROTHY CARTER
Author of "Mistress of the Air," and other popular stories

By DOROTHY CARTER, Author of "Flying Dawn"

By CONSTANCE M. EVANS
Author of "The Secret of the Brown Shed" and many other thrilling stories for girls

A series of school stories about a certain crowd of jolly Fifth Formers

"THE EDITOR REGRETS..."
by
DORIS A. POCOCK
Author of "TRIED AND TRUE" and numerous other stories

SONIA'S STOLEN DAYS
by
FRANCES COWEN

Sonia stared. It is doubtful if she knew there were such things as shillings-in-the-slot

WORRALS of the W.A.A.F.S.
BY
Capt. W. E. Johns

WORRALS CARRIES ON

by CAPTAIN W. E. JOHNS
A thrilling parachute descent over occupied France marks the beginning of new adventures

## The Robins Make Good

By ELINOR M. BRENT-DYER

*Author of "Feud in the Fifth Remove," etc., etc.*

and there are hints in abundance on how to improve one's breast- or butterfly-stroke when in the water, and one's bullying-off when out of it! Prunella Stack, the leader of the then amazingly popular Women's League of Health and Beauty, tells girl readers 'How to Keep Fit' in an article that is niftily illustrated by smiling exponents leaping about in smart white tops and black satin knickers.

The GOP, however, saved its wildest enthusiasm for the exploits of aviators, including feminine ones like Amy Johnson, Amelia Earhart and Jean Batten. The paper was not alone in this, of course; girl flyers, by their achievements and through their strength of character, were symbolic of the widening spheres of activity sought by women and girls. The media in general responded to them in prose, poetry and song, and especially to Britain's own Darling of the Skies—'Amy, Wonderful Amy'.

After Amy Johnson's Gipsy Moth solo flight from England to Australia in 1930, flying stories for girls began to catch on. The *Girl's Own Paper* echoed the popular mood and became airborne. In 1936, for example, it enthusiastically described the work of the first British air stewardess in an article entitled 'A New Career Open to Girls'. Then Dorothy Carter began to contribute stories of girl aviators like 'Lizzie of the Bush' and 'Mistress of the Air'. She was followed by Pauline Gower, who was one of the most successful women in aviation during the 1930s and 40s. She ran an air-taxi service before becoming commandant of women ferry pilots in the Air Transport Auxiliary, and a board member of the British Overseas Airways Corporation. She wrote a string of stories for the GOP about girls piloting their own biplanes, and later became its regular air correspondent.

The paper's ace contributor on flying matters, however, was not one of these enterprising women authors, but a male writer who had already created one cult figure ('Biggles') in the world of flight, and who was ready to produce another in the interests of Air Force recruitment during the Second World War. Captain W E Johns was a pilot in the Royal Flying Corps during the First World War, and a recruiting officer for the RAF during the second. When he wrote the serial 'Worrals of the W.A.A.F.S.' for the GOP in 1940, the women's branch of the service was in urgent need of recruits (when the serial was published in book form in 1941, the name was changed to *Worrals of the W.A.A.F.*). His eighteen-year-old heroine, Flight Officer Joan Worralson ('Worrals'), immediately caught the imagination of readers, and the WAAF soon received its full quota of recruits. (It is, of course, possible that the Olympian achievements of the Battle of Britain pilots also stirred girls into joining the WAAF, but Johns and Worrals must not be denied a large measure of credit.)

Worrals stories remained in great demand throughout the war, and several serials featuring her and 'Frecks', her engaging sidekick, were produced by Johns. The wartime issues of the GOP are intriguing for these items alone, even without the many other

*The World on Wings*

riches which they offer. Johns was, in a sense, pioneering with Worrals, whereas by 1940 the Biggles saga had become something of a sinecure. The girls' fiction market was new to him, and he put some of his most charismatic writing into his GOP stories, even spicing them up with lively feminist touches. Worrals starts off by ferrying battered Tiger Moths back to their makers for reconditioning; later she is parachuted into Nazi-occupied Europe to rescue British Army and Air Force personnel stranded there after the fall of France. She also grapples gamely with the Japanese enemy in the Far Eastern theatre of war.

She achieves the distinction of confronting the Gestapo, Middle Eastern gun-runners, and wild African tribes whilst always retaining her 'cool'—and her virginity! Engagingly—because Johns remembered that he was writing for girl teenagers—Worrals never lapses into obscenities or the consumption of strong liquor. After particularly nerve-shattering escapes from the enemy, for instance, she steadies herself, not with gaspers or gulps of whisky, but with chocolate or a few raisins.

Captain W E Johns became the hero of the *Girl's Own Paper* during the 1940s; his avuncular face smiled frequently from its pages, and for many issues he conducted its flying gossip column, 'The World on Wings—Between You and Me and the Joystick'. The wartime issues of the GOP featured extremely attractive cover pictures of girls in the various services. These, drawn by Mays, almost certainly encouraged recruitment.

Stories by Phyllis Cooper, Joan Verney and Frances Cowen dealt atmospherically

From *Mistress of the Air*
by Dorothy Carter

with bombing and the blackout, with evacuees, and with girls doing their bit on the Home Front on assembly lines, in servicemen's canteens or in Civil Defence. Fashions of the period are well represented. Schoolgirls wear knitted pixie-hoods and carry their gas masks in home-made leatherette shoulder bags; they are given tips on transforming their tired old gym tunics by making them look 'brand new' with boleros cut from discarded dresses. These were the days of 'Make Do and Mend', and the GOP took up the theme with a vengeance, its pages spattered with instructions on how to pep up fading garments with crochet, daisy-stitch embroidery or ric-rac braid trimmings.

There is no doubt that the 1930s and 40s represented a heyday for the *Girl's Own Paper*. Or perhaps it might be more accurate to think of it as an Indian summer, because—despite its appeal and vitality throughout the war years—decline and demise quickly followed. In 1948 it changed its name to *Heiress*, and no longer attempted to cater for schoolgirls and adolescents, but for young women. It became a tired and watered-down women's magazine, without sufficient romance of the colourful kind to attract readers. *Heiress* finally ceased publication in 1955. Few book enthusiasts now take any interest in it; but the *Girl's Own Paper* remains very much in demand.

# THE CLIFF HOUSE PAPERS

'Cliff House was a blaze of light. From the windows the lights shone far
out over the shadowed sea …'

This quotation is actually the first ever reference to Cliff House: it came in the
Frank Richards story 'The School Dance' in the *Magnet* of 27 March 1909.
Almost a hundred years on, the school and its ethos still glow brightly for
many of us. As the saga unfolded in the 1920s and 30s in the *School Friend* and
*Schoolgirl*, the exploits of its inmates, expressed in colourful language, became more
and more intriguing to young readers. For example, when tomboy Clara Trevlyn
remarked 'they stung me fearfully for the new hockey stick, but it's a real ripper', her
fans entered wholeheartedly into her mood of exhilaration. Equally, they could be
plunged into despair when she or others of the Cliff House chummery were
misunderstood, cheated or frustrated.

Bessie Bunter, Barbara Redfern ('Babs'), Mabel Lynn ('Mabs'), Marjorie Hazeldene,
Clara Trevlyn and their form-mates starred in the first issue on 7 May 1919 of the
*School Friend*. It is interesting that men as well as women now collect the Cliff House
papers, which may be linked to the fact that the school kicked off in one of the most
popular boys' papers of all time. Although the girls were only minor characters in this,
they must obviously have appealed strongly to readers, because Frank Richards kept
bringing them into the stories.

When the editors of Lord Northcliffe's juvenile papers realised that girls were buying
and wallowing in the *Magnet* as avidly as boys, they launched a girls' paper on similar

The Cliff House girls in the Edwardian setting of the early *Magnet* (left) were
sometimes precious or snooty. By the 1930s, in the *Schoolgirl*, they had become
typical schoolgirls of their period, and role-models for many readers.

lines, featuring Cliff House—which at that time seemed all set to become a feminised Greyfriars, with Bessie and her chums developing into skirted versions of Billy Bunter and Harry Wharton and Co. Frank Richards was asked to write the long 'Cliff House' tales for the *School Friend*, which he seems to have done with some relish (although he was also at the time writing a 20,000-word story every week for both the *Magnet* and the *Gem*, and another of 5,000 words for the *Boys' Friend*). He wrote his girls' stories as Hilda Richards, and the *School Friend* got off to a great start. It was the first truly schoolgirlish popular paper to be published in Britain—earlier magazines like the *Girls' Friend* and the *Girl's Own Paper* were, despite their names, designed for young women rather than children or adolescents.

With its striking red, white and blue cover the *School Friend* had a lively, inviting look. It measured 7½ x 10½ inches, and for 1½d a week offered a jolly good read of thousands of words of absorbing fiction. School stories for girls had become popular in the previous decade, especially through the hardback books of Angela Brazil; there was a new feeling of freedom for girls after the 1914–18 war (in which so many women had done 'men's jobs', and helped to establish the pattern of girls doing exciting and not merely domestic things).

In the early *School Friend* stories, Frank Richards adeptly fleshed out the skeletal Cliff House that he had brought into the *Magnet*. The buildings became more defined, and so did the denizens. The sweet but strong Marjorie Hazeldene (to whom both Harry Wharton and Bob Cherry had lost their hearts!) was already well established as a character; so too was her wonderfully robust tomboy chum, Clara Trevlyn, and Bessie, who was just as fat, gluttonous, conceited, fibbing and comically obnoxious as her brother, Billy Bunter of Greyfriars. The author also rounded out adult characters who had first appeared in the *Magnet*—like Miss Penelope Primrose, MA (the clever, benevolent but rather old-fashioned headmistress); Miss Bullivant ('The Bull'), a hefty harridan who taught maths and drill, and tended to put down any man who didn't agree with her views by walloping him with her hockey-stick or golf-club, and young and pretty Miss Locke, ex-Girton girl and sister of the revered Head of Greyfriars. Richards created a whole new set of characters to complete the Cliff House Fourth Form and, of course, their teachers.

He brought to the *School Friend* the sparkle and style which had become so characteristic of the *Magnet*—but, surprisingly, it was soon felt by the editors that his stories did not have the right touch for girls, and he was taken off the paper. Some people have advanced the theory that there was something more behind this decision, that in fact the *Magnet* and *Gem* editors wanted Richards off the *School Friend* because they felt he couldn't possibly keep up the pressure of writing for so many papers, and they didn't want to lose him.

It is said that Frank Richards wrote the first six stories in the *School Friend*, but an analysis of their style and content strongly suggests that he was only responsible for the first four. Naturally, because of his involvement, *School Friend*s 1 to 4 are the most sought-after issues of the paper today, and they are indeed rare collectors' items.

# Cliff House Celebrities

*Barbara Redfern.*

**B**ARBARA HILDA REDFERN is her real name, and, as you are all aware, she is the captain of the Junior School at Cliff House.

Cheerful, a lover of fun, a good, all-round sportswoman, Babs combines all the qualities that make a good leader, and is one of the most popular girls in the school.

"Babs" was born at Holly Hall in Hampshire, which is still her home. Her age is fourteen years and six months. She has glossy chestnut hair, deep blue eyes and a rosy complexion. Her chief hobbies are drawing and painting, and her best friend is Mabel Lynn, who shares study No. 4 with her and Bessie Bunter.

Doris Redfern, of the Upper Third at Cliff House, is her sister. Babs also has a brother, Reggie, aged three and a half years.

The girl Babs most admires in the school is Cliff House's head girl, Dulcia Fairbrother. Her favourite mistress is, of course, Miss Valerie Charmant, of the Fourth.

The girl Babs least admires is Sarah Harrigan of the Sixth, who for long has been Babs' enemy. The mistress she likes least is Miss Bullivant.

She takes size two in shoes, having rather small feet. Her height is 4 feet 10¼ inches. Her favourite colours are blue and gold, possibly because these are also Cliff House's colours, and her favourite flower the daffodil. She has no particular favourite among authors, but confesses to a weakness for Dickens and Agatha Christie. Her two favourite film stars are Joan Bennett and Robert Montgomery.

In the realm of sport Barbara has made her mark in hockey, cricket, and tennis. She is a fairly good swimmer, but not in the same class as Janet Jordan or Diana Royston-Clarke.

She is also quite a good actress and takes part in most of the Junior School plays and concerts. As an organiser she is brilliant.

She maintains a fairly good position in class, last term's examination placing her as No. 5.

Like Clara, she is enormously fond of all animals, and one of her proudest possessions is her golden retriever, Brutus, who has won many prizes.

Her great ambition is to be an artist, and have her pictures exhibited at the Royal Academy.

The Cliff House saga was taken over by different authors, all of whom were male. According to the editorial policy of Northcliffe's Amalgamated Press, men wrote better stories for girls than women managed to do. It was felt that female writers were too protective of the girl reader, and hence produced heroines who were first and foremost good examples of decorous behaviour, and therefore not particularly exciting. Whether or not this argument is true, the stories by Horace Phillips (who later, as Marjorie Stanton, created Morcove School in the *Schoolgirls' Own*), R J Kirkham and L E Ransome were written with gusto and a great deal of wit. In the hands of these writers (who continued to use the Hilda Richards pen-name), Barbara Redfern, the Captain of the Fourth, and her chums became more real to many readers than their actual friends and schoolmates.

They set standards of loyalty, strongly influencing several generations of schoolgirls. All the original Frank Richards characters were retained and developed, and of course new stars were added to the Cliff House galaxy over the years.

The *School Friend* ran from 17 May 1919 to 27 July 1929. By 1925 L E Ransome was producing all the Cliff House stories. During this period, the paper contained several short stories each week, by other authors, which were not connected with Cliff House. It had abandoned its striking red, white and blue covers (which look remarkably bold and bright, even to this day), opting for brown tones mixed sometimes with red, sometimes with orange—or green—or purple. It had an unusual and elegant look. Inside, the black-and-white line drawings of the early paper had been replaced by half-tone illustrations, but the artist remained the same. He was G M Dodshon, whose pictures were distinctive, if somewhat quirky. There is no doubt that he could draw the Cliff House girls with flowing tresses and pretty faces when he wanted to do so; often, however, he made them rather bizarre and oriental-looking (see page 114).

The new format *School Friend* was, one imagines, an effort to make the paper thoroughly up to date. It had a slickness that went well with the short skirts and bobbed and shingled hair-dos that began to adorn its pages more and more. However, it seems that Cliff House gradually began to lose its popularity. The characters who a few years earlier had been rightly dubbed 'The Most Popular Schoolgirls in the World' now began to be edged off the cover spot by other characters. Towards the end of the 1920s the *School Friend* ceased publication, and readers were urged to buy its successor paper.

This was the *Schoolgirl*, which began on 3 August 1929 and ended on 18 May 1940 (because of paper shortages brought about by the Second World War). At first its Cliff House stories were only minor features, but the paper still managed to be wonderfully attractive. It was bright and breezy, and featured, in addition to fiction, some chatty 'hints' pages on various feminine topics that make useful reading today. The group of male authors who wrote for the paper were not content merely to reflect the activities of real-life contemporary schoolgirls. They projected a new image of responsible but essentially lively girlhood in fiction that embodied the soaring spirit (despite depression and unemployment) of the 1930s. In story after story, ingenious adolescent girls debunk pompous parents and teachers—or over-assertive boys! Heroines were spreading their wings. In the early *School Friend*, for example, a girl might have had to pursue a 'baddie' by riding surreptitiously on the luggage grid of his car. But in the *Schoolgirl*, the heroines are not only more adventurous but more technically competent; they drive fast cars and speedboats, and pilot aeroplanes and service them too. The *Schoolgirl* plunged its readers (for 2d a week) into 'tales of bygone days', ghost stories, sagas of mystery and detection, exploits of gypsies in disguise, of poor little rich girls and rich little poor girls. There were also schoolgirl stories, and hazardous exploits in the outposts of Empire; plots set in film and broadcasting studios, the jungle, the Arctic and the Wild West.

With such a variety of excitements it seemed as if Cliff House had at last lost its hold on readers. It was dropped as a regular item from the paper from 12 October 1929 until the end of March in 1932. Then, surprisingly, it made a resounding comeback, in the hands of a different author—John Wheway, who, in common with his predecessor,

95

Bessie Bunter

Ransome, had also started out as a writer of boys' stories. The Cliff House adventures again became immensely popular, and Babs, Marjorie, Clara, Jemima, Bessie and Co resolutely occupied the long story spot in the *Schoolgirl* (and the whole of the cover) from then until its demise. The *Schoolgirl* had the same size page as the original *School Friend*, but there was a very new look about it. The cover was in dark blue, orange and white; the heroines in the stories were drawn as typical 'thirties' girls—no longer Eton cropped or shingled and skimpily skirted, but with crisply curling hair, and the slightly flared, gracious skirts of the period. Dodshon no longer drew the Cliff House personalities. His successor was T E Laidler (another male, of course!), whose robust line drawings were reminiscent of those of Thomas Henry (the 'William' artist), and who gave the girls a glowing, slightly glamorous and, above all, an extremely modern look.

Illustrating the Northcliffe girls' papers was quite a challenge, as editorial policy about the girls' appearances was somewhat restrictive. Although it was necessary for the artists not to make the fourteen- and fifteen-year-old heroines look too childish, they were at the same time instructed to 'play down boobs and buttocks'. This, presumably, was because many readers were only nine or ten, even though the characters that they read about were strapping teenagers. Laidler's ingenuity in carrying out his brief was astounding. He managed to make Babs and Co tremendously attractive in what can only be called a womanly way, yet there were never any obvious bulges beneath the box-pleated gymslips, and even when the girls were portrayed on holiday in bathing costumes, he niftily overcame the problem of enforced flat-chestedness by making the water come right up to their armpits!

The editorial policies of the papers, for both girls and boys, were strict, and keenly observed. Although this sometimes results in amusing moments for us (as adults reading the papers with hindsight), there is little doubt that this insistence on publishing only what was deemed suitable for fairly young children helped the papers to keep their identity: they never became ambivalent teenage/romance papers, for example. They also retained their integrity and appeal. There were healthy friendships in the stories between boys and girls, but sex was distinctly taboo. Juniors might look up psychologically as well as physically to senior girls, but there were no 'flaming pashes'. Boys might whisper admiring comments about a ripping and attractive heroine, and defend her at great personal sacrifice if ever she was threatened in any way—but attraction never went further than that. Chumminess rather than passion was always the keynote. Members of the opposite sex who cropped up in the *School Friend* were generally referred to as 'boy chums' rather than 'boy friends', as the latter expression had sexual overtones. Read now, the relationship between, say, Barbara Redfern and Jack Tollhurst, her chum from a nearby boys' school, sounds like a study in stilted chastity—although, when one encountered it as a child, it seemed utterly warm and convincing:

> 'I say, might I trot by the side of your bicycle as far as the gates of Cliff House School? ...'
> 'I shall be pleased for you to accompany me, Jack,' Babs said.

The saga of Cliff House in the *School Friend* and the *Schoolgirl* provides many insights into the lives of girls growing up in the 1920s and 30s, and some fascinating glimpses of schoolgirl fashions throughout the first half of the twentieth century. Whether the girls wore their hair and skirts long, as they did in the early *Magnet* in 'Edwardian' style, or whether they sported cloche hats like the 1920s flappers, and then 1930s film star-influenced flared shorts and 'beach pyjamas' when on holiday, they always managed to look elegant. Their stockings were never wrinkled, their ties were always set neatly under the collars of school blouses that never creased; they had gloriously waving hair, and fine complexions that owed everything to hockey and healthy exercise, and nothing to artifice. And when the bitches and bounderesses transgressed and experimented in make-up, they were well and truly chastised:

> 'You will go to the dormitory and wipe off the powder and change into your drill frock. Then, as you seem to have nothing better to do, you can write me out fifty lines.'

Bessie Bunter, of course, was the one member of the chummery who was always untidy—and often quite grubby. Her development in the *School Friend* is interesting; she was soon mellowed—in deference to the wishes of girl readers—from a grotesquely fat and greedy character into a 'plump and lovable duffer', who brought out the protective instincts of Babs and Co, and other live-wires at Cliff House. It seems that whereas boy fans of the *Magnet* were happy to accept Billy Bunter as a balloon-like buffoon, girls reading the *School Friend* were uneasy at seeing Bessie in a similar

# CLIFF HOUSE CELEBRITIES

*Diana Royston-Clarke*

AT Cliff House they call her the Fire-brand—with every reason ! Haughty, imperious, always anxious for lime-light and determined to get her own way, Diana Royston-Clarke is one of the most startling girls who has ever graced the Fourth Form. In her hatreds—ruthless ; in her affections—warm-hearted, generous, self-sacrificing.

A girl of many moods, Diana can be irresistibly charming in her good ones ; but almost frightening in her bad. A girl one can never be sure of ; who herself never knows what she will do next.

Diana is one of the most striking girls in the school. Her wealth of platinum blonde hair makes her a conspicuous figure wherever she goes. Her eyes, deep blue, set in an oval face with flawless complexion, give her an arresting beauty which few other girls can match. She is 14 years and 8 months, but likes to be thought older.

Diana was born in London but lives in Lantham, of which little town her million-aire father, Rupert Royston-Clarke, is mayor. She has no brothers or sisters, and since she is motherless, too, has always been rather spoiled.

Very rarely hard up, Diana possesses more clothes than any other girl in the Form, with a quantity of jewellery which she would certainly not be allowed to keep if the school authorities knew about it.

Clever at most things, and a brilliant all-round sportswoman, Diana would indeed be a credit to her school if only she could control her fiery temper. Her love of the spectacular, however, makes her rather unreliable.

On two occasions Diana, for short periods, has superseded Barbara Redfern as captain of the Lower School. Once she was ex-pelled and afterwards taken back. There are many girls who dislike Diana, and her only real friend is Margot Lantham, daugh-ter of Lord and Lady Lantham, with whom, however, Diana frequently quarrels.

Her favourite colour is oyster-pink ; her favourite flower the arum lily, and her favourite reading matter the latest fashion and film magazines. The film stars she likes most are Charles Laughton and Carole Lombard.

Diana has many hobbies, quickly tiring of one to take up another. Is very fond of children, and despite her loftiness, very generous to people poorer than herself. Takes size three and a half in shoes ; 5 ft. 1 in. in height.

Position in class last term was 16, though Miss Charmant says she could have been No. 1 if she had tried. Her great ambition (at the moment) is one day to become a lady of title.

light. Does this imply more gentleness in girl readers? Hardly, perhaps, when one reflects on their appreciation of the villainesses in the saga—like Marcia Loftus, a ferret-faced, sneaky, lank-haired and rather skinny girl; or, in a different category, the somewhat ruthless but fascinating 'firebrand' of the Fourth—Diana Royston-Clarke, who seemed like a schoolgirl version of Hollywood's Jean Harlow—platinum tresses, pouting lips and all. Rich and spoiled, she contemptuously dismissed the *esprit de corps* ideals of her form-mates ('I'll only play if I can be Captain!'), and had a bizarre habit (utterly intriguing to *Schoolgirl* readers) of flashing her violet eyes, dilating her nostrils and yelling 'Yoicks!' whenever she was angry, excited or even just mildly irritated.

There were so many colourful and extraordinarily competent characters that readers had high standards to live up to. Their heroines excel at horse-riding, hockey, cricket, tennis, swimming, ski-ing and ice skating. (Babs is even a skilled morris dancer—on

DIMSIE
HEAD GIRL

DORITA FAIRLIE BRUCE

FOR THE SCHOOL
COLOURS

Angela
Brazil

The HEAD-GIRL
of the
CHALET SCHOOL

ELINOR M.
BRENT-DYER

PEGGY AND THE
BROTHERHOOD

ELSIE JEANETTE OXENHAM

GIRL'S OWN PAPER

OCTOBER 1940

6ᴰ

IN CANADA 15 CENTS

GIRL'S OWN PAPER

NOVEMBER 1940

6ᴰ

IN CANADA 15 CENTS

GIRL'S OWN PAPER

DECEMBER 1940

6ᴰ

IN CANADA 15 CENTS

GIRL'S OWN PAPER

JANUARY 1941

6ᴰ

IN CANADA 15 CENTS

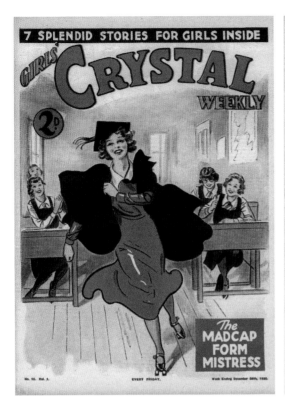

**7 SPLENDID STORIES FOR GIRLS INSIDE**

GIRLS' **CRYSTAL** WEEKLY

2D

The **MADCAP FORM MISTRESS**

Grand LONG COMPLETE Cliff House story **"THE FIREBRAND 'GROWS UP'"!** in this issue.

THE **SCHOOLGIRL**

2D EVERY SATURDAY

*Incorporating* "SCHOOLGIRLS' OWN"

**"I DON'T PLAY WITH SCHOOL KIDS!"**

The new Diana carries on with her "grown-up" pose.

*See this week's magnificent holiday story of the Cliff House chums.*

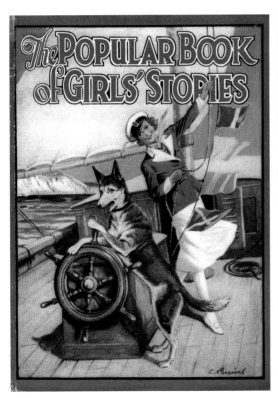

*The* **POPULAR BOOK** *of* **GIRLS' STORIES**

THE CHRISTMAS **HAPPY** EXTRA

1/-

*"Oh, Chris'mas!"*

Secret society stories were very popular in the girls' papers.

Angela Brazil wrote patriotic stories in both world wars.

ice; no mean feat this, as the lolloping morris step is hard to execute even on terra firma.) The girls could also unmask spies, baffle international jewel-thieves, resist torturers and, of course, easily defeat scheming prefects and always befriend the underdog.

The world of Cliff House was—and in fact still is for many of us—an exhilarating and satisfying one. That, of course, is why we collect the *School Friend* and the *Schoolgirl*, and the associated *School Friend Annual*, which featured our Cliff House favourites from 1927 to 1941.

# MORCOVE STORIES IN THE
## *SCHOOLGIRLS' OWN*

February 1921 marked the launching of the *Schoolgirls' Own*, a twopenny weekly paper which starred the charismatic girls of Morcove School, and was to survive for fifteen years with its price and 36-page format unchanged. It was introduced as a sister paper to the popular Cliff House weekly, the *School Friend*; and the Morcove saga not only had associations with that paper's celebrated girls' school, but also with the fictional seats of learning that had been established by Frank Richards in the *Magnet* and the *Gem*.

Morcove was the inspired creation of Horace Phillips (as Marjorie Stanton), who, with only occasional exceptions, wrote all the stories in the series until the paper folded with Issue 798 in May 1936. (Serials featuring Morcove then appeared in the *Schoolgirl* until February 1938, under the Marjorie Stanton pen-name, but inconsistencies of style and characterisation suggest that some of these were written by authors other than Phillips.) In 1921, when the *Schoolgirls' Own* began, Phillips had been for some time a Cliff House author for the *School Friend*. After Frank Richards had established Cliff House in the first few issues of the paper, Phillips (and some other writers) took the stories over. His flair was always for the dramatic and tear-jerking story. He achieved the right touch for Cliff House, attracting and retaining readers with his unusual blend of strongly emotional situations and schoolgirlish larkiness.

Before beginning to write for girls, Phillips had contributed women's stories to the *Sunday Circle* and *Sunday Companion*—papers which allowed him to give scope to his feeling for romance, which was denied him in the *Schoolgirls' Own* because of editorial taboos on the subject of sex in the girls' weeklies. However, as we shall see later, Phillips managed to charge Morcove's ambience with several romantic touches. Although he must have enjoyed creating his own characters after being saddled for some time with those that Frank Richards had originally dreamed up, several of his cast were derivations of Greyfriars and St Jim's characters.

For instance, his junior captain, Betty Barton—the humble Lancashire lass who has to overcome fearfully snobbish persecution when she first comes to Morcove—echoes the early battles of Mark Linley, the North Country Greyfriars scholarship boy.

Naomer Nakara, the 'dusky' fourth-former who is also an Eastern queen, enlivens the conventional English school scene, just as surely as Hamilton's Indian Nabob, Hurree Jamset Ram Singh, adds lustre to the Greyfriars Remove. And Paula Creel, the 'swell' of her form, seems to be a skirted version of Arthur Augustus D'Arcy, whose exquisite manners, lisping speech and sartorial impeccability she imitates.

These links with the Frank Richards papers are further emphasised by the fact that Leonard Shields, a regular *Magnet* artist, also illustrated the Morcove stories throughout their run. All this, perhaps, is why the *Schoolgirls' Own* attracted boy readers as well

as girls. Certainly today its ardent band of collectors includes men as well as women.

Horace Phillips also drew on the Cliff House characters when building up his Morcove 'chummery'. The ever-resourceful Betty Barton (whose motto is 'We'll manage!') seems set in a similar mould to Barbara Redfern, captain of the Cliff House Fourth. Betty is a touch more sedate, however, just as her bosom chum, 'merry madcap' Polly Linton, echoes the heartiness of Clara Trevlyn, the Cliff House tomboy, but is slightly less hoydenish than that much-loved character.

The intensity of Phillips's writing and the exuberance of Leonard Shields's illustrations made a perfect combination. The covers of the *Schoolgirls' Own* (blue and orange, like the *Magnet* in its heyday) were particularly appealing, with Betty Barton and Co—and even villainesses like sneaky Ursula Wade or imperious Cora Grandways—radiating vitality and charm. As well as the regular Morcove stories, the paper kicked off with two serials and a complete story. These were written by different members of the Amalgamated Press's talented team of male writers, using a variety of attractive female pseudonyms. The paper also included 'Cookery Hints', 'Needlework Notes' and, in more lively vein, 'Girl Guides' Corner'.

The *Schoolgirls' Own* was to feature the Guide movement with vigour and enthusiasm, running regular stories with Guiding themes, and offering as a giveaway in the first issue a beautifully reproduced sepia photograph of HRH Princess Mary in Guide Commissioner's uniform. The giveaway plates in the two subsequent issues were of HRH Prince of Wales, later to become King Edward VIII, then the Duke of

Windsor, and of Nurse Edith Cavell. These plates are now much sought-after collector's items.

Nevertheless, whatever other attractions the paper offered, it was Morcove that provided its long-lasting and extraordinary pulling power. The school is located on the edge of Exmoor, and the stories soon open out from the confines of its campus to the bracing atmosphere of Devon moorland mists and Atlantic breezes. Like Cliff House, Morcove stands on a high point overlooking the sea: the saga has its fair share of cliff-top dramas and rescues from watery graves, but on the whole, suspense is produced through relationships between the girls rather than by the vagaries of the elements and outside forces.

L E Ransome, who occasionally helped out as a 'holiday relief' with Betty Barton and Co's saga, specialised in inventively humorous touches. He told me that at first he felt a great deal of trepidation at being asked to write for girls—especially as the male writers' brief was to do this 'as if from the inside'! But he became increasingly adept at creating characters with whom girl readers could strongly identify.

As well as injecting some vibrant heroines into the Morcove Chummery—'In the dorm Teresa Tempest stood, radiant, with her hair up, in orange charmeuse and silk stockings'—he wrote (as Ida Melbourne and Elizabeth Chester) superb adventure stories for the paper. These featured a string of irrepressible adolescents, ranging from royal princesses to highwaymen's henchgirls. They were all early representations of girls' lib with a flair for debunking the bossy boys and pompous adults in their lives.

Of all the Amalgamated Press 'schoolgirl' writers, only Horace Phillips could—and did—manage to combine the intensity of Mrs Henry Wood's Victorian melodramas with the robust mood of 'hockey on the halfers!', and other sporty motifs. When describing chummy feelings between girls, he had no reticence in evoking deep emotions. For example, Betty tells her friend Madge Minden that she will enjoy meeting a rather delicate girl called Nell; sure enough, when 'poor ailing Nell' arrives 'with her limping step, and hand outstretched', Madge feels that 'handshakes were not good enough … She kissed Nell as if she was already quite in love with her. And perhaps she was.' (Of course, it must be stressed that this warmth of feeling between members of the same sex is, in the Morcove context, utterly innocent of homosexual undertones.)

To counterbalance this kind of intensity, Phillips kept the relationships between the girls and their boy-chums from nearby Grangemoor School under strict control, which must have been difficult for him in view of his penchant for full-blown love stories. His typical boy/girl relationship is expressed in the 'thus far and no further' friendship that exists between madcap Polly and her brother's friend Dave. His restrained but serious overtures are deflected rather than rejected by Polly. For example, after an especially hair-raising foreign travel episode (they had the most astoundingly adventurous hols!), Dave wants to sit next to Polly in the lorry which is transporting them to safety, but she declines: 'Nothing doing! I want Naomer on one side of me, and Pam on the other; then it'll be just like going home on the school bus after a match! Hurrah! Hockey next term!'

Betty Barton's chummery included—besides Polly, Paula and Naomer—Tess Trelawney (a talented painter), Pam Willoughby (stately, serene, affluent, intelligent, pretty, and Phillips's favourite of his characters), Dolly Delane (affectionately known as the Doormat, because of her obliging disposition), and Madge Minden, the musical genius of the Fourth.

With Madge, Phillips created an interesting and complex character. Being a musician, she is classed as 'temperamental', and certainly not a conformist. (Even when all her chums bobbed and shingled their hair in the mid-1920s, Madge insisted on retaining her long and flowing tresses.) Always able to withstand mass pressures, and something of a loner, Madge is nonetheless not allowed to depart too drastically from the straight-and-narrow path of sporty schoolgirlishness. Thus Phillips concocted one of his most memorable of Morcove vignettes: 'Madge Minden, a cricket bat in her hand, and carrying batting gloves, was strolling down the passage whistling a César Franck sonata.'

That colourful and atmospheric description is matched by the author's accounts of the most romantic personality in the saga—a mysterious Arab girl called Rose of the Desert, who crops up frequently, and braves the dauntingly cold Devon mists and sea-storms clad only in the insubstantial veils and draperies of her native garb! It is with Rose that Phillips gives fullest rein to his talent for the love story. She rescues Jack Somerfield, the explorer brother of Morcove's headmistress, from slow and horrible death in the desert on more than one occasion. She becomes deeply attracted to this 'Engleeshman with the heart that never quakes'. His response tends to be matey ('Well done, Rose!') rather than passionate, although he sometimes expresses himself in a flowery manner: 'I will never forget how, in the breast of my little brown maiden, there always beats a heart of gold.' However, Rose is doomed to frustration: her most axiomatic utterance turns out to be her reiteration of the famous 'East is East and West is West, and never the twain shall meet', for—after fifteen years of fancying Jack—she eventually bows out of the saga a year or two after he has married a European aristocrat who is a 'vision of radiant loveliness'.

However, Jack's involvement with Rose gives the Morcove girls the opportunity of going off to the desert for the hols on many occasions, where despite a variety of dramatic experiences (sandstorms, temporary slavery and hairsbreadth escapes from death), a good time seems to have been enjoyed by everyone!

At least, because of the Amalgamated Press's policy of playing down sex in their juvenile papers, Betty Barton and company were spared the attentions of the rapist sheiks who became so popular in light fiction after the success of E M Hull's prototype in *The Sheik*. Indeed, for the girls the camels seemed a greater hazard than the desert's human inhabitants. On one of the many occasions when they are fleeing for their lives, Jack Somerfield asks the girls 'with the cheery humour of a Britisher in a tight corner' whether they or the camels are the more exhausted. Paula Creel probably speaks for them all when she replies: 'Weally, it is cwuel! … Talk about being pwostwate, geals! This is worse than fifty hockey matches wolled into one!'

Our heroines, of course, manage to put up with privations of this kind, and many others, with splendid spirit—which is one reason why, so many years on, there are lots of us who cherish Morcove memories, and still delight in the *Schoolgirls' Own*.

The *Schoolgirls' Own* ran for fifteen years, completing its run with Issue 798 in 1936. Morcove School stories were also regularly featured in the *Schoolgirls' Own Annual*, which was issued every winter from 1923 to 1943, and many of the issues of the *Schoolgirls' Own Library* also featured the exploits of the Morcove girls.

# THE *GIRLS' CRYSTAL*

O ne of the most popular schoolgirls' papers with today's collectors is the Amalgamated Press's *Girls' Crystal*, which began life on 26 October 1935 and continued as a lively story-paper until 14 March 1953. After this, inspired by the success of its companion paper, the post-war *School Friend*, it followed the latter's format and became a picture paper until its eventual demise on 18 May 1963. It was not originally intended for schoolgirls, but as a career-orientated story-paper for young working girls.

At first it was called *The Crystal*, but by the time the tenth number appeared, the publishers realised that the paper was being bought by the under-fourteens; its name was changed to *Girls' Crystal Weekly* and the tone—from the beginning less introverted than the school story-papers—became even more light-hearted. Though it was read by schoolgirls, its heroines were generally involved in exciting and colourful jobs. The paper featured film stars, dancers, speedway motorists, female flyers, bareback riders, cowgirls and trapeze artistes. In its early days it endeavoured to appeal to girls from various strata of the community, so factory workers and shop assistant heroines were popular as well as those with more bizarre and unusual backgrounds.

The many excitements of the *Girls' Crystal* were produced mainly by male editors and authors, but a small smattering of women artists was also introduced. This was uncommon in Lord Northcliffe's publishing empire at the time; generally his girls' papers were produced by all-male teams. Female illustrators like Evelyn Flinders (who was especially adept at picturing hooded and masked members of Secret Societies) and V Gaskell (whose teenage girls looked like embryonic Hollywood charmers) atmospherically enhanced the stories, and the paper's appeal.

Several intriguing archetypes were introduced in the first issue of the paper, whose roles reflected aspirations of girls growing up in the 1930s. There was 'Nurse Rosemary', who 'brought happiness wherever she went' and whose patients called her 'a Ray of Sunshine'. In a rather more glamorous setting we find 'Tony the Speed Girl', the creation of an author known as 'Gail Western'. Gail Western was C Eaton Fearn, who also edited the paper; he specialised at this time in writing about girl racing drivers, and Tony was the first of many such intrepid speed stars to adorn this paper. When, a little later on, Fearn became bored with writing about adolescents careering around the circuits, he began to produce Secret Society stories in the *Girls' Crystal* and its associated annuals.

Another ambitious heroine in the early issues was 'Film Struck Fay'. However, poor Fay received less editorial encouragement than the speed girls. Her saga seems to have been intended as an antidote to the addictive Hollywood fantasies which many readers then regularly absorbed. Fay gate-crashes her way to an audition with her favourite screen hero only to be told that she has no acting ability. She turns down an offer of work as a junior dresser at thirty shillings a week, and only after several horrible

By GAIL WESTERN

By AUDREY NICHOLLS

By PEARL FAIRLAND

experiences—including facial disfigurement after accidentally setting the studios on fire—does Fay accept the inevitable 'back room job'. Film and theatre stories which followed 'Film Struck Fay', like 'I Will be a London Stage Star' and 'Daphne Dancing Through to the Danube', offered much greater encouragement to would-be professional actresses and dancers.

The greatest stars of the first issue of the *Crystal*, who were to enjoy long periods of popularity, were a male sleuth and a woman teacher. Noel Raymond, 'debonair detective', and Vera Desmond BA, the 'madcap form mistress' were both in their early twenties, fresh from triumphant college successes, and able to tackle with panache a variety of challenges from pepping up spineless headmistresses to solving baffling mysteries. Something else they had in common was their surprising physical agility. This was best demonstrated by their unorthodox methods of effecting rapid entries and exits: 'Noel's gaze scrutinised the ivy-covered wall and fastened on a rain-pipe. His eyes lit up. Rain-pipes were child's play to him!' The madcap mistress presented an even more engaging picture as, wearing her gown in a casual and dashing way, and with her mortar board at a jaunty angle over her unruly blonde curls, she shinned up and down the ancient walls of St Kilda's School for Girls.

It was of course Vera's breeziness rather than her BA that appealed to her pupils and to the readers of the *Girls' Crystal*. 'I must bunk back to my study. Don't forget—three o'clock in the cricket pavilion and no slacking!' Every member of the school, even the ghastly assortment of toadying and bullying prefects which all Amalgamated Press schools invariably attracted, was soon eating out of the hollow of the madcap mistress's hockey-strengthened hand! 'She's a sport, girls!' declared Pat Derwent fervently. 'A gilt-edged brick!' The author of the 'Vera Desmond' series was 'Jean Vernon', and the madcap mistress's exuberance ensured her popularity for many issues, although, as we shall discuss later, Noel Raymond's appeal was to outlast hers.

At first the *Girls' Crystal* was something of a bumper twopenny paper. It had twenty-eight 9 x 11 inch pages, which made up a larger format than any of the other AP girls' magazines. Its cover was strikingly illustrated in full colour, although this was soon simplified to red and blue on a white background. It was to become the sole wartime survivor of Northcliffe's schoolgirls' weeklies, but the paper shortages of the 1940s resulted in its reduction to a smaller page size (6¾ x 9½ inches), with only half of its cover carrying a picture. The number of pages shrank from 28 to 20—and eventually, in 1947, to only 12. However, in the late 1940s and early 50s, the paper blossomed again, and took on the characteristic and substantial appearance that had distinguished it before the war. It is to the enormous credit of the editors, authors and illustrators that, even in its most depleted stages, the *Girls' Crystal* somehow managed to seem charismatic and intriguing to its loyal readers.

Noel Raymond's popularity exceeded that of any other character in the paper. With only occasional 'rests' he survived from the first issue to No 814 in May 1951. He was an awesome example of the clean-limbed and upright young Englishmen who seemed to delight the Amalgamated Press's writers and readers. Noel was a glamorous object of adoration to many of his fans, combining manly strength with boyish frankness, and unattainability with chumminess. Perhaps because Noel was so firmly male, his creator Ronald Fleming dared to write the stories under the masculine pen-name of Peter Langley. This was an unusual practice for the AP's girls' paper authors, who nearly always assumed women's names. (Besides writing as Peter Langley, Fleming contributed many stories as Renee Frazer and Rhoda Fleming.)

INTRIGUING MYSTERIES SOLVED BY
The World's Most
FASCINATING DETECTIVE

NOEL RAYMOND *Detective*

By *PETER LANGLEY*

Many of the AP's fictional detectives were astringent, middle-aged carbon copies of Sherlock Holmes, but Noel owed more to Dorothy L Sayers's Lord Peter Wimsey, whose nonchalant manner and style of speech he sometimes adopted: 'I wonder', murmured Noel, as he slipped a Russian cigarette from his gold case and lit it thoughtfully, 'what's the correct procedure when a chappie's goin' to meet a girl he's never seen who signs herself "Yours distractedly" ... A bit awkward, what?' This slightly enigmatic investigator became more predictable and conventional with the passage of time, but he was still appreciated by the readers of the *Girls' Crystal* throughout the Second World War, towards the end of which he spent some time in the Special Constabulary, where his amazing powers of deduction served the nation's interests well. After the middle of the 1940s he no longer seemed so exciting to girl readers, who were involved in the beginnings of co-education, and becoming accustomed to easy-going friendships with boys. So Noel's teenage niece, June Gaynor, who had first appeared as early as Issue 102 in 1937 as his 'Fourth Form Assistant', began to take a more prominent role and to solve mysteries on her own. Incidentally, her habit of addressing 'the world's most fascinating detective' as 'Nunky' helped substantially to transform his image from debonair to domestic, and to take away some of his glamour.

Not every girl who read the *Crystal* in the 1930s, of course, would expect to become a famous detective. However, readers must have been gratified to learn of exhilarating careers that seemed theirs for the taking in the field of journalism. 'Stop Press Sadie— London's Brightest Girl Reporter, the Live Wire of the Daily Wire' was one of the paper's pre-war stars. She was, in the stories, usually selected by her News Editor for important assignments because of her 'tact and imagination'. She rushed here, there and everywhere with her pencil constantly poised over her shorthand notebook, epitomising efficiency and newspaper know-how. However, in spite of her up-to-date image ('Come on, spill it!'), Sadie was a simple girl at heart, frequently troubled by pangs of conscience: 'It seems so awful, somehow … prying on people …' To overcome these reservations about intruding on the private lives of others, Sadie often jollied along her interviewees by making them cups of tea and sharing her sandwiches with them. (No alcoholic tipples, naturally, because Sadie and her readers were well under drinking age!) As well as reporting, Sadie righted many wrongs, and an astounding number of famous film stars and kidnapped heiresses were deeply indebted to her for life and liberty. When Sadie's adventures came to an end in the paper, it featured news-hounds with different skills—enterprising and fetching girl photographers.

After the *Girls' Crystal*'s first few months, its career stories seemed to be taking on a distinctly middle-class flavour. Possibly realising that more of his readers came from working-class homes than from affluent families, the Editor then ran a serial about Poppy Binks—'the jolliest girl at the factory'. However, as she became the Countess of Sarfield in the first episode (no mean achievement, this!), the sociological significance of her exploits was largely negated. The stories were exuberant rather than realistic. After her sudden social elevation, Poppy was anxious to improve conditions for her former friends, and invited them to 'make whoopee' by singing rumbustious songs like 'You Can't Do That There 'Ere' around the grand piano in her newly acquired stately castle home. 'May Stevens' was the author who wrote up Poppy's adventures, which were drawn in characteristically elegant style by Leonard Shields.

Following in Poppy's wake, Elise Probyn (John McKibbin) produced a more believable mill-girl heroine in 'Susie, the Pride of the Factory'. Susie Bowling worked at a biscuit factory in the north of England, although most of her activities took place far away from the biscuit box conveyor belt. She was nothing if not intrepid. She scared an escaped convict when walking on the moors, represented her factory in an ice-skating competition against snobbish rivals, went to London to mend her sister's romance and, of course, constantly put down pretentious workmates and bullying forewomen. There is a sense of authenticity in the stories and the dialogue: 'We've earned it, duck. We've walked twelve miles,' says Susie to a chum when they are tramping the countryside in search of a cup of tea. Female acquaintances are usually addressed by Susie as 'duck' or 'dear', and (slightly older) men as 'guv'nor'.

Although the *Girls' Crystal* survived the war, historians reading issues published between 1939 and 1945 would gain little insight into the effect of hostilities on the lives of English teenage girls. The paper tended to adopt a happily escapist policy, ignoring the war completely, although a few stories were topically set in agricultural or lumber camps, to show girls doing their bit for the war effort.

Perhaps surprisingly, one of the most popular series throughout the 1940s featured 'The Cruising Merrymakers', who were, as their nickname suggested, always unashamedly enjoying themselves. Their adventures began in Issue 188 on 27 May 1939, and Sally Warner, Fay Manners, Don Weston and Johnny Briggs cruised joyfully all over the world until the series ended in 1952. German U-boats presented no problems. The author Daphne Grayson (C Gravely) reminded readers from time to time that the Merrymakers' travels, though chronicled during the war years, were supposed to have taken place earlier. The stories' settings included the high seas, South America, Hollywood, Egypt, India, Australia, France, Switzerland and, of course, England.

In London they took in the 1951 Festival of Britain, against a background of the

The Cruising Merrymakers sailed all over the world from 1939 to 1952

Dome of Discovery, the Skylon and the Islanders statue—all beautifully conveyed by V Gaskell's illustrations. (This artist stylishly reflected current fashions in teenage clothes and hairstyles.) Understandably, even the hedonistic Sally Warner and her chums occasionally tired of non-stop merrymaking, and they then had one or two spells at college, first in America and, later, on an Australasian island. All this made heady and exotic reading for girls who were prevented by the vicissitudes of war from even having the traditional two weeks a year break at an English seaside resort!

The post-war *Girls' Crystal* contained few storylines which had not previously been exploited, but boys were more frequently featured in chummy situations with the girls, and enterprising authors experimented with the 'sci-fi' themes which had begun to prove so popular in certain boys' papers. In 1949 John Wheway (as Hazel Armitage) produced a serial called 'Rosalie, Robbie and the Robot'. But fantasy got itself rather bogged down in chattiness and over-simplification:

> 'Remember the mechanical camel that Keith made?' Rosalie chuckled,
> '… and how it ran amuck and jumped the wall into the colonel's house
> next door?'
> 'And did the colonel get the hump!' grinned Robbie.

Science fiction in the paper was rather on the level of all-talking, all-walking robots: 'To start: press third button in right shoulder …' and (equally important), 'To stop: press third button in left shoulder …' Apart from these occasional flirtations with fantasy, writers for post-war readers tended merely to modify pre-war themes. Rather more realism was introduced, and holiday-camp adventures superseded world-cruising Merrymakers. Greta, a lion-taming heroine of the 1930s, gave way to the cosiness of girls who were featured in simple adventures with pets like dogs, cats and horses.

The wheel turned full circle when Vera Desmond, the Madcap Form Mistress of the mid-30s, found a ghostly echo at the end of the 1940s in Renee Frazer's 'Colin Forrest— that Amazing New Master'. Colin strode around the corridors of St Gwynn's School for Girls, and later Riversale Co-ed School, singing in 'his deep, pleasant voice, "Happy Days are Here Again"'. To his pupils he was 'a master in a million—a gilt-edged sport'. The gilt-edged heyday of the *Girls' Crystal*, however, was coming to an end, and in 1953, when picture-strips replaced stories, the paper lost its vivid identity, to become a virtual copy of the post-war picture-paper, *School Friend*. Happily its heyday lives on in the memories of many enthusiasts today.

# GIRL ROLE-MODELS IN COMICS

Brit, ritish comics before the 1950s, unlike the story-papers, featured very few female characters, presumably because publishers considered that boys formed the main readership. 'Statutory females' were introduced in the 1920s and 30s, but these, far from being role-models or heroines, were usually outrageous travesties—ranging from the curvaceous cuties of *Film Fun* or *Merry and Bright* (Flossie and Fluffie, the Fascinating Flappers) through nosey, flatfooted, skinny schoolgirls (as typified by the *Dandy's* Keyhole Kate) to mature and hefty harridans (such as police-woman Commander Clara in *Larks*).

In parallel with the stream of 1930s and 40s comics were the weekly story-papers for girls such as the *Schoolgirl* and the *Girls' Crystal*. These were rich in pictures but also provided thousands of words of text. Almost exclusively edited, written and illustrated by men, these story-papers began to create lively and attractive role-models for girl readers from eight to twelve. The tone—and popularity—of these papers influenced the creation, after the Second World War, of comics specifically designed for girls, such as the Amalgamated Press's *School Friend* (1950) and Hulton's *Girl* (1951), which established a pattern of career, sport, mystery and adventure picture-strips, introducing teenage heroines responsible for their own destinies with whom girl readers could identify. Significant examples are the sleuthing Silent Three in *School Friend* and Belle of the Ballet in *Girl*.

Girls' comics then proliferated and flourished until the end of the 1970s, when the formula began to flag. Since then the comics have had shorter runs, and the photo-strip adventures, which have largely replaced the drawn strips, have restricted the arena of the heroines' exploits. In particular the pop star-dominated teenage weekly has changed, but not advanced, the quality of role-models in girls' comics of the late twentieth and early twenty-first centuries.

In retrospect the comics from 1950 to the 1980s seem extremely rich and varied. Like the girls' story-papers of the 1920s and 30s (whose traditions they continued), they reflect to some extent the changing real-life social scene, as well as girls' fantasies about themselves. The fantasies are not only in the minds of the fictional heroines and the young readers, but, one suspects, often in the minds of the male artists and authors of the various stories and strips. Women illustrators began gradually to participate, but the genre has generally been a male-dominated one. This, perhaps, is one reason why the comics were generally more exciting than the average contemporaneous hardback girls' story book. Men were likely to enjoy putting their heroines into situations of hazard and fantasy.

*School Friend* (taking its name from the 1920s paper) started in 1950, soon after the end of the Second World War. It continued until the beginning of 1965, when it was incorporated into *June*, and it was the first girls' paper to achieve a circulation of a million copies. It carried four short text stories but was mainly composed of picture-strip adventures, which soon took it over entirely. The Amalgamated Press rightly predicted that girls who were now used to watching television, rather than reading or listening to radio, were more likely to respond to picture-strips than to text stories. No 1 of the *School Friend* included several elements which were to be repeated with variations in Hulton's famous *Girl* (the sister paper to *Eagle*) which appeared a year later, as well as in most of the comics designed for eight- to twelve-year-old girls right into the 1980s. There was plenty of mystery and suspense, notably in the front and back cover picture serial 'The Silent Three of St Kit's' (featuring a masked and hooded schoolgirl secret society) and in the adventures of 'Terry Brent, Detective', a glamorous male sleuth who combined the intelligence of, say, Sexton Blake with the magnetism and appeal of Rock Hudson or George Clooney. Terry Brent seems also to be a derivative of Noel Raymond of the *Girls' Crystal*, with sleuthing adventures transposed from text to picture-strips. (Whether or not it is coincidental, the illustrations of the handsome Terry Brent show him as having a marked facial resemblance to Stewart Pride, the Editor of *School Friend*.)

It was something of a feminist triumph that the artist given the opportunity to draw the first adventure of the Silent Three was a woman, Evelyn Flinders, and that her characters became so popular that she was commissioned to produce several other long-running serials about them. In fact Evelyn Flinders was part of a very successful team: she worked closely with Stewart Pride and with the author Horace Boyten (who wrote for girls as Enid Boyten) in planning the storylines of these serial picture-strips.

The schoolgirl heroines who made up the Silent Three were champions of the innocent and the oppressed, of a bullied scholarship girl, for example, or of some student who had been unjustly punished or even expelled. No ruse was too daring for this wonderful trio, and their courage, independence and resourcefulness influenced not only their schoolgirl readers but future writers and illustrators of girls' comics.

# "THE SPECTRE OF LYNN'S FOLLY!"

A New Story of the Girls of Cliff House.    Also in this issue : A Splendid Number of "The Cliff House Weekly !"

# THE SCHOOL FRIEND

Every 1½D. Thursday

No. 86.  Vol. 4.        Three-Halfpence,        Week Ending January 1st, 1921.

## BESSIE BUNTER'S PAINFUL PREDICAMENT!

(An amusing incident from the magnificent long complete tale of the Girls of Cliff House, contained in this issue.)

The *School Friend*'s combination of themes such as historical romance ('The Gay Cavalier', drawn by W Bryce-Hamilton), travel in exotic parts ('Jill Crusoe'), sport and tomboyism ('Freda's Daring Double Role' written by L E Ransome as Stella Stirling and illustrated by T E Laidler), and of slightly magical mystery ('Denis and the Scarab Ring') also included some knockabout comedy. The projected 'dummy' for its first issue included a picture-strip about Bessie Bunter, the fat, funny and popular schoolgirl 'duffer' from the story-papers of the 1920s and 30s, but perhaps it was decided that she was out of date for current readers, for the paper's first humorous strip did not feature her but another 'lovable duffer', Dilly Dreem, who was as skinny as Bessie was rotund.

It was not then considered 'politically incorrect' to laugh at (or with) a fat girl. Bessie, who was of course the sister of the more celebrated Billy Bunter of *Magnet*, *Knockout* and *Valiant* fame, came back into favour a little later on when the *School Friend* featured her in 1963 in a strip by Cecil Orr. Inflated to enormous balloon-like proportions, she continued to thrive when, in 1965, the paper was incorporated into *June*, and when that too suffered its demise and was amalgamated with *Tammy* in 1973, Arthur Martin continued Bessie Bunter's adventures with similar ebullience. She remained a fairly regular attraction in special numbers of *Tammy* or *Jinty* into the 1980s. It is hard to see what attracted girl readers to this overblown character, who was certainly not cast in the role-model mould: possibly her resilience was due to the fact that she essentially represented the underdog, who nearly always managed to come out on top.

When Hulton's *Girl* began in 1951, its comic relief was a character called Lettice Leefe, 'the Greenest Girl in the School', drawn by John Ryan, but the paper's emphasis was on characters who were involved in careers. *Girl* combined realism with fantasy more successfully than any other girls' comic, and it provided an interesting range of role-models. Its first front-cover picture serial starred 'Kitty Hawke and Her All Girl Air Crew'. This was boldly and imaginatively drawn by Ray Bailey, and suggestions for its creation and storyline were apparently provided by Frank Hampson, the creator

of *Eagle*'s golden boy, Dan Dare. Sadly, however, this strip was short-lived: the girl aviators were soon replaced by the more traditional 'Wendy and Jinx', a pair of sleuthing schoolgirls (also attractively drawn by Ray Bailey). Wendy and Jinx had a long run, and typified the fictional British schoolgirl at her mystery-solving and underdog-championing best. However, an older and more professional detective also graced the early pages of *Girl*: this was Penny Wise, whose main claim to fame was that she was drawn by Norman Pett, whose name was associated with Jane, the sexy strip-heroine of the *Daily Mirror*, for many years. Penny, designed of course to appeal to young girl readers, lacked Jane's sensuous charms but did inspire her readers with respect for the power of intelligence and initiative.

The most celebrated career heroine of *Girl* was Belle of the Ballet, whose exploits, pictured by John Worsley, began in 1952. Belle intrigued readers for several years, and by the late 1950s was being drawn by Stanley Houghton, with George Beardmore devising the storylines. Belle not only had to keep in trim as a première ballerina but to foil enemies who tried to undermine her troupe, and she had also to raise money to keep her dance company intact and on top form.

The two strips from twentieth-century girls' comics which are now most often referred to nostalgically are 'Belle of the Ballet' and 'The Silent Three'. These were the cult role-models: even though few of the *School Friend*'s and *Girl*'s readers from the 1950s seem to have taken up sleuthing or ballet-dancing, many were inspired by these heroines to seek challenging careers.

Despite its generally progressive mood, *Girl* took a backward step in making 'Angela, Air Hostess', drawn by Dudley Pout, a star of the paper from 1958. Surely the career of air hostess, when compared with that of an aviatrix like the discontinued Kitty

Hawke, represented a decline, and an indication that girl readers were being discouraged from setting their career sights too high. Realism was, of course, here triumphing over fantasy, but somewhat sadly.

Hulton's *Girl* ended in 1964, but IPC had the inspiration of reviving the title with a new comic launched in 1981, which enjoyed a few years of popularity. Pretty well half of this, however, was taken up with photo-strips, and neither these nor its drawn strips produced a heroine with anything like the charisma of some of the original *Girl*'s characters.

In the early 1960s D C Thomson's *Mandy*, *Judy* and *Bunty* began to take over part of the readership of the Hulton and IPC comics. *Bunty* was launched in 1958, and *Mandy* and *Judy* in the 1960s.

Their picture stories are pacey and exciting, but on the whole their heroines suffer greater social difficulties than those of *School Friend*, *Tammy* or *Girl*. Many of them are orphans who are badly treated by horrible relations or teachers: some of the leading characters are even forced into crime by wicked and grasping adults. Others are 'cripples' who yearn to become athletes, or simply girls who suffer dire poverty. Happily, however, these comics also contain stories about girls who succeed in the world of sport, and about well-adjusted schoolgirls who specialise in righting wrongs and solving mysteries. The Four Marys, who began in 1958 and ran in *Bunty* for decades, are noteworthy of this type of character. They were one of the most popular groups ever to appear in girls' comics.

D C Thomson were the first publishers to bring out a nursery comic for girls, the long-running *Twinkle* which began in 1968. It included several full colour pages, and heroines with whom small girls could identify, such as Nancy the Little Nurse (who looks after sick dolls), and other characters who convey cosy domesticity.

There were no tomboys or toughies, and adventures were variations on the theme of imitating Mummy performing household duties, spiced occasionally by magical interludes (fairies living in dolls' houses) and animal pranks. IPC tried to produce a similar nursery comic for girls with *Pixie* in 1972, but this ran for only thirty issues, despite the attractions of picture stories by Hugh McNeill. McNeill had earlier created one of the most celebrated girl comic characters, Pansy Potter the Strong Man's Daughter, who started in D C Thomson's 1938 *Beano* and ran for years.

Pansy, like Alan Morley's Keyhole Kate, her knobbly-kneed predecessor in the 1937 *Dandy*, was the statutory female character in a comic which featured mainly male personalities. Were these comic but unappealing girls simply designed to give

*Beryl the Peril*

boy readers a good giggle and a sense of superiority? They could hardly be seen as role-models for girls. Later and cruder statutory girl toughies in the Thomson comics are Leo Baxendale's Minnie the Minx, who began in *Beano* in 1953, and David Law's ferocious Beryl the Peril, who started in *Topper* in the same year.

An interesting D C Thomson innovation was their science fiction and fantasy comic for older girls, *Spellbound*, which ran from 1976 to 1978, and featured an attractive all-female interplanetary exploration team. Well-drawn and imaginative, it deserved longer-running success. It was followed by IPC's *Misty* (1978 to 1980), which echoed *Spellbound*'s interest in sci-fi and the supernatural.

Space exploits involved encounters with ghost spaceships and crews who had been dead for thousands of years, but who had magically revived. The girl astronauts—Hercula, Electra and Fauna—are also 'top space investigators', or, in other words, interplanetary detectives.

*Spellbound*, with its skilfully drawn and convincing picture stories, suggested that invasion teams from outer worlds (grisly giant spiders, etc) were at the ready, just waiting for the go-ahead from a possessed teenage girl to launch their missiles and spaceships against the earth. *Spellbound* also produced stories about an Egyptian mummy that walked the streets of Victorian London and a young girl taken over by the spirit of a beautiful concert pianist from the past; and at least one nice-minded schoolgirl whose aunt was trying to force her to become a witch!

The fact that neither *Spellbound* nor *Misty* lasted long suggests that girl readers responded less favourably to occult or fantasy themes than to the straightforward schoolgirl, sporting and career themes of the *Tammy* and *Bunty* type of comic. These more traditional weeklies also, however, included a sprinkling of stories in which magical situations or magnetised objects (jewellery that carries a curse, ballet-shoes that make the heroine dance until she nearly dies of exhaustion) set the mood.

Two memorable characters should be mentioned. Valda, the adolescent wonder girl whose adventures were featured in *Mandy*, possessed startling physical strength which got her into and out of all sorts of strange exploits.

Equally charismatic was Jane Bond, Secret Agent (no marks given for guesses at her inspiration), who was drawn by Michael Hubbard (also a one-time illustrator of the *Daily Mirror*'s 'Jane') for IPC's *Tina* from 1967.

We are concerned here with girls' weeklies that can be categorised as comics. Since the 1960s there has been a stream of a new type of paper ('for go-ahead teens') that is concerned with how-to-grab-your-guy picture stories and articles, with beauty hints, pop stars and fashion. Examples are *Romeo*, *Valentine*, *My Guy* and *Blue Jeans*. These tended to be short-lived and are beyond the scope of our present study.

It is a sad reflection that the era of the girls' comic, with its emphasis on adventure, careers and initiative, seems to be over. *Judy*, *Mandy*, *Jackie*, *Bunty*, *Debbie* and similar comics have long been defunct. It seems unlikely that today's papers (now hardly qualifying as comics, and concentrating on clothes, cosmetics, and celebrity culture) will remain long in the imagination of readers. It is also hard to believe that they (as some of the old comics did) will encourage readers to feel that every girl has a significant part to play in contemporary society. Where are the role-models who have replaced the Silent Three or Belle of the Ballet? Presumably some now come from other areas of popular culture—from television, the world of the pop star or, of course, computer games and activities.

# FRANK RICHARDS AND FEMINISM

The heroines of Charles Hamilton (Frank Richards) may stand low on the ladder of liberation according to the ideals of Germaine Greer, but at Greyfriars and St Jim's a few joyful blows *were* struck for the women's movements. At the same time Frank enjoyed swiping them occasional back-handers, especially during the days of suffragette militancy. He was always sympathetic with characters like Cousin Ethel and Marjorie Hazeldene, whose sturdiness never eclipsed their femininity: an aura of graciousness surrounds them, surviving from the Edwardian days of their creation until the *Gem* and *Magnet* ended. Conversely, he relished writing about burly characters like Miss Bullivant, gym mistress of Cliff House School, and her fictitious fellow-campaigners for women's suffrage.

In 1908 (*Magnet* No 28), Frank champions Dr Locke's young sister, Amy, who volunteers to become temporary 'master' of the Remove so that Mr Quelch can extend his much needed sick-leave. Fresh from Girton, '… there was nothing of the "blue-stocking," the learned miss, about Amy Locke … a young and graceful girl with a

From the *Gem*

sweet face, and soft, brown eyes.' Needless to say, she is in for a tough time from the wilder spirits of the Remove. Even Harry Wharton and Co, whose natural chivalry is heightened by Miss Locke's youthful prettiness, are aghast at the prospect of 'knuckling under' to a woman, knowing this would make them the laughing stock of other forms. The Head's sister, during her first morning in class, soon proves herself mistress of the situation, in spite of persistent insults from Bulstrode (the form's bully), Levison, Skinner and Billy Bunter.

> There was a painful silence in the Form. The Remove had chafed at feminine government, but now that there was actual rebellion, some of them began to think that, after all, it was not very manly to 'rag' a woman … Wharton's eyes were beginning to sparkle. He was strongly inclined to back the Girton girl up.

Bulstrode receives his just deserts from 'that confounded suffragette'—a sharp cut across the palm from Miss Locke's pointer. This humiliation takes the fire out of his revolt against the despised 'petticoat government', and Harry, as form leader, is implored by the Removites to find a way out of their embarrassing predicament: falsetto-voiced jibes from other forms about 'good little girls' have to be endured because Amy Locke has forbidden the Remove to engage in fighting!

> The Girton Girl … looked very fresh and pretty in the dull old classroom, and it struck Harry that she brightened the place very much, and was a much more picturesque figure than Mr Quelch.

Her charm, however, does not prevent Skinner from releasing a clockwork mouse which instantly undermines her independence and sends her leaping up on to the nearest chair, clutching her long skirts about her. This prompts Bunter's fatuous observation, 'Look there, Levison! I told you she hadn't blue stockings!' Wharton helps to restore order and repress Skinner's malevolent schemes.

> As the Form filed out, the young lady from Girton signed to Harry Wharton to come to her. Somewhat wondering, Harry obeyed. Miss Locke detached a rose she was wearing, and pinned it to Harry's coat. 'In recognition of the good example you have set the class, Wharton,' she said, with a sweet smile.
> Wharton was crimson and dumb.

Too considerate to refuse the rosy tribute, he has to resort to 'wild and whirling conflict' with those who jeer at him, in defiance of Miss Locke's veto on fisticuffs. Strengthened through battle, Harry decides he will give every support to his temporary form-mistress.

'My hat! ... I say, you'll be giving the women seats in Parliament next!' exclaimed Bob Cherry.

Though doubtful, Bob and the rest of the Co back up Wharton, and Amy Locke is eventually accepted by the Remove.

Very different exchanges take place between conventional schoolboy and blue-stocking schoolmistress in *Gem* No 756, 'Gussy among the Girls'. Arthur Augustus D'Arcy ('Gussy') is in hiding at Cliff House, one of his several refuges on the notorious occasion of his 'retirement' from St Jim's, to avoid the indignity of an unjustified flogging. Gussy, concealed in a woodshed, is discovered by Bessie Bunter, who ventures there to devour a bag of jam tarts appropriated from Clara Trevlyn. Bessie's screams rend the air and bring the gym mistress to the scene.

> Miss Bullivant was a determined character. In younger days she had helped to wring the Vote from terrified Cabinet Ministers, whom she had waylaid with golf clubs.

Now, with her club at the ready, she commands Gussy to come forth.

> Arthur Augustus did not come forth.
> 'Oh dear! S-s-suppose he rushed at you, Miss Bullivant!' exclaimed Barbara. 'Hadn't we better all go away, and—and send the porter ...'
> 'Nonsense: What a mere man can do a woman can do—better!' said the Bull.

When her repeated commands to the 'ruffian' to come forth are ignored, Miss Bullivant announces her intention of stunning him with one blow, and, swinging her golf club through the air, she crashes it down on the stack of faggots sheltering D'Arcy. Crumpled and dishevelled, he has to emerge, to a chorus of laughter from the girls and fury from Miss Bullivant. At first she suspects him of criminal intent and then of 'holding surreptitious communication with a girl belonging to this school.'

> 'You are a young rascal! ... An unscrupulous and precocious young scoundrel!' continued Miss Bullivant, who had learned a fine flow of language in her early days of the struggle for the Vote. 'Well may you cringe before me ...'
> 'Bai Jove! I was not awah that I was cwingin' ...'
> 'I look upon you with disgust, detestation and abhorrence!' said Miss Bullivant. 'Wretched interloper!'

Gussy's gorgeous manners and niceties are utterly lost on the Bull who, after lacerating the St Jim's boy with her tongue, propels him protesting to the gate. With an

iron grip on Gussy's collar, the ex-suffragette yanks him along so vigorously that he has to trot to keep pace with her.

'Wretched boy, take that as a punishment!'
Smack!
'Yawoop!' roared Arthur Augustus, staggering to one side as Miss Bullivant gave him a powerful box on the ears.
Smack!
A box on the other ear righted the swell of St Jim's.

D'Arcy, discomfited and muttering about the 'feahful thwashin' he would administer if only Miss Bullivant were a man, 'stood not upon the order of his going—but went!'
Gussy has a delicious knack of involving himself in skirmishes with suffragettes and the 'new woman'. In *Gem* No 78 (in 1909) he determines to talk Cousin Ethel out of the 'Gal Scouts'—the Guide movement had not then been officially recognised, and Baden Powell-inspired female pioneers had dubbed themselves Girl Scouts. Arthur Augustus confides to his chums … 'A man bein' so much supewiah to a woman in intellect is bound to look aftah her and give her fwiendly advice.' Tom Merry, Figgins and most of the St Jim's juniors do not share Gussy's convictions and are inclined to think the Girl Scouts an excellent innovation. Undeterred, D'Arcy continues his crusade …

'There is an old maxim about wesistin' the beginnin's. I wegard it as necessary for a woman to wemain in her place … It would be absolutely howwid for women to get into Parliament, you know, when you considah what kind of boundahs they would have to mix with there …'

Gussy favours a view widely held by men of the period that women were too noble—or too foolish—to participate in government! His attempts to point out to his cousin Ethel the error of her ways are somewhat emasculated by the fact that, when going to meet her in Rylcombe woods, he is attacked by Grammarians and ignominiously 'rescued' by Ethel and her Girl Scout Curlew Patrol. With his customary exquisite tact and delicacy Gussy explains to Ethel that she should stay quietly at home and set a good example to her sex! She suggests that she can best judge her own needs, and Gussy, exasperated, declares that she will be wanting a vote next. Ethel proceeds to challenge the St Jim's juniors to a scouting contest—which the girls win! However, this victory is achieved as much by Mellish and Gore's sabotage against Tom Merry's patrol as by the girls' skill, so honours are declared even, and the story ends with Gussy converted … 'An assuahed and convinced supportah of the idea of patwols of Gal Scouts.'

His further struggles with the fair sex are described in *Gem* No 274, 'D'Arcy the Suffragist', in which Frank, as Martin Clifford, tilts at feminist militancy. (Another Amalgamated Press author once told me that when he was five years old he was kissed by a suffragette; he found this a terrifying experience, as the rating of these ladies was then much the same as witches and vampires.) Violence was increasing in the Women's Suffrage campaign when, after more than fifty frustrating years of constitutional agitation, there still seemed no hope of gaining the Vote. Frank was doubtless horrified by the suffragette who took a horse-whip to Mr Churchill in 1910, and presumably equally appalled at the beating-up of Mrs Pankhurst by roughs at an election meeting in 1908. Ironically, a few weeks after 'D'Arcy the Suffragist' was published in May 1913, the hideous climax of violence came: Emily Davison, just released from six months in prison for setting fire to a letter-box, went straight to the Derby and threw herself under the King's horse, to die a few days later.

In *Gem* No 274, D'Arcy's involvement with the 'Feminine Liberty League' is pure farce. Its leaders, Mrs Jellicoe Jellicott and her daughter, Miss Gloxianna Jellicott, are tyrannical termagants in true Frank Richards tradition. Arthur Augustus, now a convert to the cause, is ambushed by Figgins, Kerr and Wynn on his way to a suffragette meeting. Disguised, they claim to be Asquith, Winston Churchill and Lloyd George, and strip Gussy of his clothes. He has to dress in a weird assortment of feminine attire, daubed with suffragette slogans. D'Arcy is then pelted with rotten eggs and thrown into the horse pond by local residents, who resent the window-smashing and letter-box-burning activities of Mrs Jellicott and her League. All this is mild compared with the shrieking vehemence of the suffragettes who consider that Gussy, a male impersonating a female, must be a spy! Their ferocity ends his determination to help the fair sex in their struggle for freedom: from then on they have to go it alone, minus his invaluable assistance!

Frank Richards describes a happier aspect of feminine independence in another of his creations—Clara Trevlyn. She is typical of the Edwardian new woman, the 'sport' or 'tomboy' who gets on well with the opposite sex and would rather play a vigorous round of golf with a man than have a romantic relationship with him! Clara occasionally dumbfounds Harry Wharton and Bob Cherry by her daunting observations, particularly concerning their obvious devotion to Marjorie. In *Magnet* No 1535, after estrangement and suspicion, Bob is reconciled with Marjorie; Greyfriars and Cliff House parties meet at the Old Priory for a picnic. Bob has suffered long agonies for Marjorie's sake, and Clara's unsentimental comment is characteristic.

> 'So you've got over it?'
> 'Eh—what?' stammered Bob.
> 'You had your back up about something ...'
> 'I—I hadn't ...'
> 'Bow-wow!' said Miss Clara. 'Think I didn't know. So did Marjorie! Didn't you, old bean?'
> Marjorie coloured. 'Nonsense, Clara!' she said.
> Miss Clara laughed and ran on into the priory ...
> Marjorie lingered in the old gateway and Bob remained with her.

And we can leave them there, standing together in sunlight and serenity, undisturbed by echoes of Emmeline Pankhurst or the clarion calls of Women's Lib!

# PART FOUR

# DETECTIVE, SECRET SOCIETY AND GHOST STORIES

# SISTERS-IN-LAW

After we had co-authored *You're a Brick, Angela!* and *Women and Children First*, Patricia Craig and I began to work on *The Lady Investigates*, a study of fictional women sleuths and spies. Whenever I mentioned this to anyone, the usual response was: 'Oh yes, of course … there's Miss Marple—and Miss Silver—and …' Not many names came readily to people's minds after these, but of course there have been hosts of female investigators in fiction, in both hardback books and the periodicals.

For nostalgic reasons, and because the Amalgamated Press (AP) papers produced so many attractive girl detectives, we used as the model for the dustjacket of our book a 1930s *Schoolgirls' Weekly* cover drawn by Leonard Shields. It seems that it was never too young for girls to embark upon the sleuthing process, and in comics as well as story-papers, female 'snoops' abounded. It is interesting that as far as women and girls are concerned, a strong image of 'nosey-parkering' has always been attached to the business of detection. Keyhole Kate was created by Allan Morley for the *Dandy* in 1937; this unglamorous, skinny, wrinkled-stockinged anti-heroine was not exactly a sleuth—but she was certainly a snoop! Her obsessive curiosity got her into hot water more often than it ever helped her to solve mysteries—but she did occasionally come across some keyhole clues to bits of nasty practice and double dealing, to give a kind of comic justification to her prying pranks.

The pre-World-War II comics did a nice line in lady police constables of the uniformed rather than plain-clothed variety. Peggy the Pride of the Force in *Larks*, brilliantly drawn by George Parlett, began her exploits in 1932, and these continued for many years. She strode purposefully across the pink-tinted pages of the comic on one of the strongest and most shapely pairs of legs ever to have graced a periodical. She also had wide eyes, and a froth of blonde curls that engagingly peeped out from under her Metropolitan Policewoman's big-brimmed hat. Peg's pretty appearance and attractive personality present a vivid contrast with those of her superior officer, the

## PEGGY, THE PRIDE OF THE FORCE!

hefty-footed and hatchet-faced Commander Clara. Unlike Peggy's streamlined garb, Clara's uniform sagged and bulged unflatteringly. Clara was not only plain but lazy, spending most of her time guzzling tea at the nick, and leaving all the criminal catching to Peggy—who, of course, conducted this with charm as well as panache.

Peggy's success must have prompted the *Butterfly* to follow up with another police girl Peg—a mobile speed-cop this time, who struck echoes perhaps too of the musically celebrated real-life Gertie, the Girl with the Gong. However, Peggy the Pretty Police Patrol, created by Ray Bailey in 1936, didn't pursue her quarry in a car, but with dash and dazzle on a motor bike.

Crime fiction for adults was enjoying a long golden age during the 1930s, and the popularity of the theme spilled over with gusto into the girls' papers. In the Cliff House periodical, *Schoolgirl*, most of the leading characters tried their hands at sleuthing in one adventure or another. As Hilda Richards, John Wheway created many superb and suspense ridden stories of detection, starring Barbara Redfern, Clara Trevlyn, Marjorie Hazeldene and even duffer Bessie Bunter, whose investigations succeeded—like Billy's occasionally in the *Magnet*—far more by luck than judgement. Without doubt the most efficient of the Cliff House girls in the sleuthing field was Jemima Carstairs, the monocled, Eton-cropped 'enigma' of the Fourth, who hid her brainy astuteness beneath a burbling and indolent persona. (Wheway, who developed Jemima from a character produced originally by L E Ransome, told me that she was inspired partly by elements in the Bulldog Drummond canon, partly by Dorothy Sayers's Lord Peter Wimsey, and also by the 'silly ass' character that possibly derived from Wodehouse's Bertie Wooster and was so popular in the books, plays and films of the 1920s and 30s.)

However efficient they might have been at the sleuthing business, the Cliff House personalities in the *Schoolgirl* of course had to pursue their investigations in their spare time—in between history and hockey, domestic science and dormitory routines. The full-time professional girl detectives were prominent in the *Schoolgirls' Weekly*, a different AP paper with a stronger career bias than *Schoolgirl*. For this, John Bobin (a Sexton Blake author), writing as Katherine Greenhalgh, created Sylvia Silence in 1922. Fifteen-year-old Sylvia was heralded as 'The Girl Sherlock Holmes', though it was really her father who slightly resembled Conan Doyle's renowned character. He, also a detective, sits around in an ancient dressing-gown playing a violin—though, in the wholesome context of the schoolgirl papers, he does not inject himself with cocaine! Sylvia has, we understand, learned her trade from Dad, but by the

Sylvia's plucky leap

time of her debut in the *Schoolgirls' Weekly* she is solving crimes on her own, except for some help from her animal assistants—her monkey Jacko, and her Alsatian, Wolf. Sylvia thus sets the pattern for many subsequent girl sleuths in the papers who were helped by Alsatian assistants (it is worthy of social note that American teenage 'tecs didn't have doggy helpers but boyfriend assistants). Sylvia was a trend-setter too in having a wealth of 'bronze-brown' hair, because for adolescent girl detectives afterwards in the 1930s and 40s, red hair seemed a statutory requirement. In England they sported every shade of auburn from dull rust to frightful flame, and across the Atlantic Nancy Drew abandoned blondeness for Titian tones early in her saga.

Sylvia was intelligent and intrepid but, despite her colourfulness, slightly staid in certain ways. Bobin had another attempt at a girl detective in the 1930 *Schoolgirls' Own*. As Adelie Ascott he produced Lila Lisle, who was rather more stylish than her predecessor, wearing artificial silk stockings, court shoes, smart hats and well-cut fur-trimmed coats. Her hair was 'red-gold'—of course—and shingled. Lila was described as 'the Girl Problem Investigator', which somehow made her sound like the sympathetic 'auntie' of a women's magazine letter page rather than a fearfully efficient sleuth. She was, however, adept at bringing criminals to book, though more, it has to be said, by semi-psychic guesswork than brilliant interpretation of events and evidence.

Bobin finally hit upon the right formula with Valerie Drew, whose regular adventures in the *Schoolgirls' Weekly* from 1933 were addictive for many thousands of girl readers. (After Bobin's death in 1937 the series was continued by other writers, and eventually Valerie was transferred to *Schoolgirl* when the *Schoolgirls' Weekly* folded in 1939.) Amber-haired, violet-eyed Valerie was adept not only in the business of investigating, but in a range of other skills. She could understand 'deaf and dumb language', read with unerring accuracy the messages of signal flags hoisted on ships, effectively manipulate her 'trim sports car', successfully navigate speedboats or yachts, and—of course—pilot aeroplanes. Her Alsatian helper Flash was pretty efficient too. He could not only bring help to Valerie when her enemies had, for example, holed her up in some disused

VALERIE AMONGST
THE MYSTERY
MAKERS

coal mine or crumbling clock tower, but towards the end of his career, he was promoted in one or two stories to solving mysteries pretty well entirely on his own. So effectively were the stories written that this seemed credible to girl readers at the time.

The AP tales of girl detectives were satisfyingly rich in inventiveness, atmosphere and suspense, but the same cannot always be said of Nancy Drew, the American perennial created by 'Carolyn Keene' (the pen-name for a group of authors in the

Yvonne Cartier

Stratemeyer syndicate). Nancy preceded her namesake Valerie by four years, although of course the distinction of creating the first long-running teenage girl sleuth can be claimed with pride by the English AP with its 1922 Sylvia Silence. Flaming-tressed and efficient, Nancy still inspires new adventures today, though these are bland indeed compared with the AP stories, even though she has the glamour of good clothes, flashy accoutrements and a boyfriend (with the rather quirky—for a man—name of Ned Nickerson!). Nancy's success triggered off the production of other American girl detectives—Margaret Sutton's Judy Bolton, Carolyn Keene's Dana sisters and Frances Judd's Kay Tracy, to name only a few. They all fit into the same glossy slot occupied by Nancy Drew. Without doubt the least attractive of all the American juvenile feminine mystery-solvers was Helen Louise Thorndyke's Honeybunch, an eight-year-old created several years before Shirley Temple, and uncannily presaging the film star's sugar-pie charm but not the sturdiness or likeability that also characterised Shirley.

Reverting to the English scene, Bobin not only specialised in girl detectives but in secret societies. His hooded helpers began in 1934 with the Silent Six in *Schoolgirls' Weekly*. They were an instant success, copied wholesale by other authors, and the pinnacle of secret society adventures was reached in 1950 with the post-war *School Friend*'s picture story by Evelyn Flinders of the Silent Three. This trio of schoolgirls who donned hoods, masks and long robes in order to put down conniving prefects, crooked headmistresses and dastardly criminals became cult figures for more than one generation of girls. (Posy Symonds transmuted the threesome from schoolgirls to housewives in her 1970s *Guardian* cartoons.)

The *Girl's Own Paper* got away from conventional sleuths and secret societies, and featured a different kind of detective-cum-secret-agent in 'Worrals of the W.A.A.F.S.' by Captain W E Johns. She was launched in October 1940 and conceived after the Dunkirk retreat, as part of the Women's Auxiliary Air Force's 1940s recruiting campaign. For girls growing up during the 1940s who were inspired by the legendary valour of the 'Few', there could have been no more potent symbol of patriotic idealism or endeavour than Worrals. She was also attractively liberated, with intelligence that matched her courage.

Worrals was designed for teenage readers, but the heroine of many Sexton Blake adventures, Mademoiselle Yvonne Cartier, must have appealed to adults as well as juveniles. The creation of G H Teed, she entered the saga in 1913 and was afterwards frequently featured in the *Union Jack*. At first she operated on the wrong side of the law, to avenge dreadful wrongs done to her family by a gang of crooks, and she was sufficiently quick-thinking to outwit Blake and, naturally, the 'plodders' from the Yard! Later she frequently assisted Blake in his cases, but whether committing crimes or solving them, she worked with 'mathematical precision', and proved herself also to be a dab hand at physics and chemistry, and at disguising herself. Although her exploits were extremely exciting, Yvonne emerged as a compelling and credible character, attractive enough to make not only Sexton Blake but many of her readers fall in love with her. She combined glamour and dependability, astuteness and niceness. Of course, because the series could hardly have been sustained if Blake and Yvonne had settled down into domesticity, though 'her pulses throbbed with exquisite pain' in the presence of the supersleuth, Yvonne could never become his wife, and had eventually to fade out of the stories.

Later on, other girls in the Blake adventures seemed to be modelled on Yvonne, but her natural successor is from another AP paper. Eileen Dare entered the *Nelson Lee Library* in 1916 as Lee's 'Lady Assistant'; E S Brooks created her, but sadly her career was brief as, apart from a one-off reappearance twelve years later, she was written out in 1917 when she had found her 'perfect specimen of English manhood'. She was a very lively heroine, who thought nothing of taking a several-storeyed leap from blazing buildings or, when the need arose, of shinning swiftly up a six foot wall, in spite of her fashionably long but cumbersome skirts.

She was extremely pretty, but tough too—able, for instance, to half-carry an injured man several yards from a woodland clearing to her car. She was also, we are told, 'as clever as ten Scotland Yard detectives put together', and she 'could ride, drive, swim and run like a deer'.

Edith Dexter

Janet Darling

Girl detectives, and sometimes spies, were popular in a vast range of magazines. For the *Strand Magazine* of 1893–99, Grant Allen wrote serials featuring Lois Caley, the ex-Girton girl investigator, and Hilda Wade, the nurse detective. (Hilda's great claim to fame is that as her creator died before the serial finished, Conan Doyle wrote its last chapters.) Lois and Hilda were fairly emancipated, and as well as solving mysteries they both did a lot of globe-trotting before finding their respective Mr Rights.

Soon after the *Strand Magazine* published their adventures, *Harmsworth Magazine* produced Miss Van Snoop (the name again suggesting noseyness, please note), a member of the New York Detective Force, who apprehends a criminal outside London's Café Royal. The story was written by Clarence Rook, who contributed several tales of 'Underworld' situations to the *Strand* and other periodicals. The romantic papers were not to be outdone; they realised that female sleuths pulled in the readers and so decided to sandwich inventive stories of crime-solvers in between 'charming' love episodes like 'A Mid-June Bride' or 'The Torments of Tessa'. The AP's *Forget-Me-Not* began in 1909 to feature Janet Darling, 'the Girl Detective Who Will Only Help Lovers'. This selectivity, one feels, must have seriously cut down her scope; still, she coped, and always managed to look very fetching too. Janet had an Edwardian-lady-like quality. She was followed up in 1910 by a robustly working-class sleuthess—Edith Dexter, 'the Mill-Girl Detective'—in the AP's *Golden Stories*. Edith began as an amateur, but was quickly promoted to full-time and professional status. She was at this time unusual for a girl in being allowed to tackle industrial mysteries as well as the more domestic run of jewellery thefts and missing will cases that were the customary lot of the female investigator.

Although the magazine lady crime-solvers make a dazzling array, it was actually in books that their tradition had begun when W S Hayward created Mrs Paschal in *The Revelations of a Lady Detective* in 1861. Andrew Forester Junior then produced a nameless sleuthing heroine in *The Female Detective* (1864), and it is interesting that these intrepid and convention-defying Victorian ladies are neatly balanced in time almost midway between the first fictional sleuth (Edgar Allan Poe's C Auguste Dupin in 1841) and the most celebrated (Conan Doyle's Sherlock Holmes, whose adventures started in *Beeton's Christmas Annual* for 1887). Mrs Paschal, a widow 'verging on forty', took up sleuthing as an escape from genteel poverty. She did not suffer from false modesty, and liked to talk about the capacities of her 'vigorous and subtle brain'. Nevertheless, she proceeded in the matter of investigation by the use of 'female intuition', and a laboured stumbling from clue to coincidence, rather than by intelligent deduction. My favourite moment in her saga is when, pursuing a criminal into a damp and slimy underground vault, she uninhibitedly throws off her crinoline ('that obnoxious garment'), in order to race more quickly down the ladder. She took most things in her stride, from grisly, gothic and unbalanced abbesses to nefarious secret societies, and what she lacked in logic she made up for in flair.

Mrs Paschal had a string of successors in late-Victorian and Edwardian books. One of the most notable was Baroness Orczy's *Lady Molly of Scotland Yard* (1910). Lady

Molly, like so many of the early lady investigators, took up detection mainly in order to vindicate the honour of the man in her life. (Her husband had unjustly been sentenced to life imprisonment for a murder that he did not commit.) She cuts her sleuthing teeth, so to speak, on a series of less important cases, and only in the last chapter manages to redeem her husband's reputation. The 'Lady Molly' stories (though not half so compelling as Baroness Orczy's tales of her male secret agent, the Scarlet Pimpernel) now have a vintage charm. Lady Molly, despite her pluck and braininess, trails an aura of discreet scent, elegant gowns and earnest tea-room tête-à-têtes. She is insular and snobbish, making frequent nasty remarks about the native 'peasantry', foreigners, trade-unionists and socialists (whom she loosely equates with the Mafia). Being highborn and richly invested with fanciful feminine charm, she is surrounded by adulation. Her exploits are chronicled by her former maid (now her sleuthing assistant), who cannot keep her admiration in check, declaring, 'I of course was her slave!' and that Lady Molly 'could do anything she liked with the men' (including, apparently, the whole police force, who were 'invariably deferential' towards her). Lady Molly represents the Edwardian female detective *par excellence*.

Spies are sleuths of a kind, and it is fascinating to take a glance at some of the women espionage agents of this period, who tended to fall into two distinct types—the actress spy of dubious morals who worked for money rather than love of country; and the noble patriot who had no interest in financial remuneration. Fiction in this sense anticipated fact, and the First World War produced two real-life embodiments of these types: Mata Hari, the seductive betrayer-dancer, and Nurse Edith Cavell, whose career as well as character emphasised her self-sacrificing qualities. Naturally the fictional female spy is always at her most potent during a time of war. (Bernard Newman's Belgian prostitute character Regina, who could adeptly blink out messages in morse code whilst engaged on other activities, could for example *only* be a wartime product!)

1914–18 spying 'vamps' had a stylishness that quickly evaporated during the interwar years, but came into their own once again after 1939.

We see then the beginnings of the female equivalents of James Bond, the adventuress/investigator type that has, since the Second World War, been refined (not quite the correct word in this context, perhaps; developed might be better) into the 'Avengers' and 'Charlie's Angels' heroines of more recent television series. Modesty Blaise

Peter O'Donnell's Modesty Blaise and
Willie Garvin

in stories and picture-strips is the apotheosis of this kind of character. With lethal weapons concealed in her deep cleavage and high chignon, and mental capacities to match, she is indeed a force to be reckoned with as a secret agent. One should thank heaven that she—like Bond—worked for and not against the democracies!

However, a different kind of female spy emerged in the shape of Mrs Pollifax, the New Jersey widow and grandmother created by Dorothy Gilman in the 1960s. Emily Pollifax wears flowery dresses and hats, loves gardening and has become one of the CIA's most efficient freelancers, who still worked for them (in fiction of course) into the 1980s. She progressed from influencing the course of the Cold War to working alongside Russian agents to prevent crazy and unaligned scientists from destroying the societies of both East and West. Mrs Pollifax can be seen as the spy equivalent of the elderly spinster detective, of well-meaning busybodies like Patricia Wentworth's Miss Silver and Agatha Christie's Miss Marple, who, though fluffy, are not quite so soft-centred as they initially appear.

The variety of female sleuths and spies, since Mrs Paschal first took up this 'curious career for a woman' in 1861, has been so tremendous that it cannot be covered by just one chapter. The twentieth century has produced the hard-boiled 'she-dicks', the secretary- and spouse-assistants to famous male detectives, the lesbian butch, and the aggressively liberated women sleuths. And there are many other types. But—to end this chapter as it began—it is the ladies on the wrong side of middle age who have most enduringly captured the imagination of readers; and, of these, it is surely Jane Marple, the dear old lady of English popular fiction in a direct line that runs from 'Cranford' to 'Miss Read', who will never die. In some fictional or cinematic form she will be sleuthing in the future as vigorously as she has always done. In Agatha Christie's own words: 'There is no detective in England equal to a spinster lady of uncertain age with plenty of time on her hands.'

# SPOTLIGHT ON SOME SECRET SOCIETIES

The hooded helper or secret society theme turned out to be an extraordinarily potent one in the Amalgamated Press's schoolgirl papers over several decades. Much of the credit for this must be given to the Sexton Blake writer, John William Bobin, who as Gertrude Nelson created the first really charismatic clandestine group, the Silent Six, in the *Schoolgirls' Weekly* during the early 1930s. In the same paper, of course, as Adelie Ascott, he had produced the resiliently appealing girl detective Valerie Drew and her magnificently intelligent Alsatian assistant, Flash.

Valerie's adventures began in No 533 (17 January 1933), and for No 651 (13 March 1935), Bobin—or his editor—had the bright idea of bringing together Highcroft School's righting-of-wrongs sextet and the young but seasoned female sleuth. (This was the only time that such a meeting occurred; Bobin died at the early age of forty-five, just four days before this story was published. The last of his 'Valerie Drew' tales appeared in the *Schoolgirls' Weekly* in No 653 published on 27 March 1935. For some time after that her exploits were published anonymously, and later in the name of Isobel Norton.)

The story 'Valerie Leads the Silent Six', published under the Adelie Ascott byline, opens with Miss Spence, Highcroft's headmistress, sending for the detective and seeking her help in ending the 'escapades' of the Silent Six, whose members have 'for a very long time defied all authority in this school … They have now been responsible for something too heinous to be tolerated or overlooked'.

The Head goes on to explain that the Silent Six have broken a beautiful and extremely valuable Italian statue in the garden of Major Fortescue, who is one of the school governors. His home and grounds adjoin those of the school, and, on the night when the damage was done, a long-robed and cowled figure was seen to be 'running frantically' away from the broken statue.

The girl's garb immediately suggested to the Head that the culprit must be one of the Silent Six. Valerie (by intuition) and the *Schoolgirls' Weekly*'s readers (from previous knowledge of the stalwart Six) know better! The girls of that Secret Society would never have done anything dishonourable, and if one of them *had* broken the statue accidentally, she would have owned up, even at the expense of blowing the anonymity of the group.

Most of Valerie's investigations there seem to take place at night, and the author makes good use of nocturnal atmosphere and suspense: 'The clock of Highcroft

Enthralling LONG COMPLETE Valerie Drew Story, dealing with the thrilling things which happen when—

VALERIE LEADS THE SILENT SIX

THE CELEBRATED GIRL DETECTIVE
—sent to trap the Silent Six—
LEADS THEM INTO ADVENTURE !

By Adelie Ascott

Illustrated by C. PERCIVAL

School chimed the hour. A disturbed bat flitted eerily round the tower … A moon glimmered fitfully from a cloudy sky, throwing the black mass of the school buildings into silhouette. A faint wind disturbed the trees …'

In fact, Valerie doesn't have to stretch her deductive skills too tautly in order to discover the Silent Six's secret hideout. She sees an 'uncanny' hooded and robed figure darting through the woodland at the edge of the school grounds: 'Jingo! One of the Silent Six! What a stroke of luck,' she breathes; and, 'her pulses thrilling and her violet eyes bright and excited', she trails her quarry to an oak-panelled room in a ruined manor house in the wood.

Here the Silent Six conduct their meetings with solemnity and all the appropriate trappings. Their candlelight confab is abruptly disturbed by Valerie's sudden entrance as she drops into 'the hitherto secret meeting-place' through a window. In 'utter consternation' the Six try to escape (concealed passages, crypts and stairways are never far away in secret society stories!) but are stopped in their tracks by the reasonable tone of Valerie's questions. She makes it clear that she believes in their innocence, and intends temporarily to become one of their number so that she can more easily pursue her investigations. Naturally, gratification and relief are felt by the six strangely assorted members. Shirley Carew, 'the fair-haired and madcap leader of the group', had founded it 'to cleanse Highcroft of sneaking and injustice on the part of the prefects'. Her colleagues are Inez Lawton, Pam White, the twins Margaret and Dolly Downer, and 'the flaxen-haired, rather dumpy Dutch girl, Gretchen van Houten', whose severely fractured English ('und ve thought dot you vere going to put der tin hat on things for us, aind't it?') would surely have provided a disastrously strong clue to her identity, should anyone in authority have come within earshot of the group.

Valerie dons a spare robe and hood, and takes the oath of allegiance: 'I, Valerie Drew, do solemnly vow to observe the mottoes and rules of the Silent Six … Each for all. All for each. Nothing too good for Highcroft!'

But where, you may ask, while all these rites are going on, is Flash, Valerie's canine assistant? Valerie has, in fact, left him in the temporary—but inept—care of the school porter at his lodge, because she knows that if the inmates of the school see her with the Alsatian they will guess that she is Valerie Drew, the famous detective, and the baddy or baddies will be put on guard.

Flash, of course, takes a dim view of being separated from his beloved mistress. 'Humph!'—he thinks, in his characteristic, half-human way—'I wonder what she's up to!'

While the porter dozes, Flash chews through his leash, grips the handle of the door between his teeth and opens it (an easy matter for this multi-talented animal). Unfortunately, he is not at first helpful to Valerie and the Silent Six. His enthusiastic intervention almost causes Gretchen to be caught, in her incriminating robes, by Major Fortescue. Later, however, the girl detective's doggy helper comes into his own. When Valerie and the Six have been trapped and shut up in the tower, Flash responds to Valerie's rescue call: 'He looked up at the door. His eyes were bright with intelligence.

He saw the bolt, rose on his hind legs, and seized it between his teeth. Flash tugged and strained at it … the bolt shot back.' (This kind of canine behaviour was very thrilling to me when I first read the Valerie Drew stories. None of our family dogs was particularly responsive to training. Once let off their leads they were more likely to dash off over the horizon than to obey injunctions to sit, or come to heel. Flash was a revelation. Not only was he astoundingly sensitive to Valerie's wishes, and physically able to carry these out, but he could weigh up complex situations, make accurate human character assessments and, indeed, solve mysteries on his own!)

Once he releases his mistress from the tower, all is calm and bright. She has already worked out the identity of the statue-breaker who has discredited the secret society. It is Laura Norton, a prefect, who is in the habit of taking a short cut across Major Fortescue's grounds on her surreptitious nocturnal visits to the local palais de danse!

Valerie persuades Laura to confess to Miss Spence, and the story ends rather tamely with the girl sleuth explaining that the Silent Six have 'got away': 'I'm afraid they're too elusive even for me to catch, Miss Spence. But as they are innocent, it makes all the difference, doesn't it?'

Apparently it does, and the Head is content to allow the high-minded hooded helpers to continue their activities unmolested within the school precincts.

Despite the weakness and predictability of the plot, 'Valerie Leads the Silent Six' is intriguing on many counts. First, of course, there is the coming together of those two popular casts—Valerie Drew and Flash, and Shirley, Gretchen, Inez, Pam and the twins. Then Flash's contribution to the tale provides many satisfying moments; Valerie manages as always to be crisply charismatic; and—as a bonus—there are delightful pictures of the robed and hooded girls by C Percival, who was at this time the regular Valerie Drew artist, though not the usual Silent Six illustrator. The early adventures of the secret society were drawn by B Hutchinson; later S H Chapman took over. I think Percival was the best of these three artists in conveying the charm and robustness of the Silent Six, even though, for him, this assignment was a 'one off'. He also did his expectedly excellent job with his depiction of Valerie and Flash.

Let us now look at the secret societies of the 1940s and later, and particularly at the Silent Three. This featured extremely attractive artwork by Evelyn Flinders.

Nostalgic enthusiasts knew little about this artist, nor indeed that she was the original illustrator of the Silent Three, when I first became a collector in the late 1960s. It was only through attending the London Old Boys' Book Club that I 'discovered' her. One or two members occasionally referred to 'Polly' Flinders and her particular love for the boys' school, St Jim's, which was created by Frank Richards in his second most famous pen-name of Martin Clifford.

I was shown a picture drawn by Evelyn Flinders of Arthur Augustus D'Arcy—one of the leading lights of St Jim's. It had a familiar look, and when I contacted her, I found that she was the artist who had created the visual images of those hooded heroines, Betty, Joan and Peggy, as well as having also drawn for many of the stories in earlier girls' papers such as the *Schoolgirl*, *Schoolgirls' Weekly* and *Schoolgirls' Own* of the 1930s.

Evelyn and I met several times; we corresponded for a decade, and she was kind enough to give me several pieces of original artwork by herself, and by other illustrators of the popular papers.

She was a lady of robust and lively opinions and was something of a pioneer, being one of the very few female illustrators employed on the Amalgamated Press's pre-Second World War girls' story-papers. She studied at the Hornsey Art School from 1925 for three and a half years, and continued there as an evening student for two further years. Her first professional assignment was to illustrate a story about a boy prince; she later found this in what she describes as 'a paper book in Woolworths'. Her ambition was to work on the Amalgamated Press girls' papers and she 'just kept on badgering and worrying them' until she got a foot—or rather her two very competent hands—through the door!

During the war, she worked as a semi-skilled joiner making shell-cases for four years and, happily, had no trouble afterwards in getting assignments from the Amalgamated Press, which led to her illustrating 'The Silent Three'. Her work on this addictive picture-strip story, covering both the front and back pages of the *School Friend*, continued for eight years and represented the pinnacle of her career.

Detectives had been popular stars in the Amalgamated Press girls' papers in the 1920s and 30s, but during the 1940s sleuths were superseded by heroines of various secret societies.

Girl readers responded to the romantic atmosphere of clandestine meetings in ancient crypts lit by flickering candlelight, and the thrill of dressing up in long hooded robes (particularly at a time when wartime clothes rationing still continued). Secret society stories also continued the psychological attractions of solving mysteries and righting injustices. These vivid ingredients proved a winner for the Amalgamated Press, first in several unconnected stories in the post-war annuals, then in serials in the weekly *Girls' Crystal*. The secret society theme was eventually to become most clearly delineated, and most popular, in the 1950s with the Silent Three serials in the new *School Friend*.

One of the Silent Three's forerunners appeared in the 1945 *Girls' Crystal Annual*: 'Hilary and the Phantom Three' was written by the Editor of the *Girls' Crystal*, C Eaton Fearn, under the pen-name of Gail Western. The Phantom Three, wearing long grey robes, with tasselled girdles at their waists and owl-like hoods and masks, are conducting a vendetta against an unscrupulous Senior Prefect, and they are aided by new girl Hilary, who at first does not know their identities. (Of course they turn out

Evelyn Flinders with *School Friend* No 1,
showing her first 'Silent Three' picture story

to be her study-mates, and the Phantom Three become the Phantom Four when Hilary is later officially allowed to join them.) Gail Western exploited the secret society idea again in the 1947 *Girls' Crystal Annual* in 'Her Feud with the Secret Three'. This society, too, is operating against an unpopular prefect, and it consists of Linda Hale, Mary Walton and Patsy O'Dare (whose 'shures', 'darlints', 'bedads' and 'spalpeens' would quickly have announced her identity to the world at large, despite concealing dark dressing gown, white hood and mask).

A common factor in almost all the stories is that the headmistress bans the secret society, whose members are then under the threat of expulsion on discovery. (They are usually brought into temporary disrepute by the villainess of the piece, whose nefarious schemes they are frustrating. She 'frames' the society with dirty tricks—like study-wrecking, petty thefts and booby traps—by leaving notes at the scene of the crime saying WITH THE COMPLIMENTS OF THE HOODED FOUR, etc, etc.) Generally, too, the secret society is formed by three or four girls who actually share the same study; the percipient reader might sometimes feel they would have functioned more efficiently through quiet, uninterrupted study confabs which would have spared them the problems of getting trapped at midnight by prefects in draughty crypts from which escape is hampered by the paraphernalia of floor-length robes. Of course, the secret, if awkward, meeting place becomes perfectly justified when one member of the society has been expelled unjustly during the previous term and is hiding on the school premises. She then can only meet her confederates somewhere outside run-of-the-mill school confines. Happily all the Amalgamated Press fictional schools were well equipped with underground passages, ancient towers with secret escape routes, and fountains in whose ornamental gargoyles important and confidential messages could be concealed.

Stewart Pride, who edited *Schoolgirl* from the late 1930s until its end in 1940, made a big contribution to the secret society story's popularity. As Dorothy Page he wrote 'The Fourth Grey Ghost', a serial beginning in the *Girls' Crystal* on 14 August 1948. He produced further variations on this theme, and when he became Editor of the post-war *School Friend*, the first issue in 1950 introduced 'The Silent Three', whose stories were written collaboratively by Pride and Enid Boyten (Horace Boyten). 'The Fourth Grey Ghost' featured a new angle—the girl helper to a boys' secret society. Penelope Cartwright, daughter of the Headmaster of Harcourt Abbey Boys' School, is of seemingly meek demeanour, symbolised by the knitting bag which she constantly carries. (This comes in handy for concealing her robe!) She is actually quite intrepid and saves the day for the boy members of the society, who are working against a crooked Senior Master. She is then officially made 'number four'. This serial was illustrated by Evelyn Flinders. Stewart Pride, writing as Joy Nesbit, produced a similar story for the *School Friend Annual* which came out in 1948 (dated 1949) and this was called 'Secret Member of the Silent Six'.

Once again, a headmaster's daughter—this time Vivien Locke—helps a group of boys 'to crush the tyranny of the head prefect', and like Penelope in 'The Fourth Grey Ghost', she becomes adept at whisking off her long black hooded cloak and stuffing it into her knitting bag whenever occasion demands.

Grey Ghosts are at it again in the *Girls' Crystal* weekly of 1949—only a year after they were previously featured. In 'The Elusive Grey Ghost' Dorothy Page has removed Penelope from the boys' school: she now lives with an aunt nearby. The Grey Ghosts are trying to overthrow the new, tyrannical and usurping headmaster, who is not only engaged in smuggling activities but is also keeping the Head prisoner in a disused mine. Of course there is also the statutory bullying prefect, Paul Crombie.

In the middle of this serial (*Girls' Crystal* No 726, 17 September 1949) the paper at last shed its wartime austerity appearance. The cover became one large coloured picture again, as in pre-war days; and this was an Evelyn Flinders illustration of robed and hooded Penelope—the elusive 'ghost'—escaping on a bicycle from two boy prefects. The story, however, still evoked a slightly wartime atmosphere because the Grey Ghosts held some of their meetings in an air-raid shelter. They were back again later in 1949 in the *Girls' Crystal Annual* (dated 1950)—with 'The Grey Ghosts' Secret Enemy'. This time Penelope was living with her aunt in the country, and the boys' school were allowed to camp on their land. The secret society outwitted a schemer who was trying to end the camping concessions because his father wanted to buy the land cheaply. The *School Friend Annual* for the same year introduced a new line in hooded secret societies with Enid Boyten's 'Their Secret Task at St Claire's'. This featured 'The Adventures of three Daring Schoolgirls in the days of Nazi occupied France'. The girls are organising a pageant '… if only to show those Nazis that we're not down-hearted. That we're keeping our spirits up, in spite of all they can do!' The pageant is based on the historical exploits of a group of real-life bandits who had been known as the Hooded Owls. In their grey robes and hoods the girls are able, under the noses of the slow-witted, bemonocled Nazi officers, to smuggle Louis Gerard, a young boy resistance worker, to the beach and an awaiting British torpedo boat.

This story provided an example of a girls' society helping a boy. A more usual pattern was that of a girl joining a boys' secret society, and this was well expressed in 'Girl Helper of the Hooded Four', by Jane Preston (Reg Thomas). When Rita Marsden was not enveloped in her green monk-like garb she made 'a trim, workmanlike figure in sweater and jodhpurs', helping at her father's riding stables. This secret society adventure is enlivened by its equestrian atmosphere as, when things begin to flag, the leading characters can participate in desperate horseback chases and escapes across the moors. The Hooded Four (eventually Five, when Rita passes her nerve-racking initiation test) are up against an unpopular master who has engineered the expulsion of one of their members during the previous term. As soon as Rita sees the wronged boy for the first time minus his mask, she knows, without a shadow of doubt, that 'it was utterly impossible that a boy who possessed such steady eyes could ever do anything underhanded'. Her fellow society members are eventually equally appreciative of her: 'Here's to Rita! … To the very best little friend and helper we shall ever know … To Rita. Our very best pal.'

The Silent Three, on the whole, were firmly not co-educational, though occasionally

## THE SILENT THREE AT ST. KIT'S.

*(Continued from page 1)*

How excited and mystified Joan and Peggy were! They were confronting the unknown person who had sent them the intriguing note. Why was the figure so strangely robed? And what message had she for them?

So there in the crypt the solemn vow was made. The Silent Three was formed — Joan, Peggy — and the Unknown No 1......

But danger was threatening the Silent Three! No sooner had Peggy and Joan put on their robes than there came a clatter of footsteps on the stone stairs as Cynthia and Mildred rushed down. Would they be discovered?

they helped, or were helped by, a member of the opposite sex. Their first story begins in the post-war *School Friend* No 1, dated 20 May 1950, and ends in No 20 (30 September). At St Kit's School the fourth formers are unhappy under the harsh rule of tyrannical Head Prefect Cynthia Drew. Betty Roland (another of those unfortunate characters who has been wrongly expelled) decides to hide at the school and form a secret society to prove her innocence, and to outwit Cynthia—who with her father is engaged in illegally salvaging bullion from the wreck of a ship sunk during the war. The Silent Three's other members are Betty's erstwhile study-mates, Joan Derwent and Peggy West—and very fetching they all look too—with impeccably curly hair and red-and-white striped blazers. They are equally appealing in their well-fitting green robes, hoods and black masks. Evelyn Flinders produced extremely attractive work: she drew the cover picture-strip story from the *School Friend*'s first issue in 1950 until she eventually gave up her Amalgamated Press commissions in 1959. She, perhaps even more than Stewart Pride and Horace Boyten—who were responsible for the storylines of the series—created the wholesome yet intriguingly mysterious atmosphere of the Silent Three's adventures. Miss Flinders says, 'I had no holiday during these years, as I couldn't get far enough in front of the printers.' She put as much care and effort into every one of the dozen or so weekly Silent Three pictures as she had done with the single illustrations she used to make for pre-war Amalgamated Press stories.

During the course of the first story, the society is discredited by Cynthia's scheming, and outlawed by the headmistress. But at last Betty, Joan and Peggy triumph, and the headmistress at assembly calls for 'Three Cheers for the Silent Three'. As they put their robes away, Peggy says, 'Perhaps one day we may need them again, who knows?'

Of course they do—frequently—in spite of the fact that unfortunately the authors had allowed the identity of the girls to be revealed to the school towards the end of this first adventure. Realisation soon followed that without the clandestine element the Silent Three would lose a substantial part of its effectiveness and dramatic appeal. They were therefore removed to another school, where their society could start up again—with secrecy preserved. So several subsequent exploits, in the weekly and the annuals, took place at Island School. Wherever they operated, the Silent Three came across an abundance of crypts, caves and ivy-covered towers, as well as positive labyrinths of underground passages. (They also had an extraordinarily plentiful supply of excellent candles.) Apart from their aptitude for solving the problems of the underdog and bringing rogues to justice, the Silent Three were fearfully efficient at concealing their robes under their blazers without even a minimal lump to make this obvious to all and sundry. One story informs readers that they always carried their Silent Three robes around with them, on the off-chance of the secret society having suddenly to spring into action. The stories were dashingly told in 'balloon captions' and pictures, occasionally amplified by small blocks of narrative text. Evelyn Flinders managed to convey in her illustrations not only pace, but a sense of character not often achieved in picture stories. The sheer competence of the Silent Three is breathtaking. When threatened with discovery, they blow out their candles in a concerted movement, as their leader raps out, 'Escape plan "B" in operation! Make for the secret door!'—and like lightning they have hopped out of the crypt and vertically ascended 'through the walls' to the roof of the old clock tower, and safety. It is easy to see that the Silent Three, though rooted in the Amalgamated Press's earlier juvenile detective and mystery stories, also owed a lot to the supermen and -women of films and television. They cropped up in several long serials—always across the front and back covers of the *School Friend*—throughout the 1950s, and their venue was often changed. One of the last stories in the weekly was 'The Silent Three in Switzerland' (1956–1957). In the *School Friend Annual* they continued to appear—sometimes in repeats—until the early 1960s, and were given 'star' positions. Perhaps they were dropped eventually because Evelyn Flinders was no longer working for the Amalgamated Press (and IPC), and readers might not have readily accepted other artists' portrayals of Betty, Joan and Peggy; or perhaps the planners felt that girls growing up in the 1960s found pony-riders, ballet stars and pop singers more attractive objects of identification than the earnest, intrepid but unashamedly schoolgirlish Silent Three of the 1950s.

# BUT FLEUR HAS OFTEN WONDERED

In the September 2001 *Collector's Digest* Ray Moore wrote: 'Given that so many of the old AP papers had a fascination with printing "ghost" stories, are there any examples in *Magnet*, *Gem* or any of the girls' papers where one of these Yuletide spectres turned out to be exactly that, and not a spy, thief, smuggler or whatever?' There is no doubt that ghost stories in both boys' and girls' papers generally turn out to have nothing to do with the supernatural but to be tricks or hoaxes, usually, as Ray suggests, carried out by ordinary human characters who are up to no good.

However, prompted by a memory of a story in one of the 1930s girls' annuals, I decided to look further into this. Ever since I read that particular tale as a schoolgirl, it has niggled at my memory, and I've carried in my mind its closing line: 'But Fleur has often wondered ...' I couldn't recall much more about it, and sometimes wondered if I'd simply imagined that this was a particularly compelling spectral story; but, a year or so ago, I rediscovered this closing line—and of course the whole story—in the *Golden Annual for Girls* of 1938. So—for the purpose of this chapter—I read it again, and decided also to read all the ghostly stories that appeared in the *Golden Annual* and the other prominent girls' annuals of the same year, 1938 (actually 1937 but dated 1938).

I will describe here the ghostly exploits of the *Schoolgirls' Own* and *School Friend* annuals, the *Popular Book of Girls' Stories* and the *Golden Annual for Girls* of that year, saving the 'But Fleur has often wondered ...' story to the end!

The *Popular Book of Girls' Stories* for 1938 had no truck whatsoever with supernatural happenings, real or imagined, so we can quickly dismiss that.

The *School Friend Annual* carried one story which promised a ghostly element: this was 'The Unexpected Witness' by Denise Hope, which was subtitled 'A Gripping Mystery Story'. It features two cousins, Mavis and Janet, who are invited to stay at a house acquired by a young aunt whom they've never met, as she's only recently returned from abroad. However, the house, Moor Manor, far from being the luxurious residence which they anticipated, turns out to be old, draughty, creepy, creaking and neglected, with decaying furniture, and lit only by candles.

An elderly, apparently deaf, servant is in attendance, but there is no sign of their aunt. Mavis, always cheerful, makes the best of things and is considerate towards the aged retainer, while Janet—a bit of a bitch—moans constantly and is rude and unpleasant to the servant. She is obviously only staying on at Moor Manor in hopes that the unknown aunt will turn out to be rich, and generous towards her nieces.

The two girls notice that the eyes in the portrait of a beautiful young female ancestor appear to move. Later, Janet becomes hysterical with fear when she sees this same ancestor's face at an upper window. Convinced that Moor Manor is haunted, she leaves without ever meeting the aunt who has invited her there. Mavis—less certain that there is a ghost—stays on, and her young and pretty aunt soon puts in an appearance. She bears a strong resemblance to the ancestor in the portrait, and it is she, of course,

Illustrations from 'The Unexpected Witness'

whom Janet has mistaken for a ghost. (Actually the aunt has been disguised for most of the time as the old, 'deaf' servant in order to find out what her nieces are really like.) Mavis's good nature and kindness to the supposed servant are rewarded as her aunt whisks her off to her *real* home—a well-appointed and luxurious house nearby—for a great and memorable holiday. So, as in most ghostly tales, there is nothing truly eerie about 'The Unexpected Witness'.

The *Schoolgirls' Own Annual* features the traditional Christmassy house-party in a warm and welcoming mansion with lashings of snow outside, in 'The Ghost Play' by Louise Carlton (Lewis Carlton). The author was very good at creating stories of mystery and suspense (in the Sexton Blake saga and elsewhere), and this girls' tale makes rewarding reading.

Kay Warren is in the throes of producing a play 'in the huge baronial hall' of her father's house (Normanhurst), but on the night before the performance she sees the 'dreaded grey spectre' outside in the cloisters. The tradition is that whenever the owner of Normanhurst or one of his family sees this ghost, it heralds death or monetary loss. Kay is also worried, naturally, that her play might be doomed, and with ambitions for a theatrical career, this would 'spell disaster' for her.

She keeps quiet about sighting the spectre in order not to upset her friends who are staying at Normanhurst and are in the cast. However, one of these guests, Renee, also spots the ghost and makes its appearance widely known. She is suspected of 'playing ghost', although there are various spooky signs for which she does not seem to be responsible—strange tappings, and a distant greenish glowing light through which a grey figure is moving.

Kay and her friends go ahead with the performance, despite any fears which they may have about ghostly happenings. Kay has written into the play an episode in which the Normanhurst ghost walks—all done by tricks of lighting. But she gets more supernatural atmosphere than she bargains for. When her planned spectre appears on stage, to suitably weird music played by the orchestra, a second totally unexpected apparition also treads the boards. When these two ghosts are seen simultaneously there is horror and uproar from the audience, but Kay has sufficient presence of mind to pursue the interloping ghost and unmask it. She finds (rather anti-climactically) that it is their housekeeper, Mrs Hannington. This otherwise impeccable lady is playing ghost to prevent guests and the audience for the play from going into the east wing, because she is hiding the previous owner of Normanhurst and his wife, who are now penniless, there.

Of course Kay's wealthy father agrees to help the impoverished pair, so there is no need for Mrs H to carry on her spookish tricks. The performance of the play is resumed— and Kay's future on the professional stage is assured by the warm approval of a theatrical dignitary who is in the audience.

It is a pity that this story ends with a touch of banality, because the ghostly suspense is, for most of the narrative, well sustained. The second of the 1938 *Schoolgirls' Own Annual*'s flirtations with the supernatural is called 'Rona Films a Phantom' by Muriel Holden (Roland Jameson). Rona, an enthusiastic amateur film-maker, goes with her cousins Joan and Belle to Bilbury Manor where she's been given permission to make a historical film, in which a ghost is to be featured. Of course, during the proceedings an unexpected 'spectre' (a lady from the Stuart period) turns up and Rona, by chance, films her. The three girls revisit the Manor by night to try to lay this ghost. It transpires that this 'phantom' is one of a gang who have, by their spooky stunts, scared off the housekeeper who is supposed to be looking after the house while the owners are away. Rona's film helps the police to identify the gang who, we are told, were using the Manor 'for a gigantic swindle connected with the sale of bogus shares'!

Nothing supernatural about that, of course.

So now we come to the *Golden Annual for Girls*. It included three ghost stories. The first, 'The Weird of Weirdslea Grange', was by Joan Inglesant (Draycott M Dell), a writer who was particularly good at creating strongly atmospheric mysteries. Audrey Morton lives with her parents in Weirdslea Grange, and sees what appears to be a great band of white and ghostly figures in the grounds at night. Their presence has become known in the village and further afield, and is scaring away visitors from Weirdslea Grange, which Audrey's parents are now running as a hotel. (All their money has been invested in it.)

The ghosts are reputed to be those of knights killed in a battle that had taken place nearby during the Wars of the Roses. The villagers (and Audrey's parents) seem too craven to investigate the mystery. However, plucky teenage Audrey takes things in hand. She looks up the Morton family history and finds that the legend of The Weird (a

## A Story of a Strange Mystery
### By JOAN INGLESANT

headless spirit) has existed from the time of Charles the First, although no-one has ever claimed to see it. She ventures outside at night and sees the mass of ghostly figures—but, revisiting the garden by day, finds a well-polished military brass button on the ground. Locating a nearby army camp, Audrey finds that after dark the soldiers are using a machine (a 'kind of cinematograph') which 'can suggest an attack at night by troops when … there are no soldiers there …'

Audrey explains the difficulty these manoeuvres have made for her family, and to make up for the loss of business at their hotel, a kindly officer arranges for 'a number of regiments' to seek accommodation there—and, as the 'ghosts' are no longer seen, all is well again for Weirdslea Grange. A good story, but, once more, nothing truly supernatural takes place.

The *Golden Annual*'s 'A Test for Tessa' is by Bertha Leonard, and from its first, full-page illustration we know we are in for encounters with something spectral. Tessa and her brothers and sisters answer a newspaper advertisement offering a free holiday to a family which will help a man who wants a mystery unravelled. The advertiser is Captain Wynflete of The Monastery at Clinton-by-Storrbury. He is wheelchair-bound as the result of disablement caused by an air crash. He also has failing sight (because of cataracts, and readers are reassured that eventually an operation will save his sight), and his double handicap renders him incapable of solving the puzzle connected with his home. He has restored the old monastery and uncovered cryptic clues carved in the old walls:

> 'By fire and air go find the lair
> Nor step nor stair shall take ye there …'

Tessa and her family explore The Monastery in the light of the clues, and one night Tessa decides to search around the great fireplace in the kitchen. From the cavernous depths of this 'a cowled figure that shone with an unearthly glow came gliding into view'. A monkish spirit? No—it turns out to be a burglar who is after Captain Wynflete's silver! Tessa hides from him by climbing up the chimney on its jutting brick ledges: she then terrifies the intruder by emitting a series of blood-curdling yells and wails. Rooted to the spot, he is soon apprehended and handed over to the police.

Meanwhile, up in the chimney, Tessa has uncovered a brick aperture which contains an iron canister of 'old folios and missals' that make the Captain, 'an archaeologist at

heart', so happy that he gives Tessa a cheque for a hundred pounds. So the main mystery of the whereabouts of the monastery's particular treasure is solved—although the 'unearthly glow' around the cowled figure is not referred to again or explained.

The third ghost story in the *Golden Annual*—the one which stayed in a niche in my memory for so long—is 'In the Dark' by Dorothy Vernon (C L St John Pearce). Its heroine is Fleur, who is staying at Cranleigh Towers, the home of her school friend, Bell. They find a secret drawer in an old bureau: it contains a faded note from a previous occupant of the house recording the fact that he had seen, in that very room, the figure of a man in 'the costume of the second Charles, with frills and ruffles, a large wig on which was a plumed hat … It stood there … gazing up at the painting of Lady Honoria …'

This portrait still hangs in the room, and Bell explains that Honoria is an ancestor who died in 1690. She adds that 'the picture's worth a ton of money'.

Before the two girls have read the rest of the note, they go out into the garden, and Bell loses the piece of paper. She seems very disturbed, and after Fleur goes fruitlessly in search of it, she finds Bell talking agitatedly to a young man, who quickly takes off. Bell offers no explanation of this, or of her strange mood, but later that day Fleur hears her crying in her bedroom.

Bell still refuses to tell Fleur why she is so upset, but she enlists her help for a task that *must* be performed that night, when everyone else is in bed. Fleur finds that she is to help Bell take Lady Honoria's heavy picture down from the wall and upstairs into Bell's bedroom, where Bell locks them in with the portrait. They are supposed to take it in turns to sleep or keep awake, and, while Bell is asleep, Fleur looks out of the window. She sees the stealthy figure of the man who had been earlier in conversation with Bell mounting the steps to the room in which Lady Honoria's picture is usually hung.

As he does so, something extraordinary happens. Wildly waving his arms as if warding off an attack, the young man wheels in his tracks and, terrified, flees to the end of the garden. It seems that some fearful enemy—invisible to Fleur but seen by him—is pursuing him. When the young man eventually disappears into the trees beyond the garden, Fleur, whose hair has literally stood on end, breathes, 'The spectre of the cavalier was after him!'

The next morning there are some explanations. The local doctor calls to say that Bell's brother has been brought to him in a delirious state and he is 'in for a bad bout of brain fever'. He's been hospitalised and keeps on mumbling about being pursued by some ghostly cavaliers, and he also mentions a picture. Apparently he was carrying his passport and a ticket to France.

Bell breaks down and tells Fleur that her brother, Philip, had told her he was going to steal the picture and sell it abroad (we gather that he has always been 'a bad lot'). That, of course, is why she took the picture into safe keeping for the night into her bedroom.

Bell also explains to Fleur that she never actually lost the note they had found in the secret drawer, and that this in fact described not one but two ghostly cavaliers who, both in love with Lady Honoria, had fought a desperate duel. Apparently Bell had told her brother about this when she met him in the garden. At first she and Fleur believe that, suffering from a guilty conscience about his proposed theft of the picture, Philip simply imagined those two fighting spectres and thought that they would stop at nothing to prevent him from taking away Lady Honoria's portrait.

This explanation satisfies Bell, but on reflection Fleur cannot accept it. She is anxious that her friend should not be upset, so does not voice her doubts, but she feels that there could have been some supernatural intervention to keep the picture where it belonged, in Bell's family home.

'In the Dark' ends dramatically with the unfinished sentence:

'But Fleur has often wondered …'

And sometimes I wonder too. I think that just once in my life I have seen a ghost; at any rate it was something that could not be explained by logic or rationality. So, like Fleur, I have often wondered …!

# PART FIVE

# MISCELLANEOUS GIRLS' FICTION

# JOLLY HOLLY JINKS

In the run-up to Christmas there is generally a lot of complaining about growing commercialisation, and we occasionally look back longingly from our consumer-orientated and computer-monitored society to the vivid yuletide festivities of our Victorian forebears. It seems that somehow, among the proliferations of turkey and toys, presents and plum pudding, they managed to strike the right balance of rumbustious fun and religious feeling.

The family was all-important, and Christmas conviviality prompted stern papas and staid mamas slightly to relax normal disciplines and encourage their young offspring to be heard as well as seen. But a browse through some of the books and magazines published for girls over the past 140 years suggests that despite these relaxations of parental restraints, Christmas remained a much more sober affair for girls than for their brothers; at least, until the beginning of the twentieth century there was little whooping-it-up for the good, sweet maids. The festive season, like many other things, has been shaped by changing fashions and social attitudes. Its evolution from spiritual celebration to merrymaking at a more material level is accurately reflected in girls' fiction—from *Aunt Judy's Magazine* in the mid-1860s to *Blue Jeans* or *My Guy* towards the end of the twentieth century.

*Aunt Judy's Magazine*'s first Christmas number (December 1866) reminds readers that their family reunions and rejoicing should be seen as foretastes of that more perfect future in which sin and avarice (and life itself) are swept away: 'Children cannot be too soon told that they are born into the world to be of use and to do God's work.' To punch home its daunting version of Christmas cheer, *Aunt Judy's* devotes much of this issue to the theme of early death, which is euphemistically expressed as 'a longing for Heaven'.

Across the Atlantic at about the same time, emotional uplift and daughterly duty in a seasonal setting were being presented far more palatably. Louisa Alcott's *Little Women* was running as a serial in *Merry's Museum* during 1867, prior to its publication as a perpetually best-selling book, and today thousands of little girls and grown women still remember the story's opening lines:

'"Christmas won't be Christmas without any presents," grumbled Jo, lying on the rug …' Tomboy Jo March does not in fact grumble for long. Though chronically hard up, she and her sisters Meg, Beth and Amy each use their cherished last dollar to buy gifts for their mother, Marmee, and spend nothing on themselves. They further demonstrate self-sacrificial goodwill by giving up their own Christmas breakfast to a really hungry family. But Louisa Alcott brought jollity as well as duty into girls' fiction, and there is vitality and humour in the effort of the March sisters to put on their Christmas play.

Susan Coolidge, in *What Katy Did at School* (1873), also conveyed the warmth of family Christmas celebration. Katy and Clover Carr, who are away from home at boarding-school, receive an enormous box: it is full of specially cooked cakes and carefully selected gifts, most of which have been lovingly made by their small brothers and sisters. 'Never was such a wonderful box. It appeared to have no bottom whatever. Under the presents were parcels of figs, prunes, almonds, raisins, candy; under those, apples and pears. There seemed no end to the surprises.'

Katy and Clover, in true Christmas spirit, share the edible goodies not only with their school friends but also with the waspish teacher who has fairly recently unjustly punished Katy. Goodwill and harmony then abound!

A rather high-minded Christian helpfulness was the guiding spirit of the early *Girl's Own Paper*. In its first Christmas issue in 1880, the Archbishop of Canterbury set the mood by contributing a full-page article on 'the general lessons' of Christmas, whose only hint of frivolity came in the graphics. Snow drips off the blown-up initial letter of the article in a style reminiscent of that of the Christmas numbers of the comic papers. The main drift of the Archbishop's message is bleak because he is preoccupied with sectarian divisions and rivalry rather than with spiritual joy; but he ends with a touch of warmth and wonder, meditating on the Christ Child and the benefits accruing from 'holy homes'.

The issue perks up with a page of seasonal puzzles and some beautiful black-and-white Christmassy illustrations. There is a promising note of liveliness, too, in the title of the fashion article, 'Seasonal Clothing and How to Make it'. Soon, however, the text begins to underline the paper's stern rejection of fripperies. Even for Christmas, the sartorial keynote was to be serviceability and sedateness: 'I heard of a young lady the other day, who wore the fashionably pointed toes and high narrow heels, who had a succession of violent nervous headaches, which ended in floods of tears and hysterics.'

*Atalanta*, a girls' magazine edited by the celebrated author L T Meade, seemed in 1891 to be addressing itself at Christmastime to 'perplexed ladies bountiful'. In a feature on 'Our Christmas Entertainment' there are useful tips about how to make up bundles of clothing for cottagers, plus a run-down of suitable toys that might be bought for their children at a penny each. These represent incredible value in contrast with today's expensive toys. *Atalanta's* list includes 'paint-boxes, with six real paints, two brushes, etc, boxes with six wooden soldiers, boxes of dominoes complete, three varieties of dolls, whips with whistles, tops, a jack-in-the-box', and so on.

In Victorian days entertainments had largely to be made at home, so *Atalanta* thoughtfully provided a seasonal play for girl readers to produce for estate workers and villagers. In its 1902 Christmas number another magazine, *Girl's Realm*, had suggestions to offer its readers on the subject of do-it-yourself entertainment. In an article aptly headed 'Conjuring Tricks From a Work Basket', David Devant emphasises the popularity of 'magical' performances, but remarks: 'I do not remember ever having seen a girl entertaining her friends in this way, and yet there is no reason why a girl should not be as clever a conjurer as her brother.' None indeed—and to make his point the author describes some natty tricks, neatly illustrated by photographs of broderie anglaise-clad young girls doing odd but intriguing things with balls of wool and twirling thimbles.

*Girl's Realm* really went to town on Christmas: in this bumper issue there are many lovely pictures and stories with an old-time flavour. Christmas was a nostalgic business, even in 1902; there is a lot of looking back to yuletide pictures from the past and to ancient traditions. In this paper, as far as girls' participation in the festivities is concerned, there is a flavour of progressiveness and of letting one's hair down.

Angela Brazil, whose school stories gave pleasure to so many of us, was also adept at painting word pictures of Christmas. The American heroine of *A Harum Scarum Schoolgirl* (1919), Diana Hewlitt, when unable to be with her parents, is invited to spend the festive season in an English vicarage. Here, she joins the family in cutting evergreens and berries to decorate the church, and in arranging a big Christmas party for the children of the village. But for Diana, the climax of her traditional English Christmas is a carol-singing expedition: 'It was a unique experience, trudging along country lanes with a cart and lanterns, with hoar frost under foot, and a few stars winking in a misty sky, then standing in the cold night air to sing their carols. Diana felt that she could never forget it …'

There is a colourful seasonable chapter in Elinor Brent-Dyer's *Jo of the Chalet School* (1926). It focuses on the warm and wonderful Christmassy trappings of presents, rich food, lovely new frocks, and the singing by Joey Bettany of traditional Christmas carols, from the Coventry Carol to 'Away in a Manger'. There are additional Tyrolean touches, like sleigh-rides in the snow with bells on harnesses 'making silvery music'. However, the most memorable moment is an act of charity on Christmas Eve:

> 'Madge! Wake up, old thing! It's Christmas morning! Merry Christmas to you!'
>
> Madge rolled over and blinked sleepily up at the excited face Joey bent down to hers. She had been dreaming of the wonder-music they had heard in the great Hof-Kirche the night before, when the boys' voices, soaring up and up in almost angelic melody, had brought tears to her eyes with their poignant sweetness. Then had come the walk home through the gay, lamp-lit streets, across the old bridge, beneath which the frozen river lay silent—*dead*, as Joey said—and up the much quieter streets of the suburb.

Sometimes, as they passed the lit-up windows of the houses, gusts of melody came out to them. Through one, where the shutters had not been closed, they could catch a glimpse of a Christmas-tree, and there floated out to them the sounds of merry voices and gay laughter. By this house stood a little girl, listening to the gay noise with a wistful face. With a vague remembrance of dear Hans Andersen's Little Match Girl, Joey the impetuous ran to her, and pressed what was left of her money into the purple hands. 'Run!' she cried eagerly. 'There are *heaps* of shops open still! Do go and get something to eat *now*!'

Joey spoke in English, but her tones and actions were unmistakable. The child gasped; then caught the kind little fingers pressing the paper into her own, and kissed them. 'God bless thee!' she cried, before galloping off at full speed.

Most of the stories discussed so far were intended for older girls, but small children were catered for in magazines like *Little Folks*, *Children's Friend* and *Books for the Bairns*. These featured superb illustrations full of Christmassy trappings and moments of cosy magic, but there was plenty of moralising, too, in tales of juvenile death and deprivation. As the twentieth century progressed, a more consistently happy note was established for small children; in *Young Folks' Tales* a pretty little golden-haired girl called Mabel usually contrives to find her way into Fairyland every week. She is a sturdy character, and one of her Christmas achievements is to give an interfering and bossy dwarf his come-uppance when he tries to strip the toys off her Christmas tree and hang it with 'useful things like coal, cauliflower and castor oil'.

*Tales for Little People* was even more vivid both in appearance and text. It offered seasonal cheer in attractive full-colour covers, tales of zany enchantment and some jokey cartoons. The traditions of these nursery story-papers were continued in Enid Blyton's *Sunny Stories* during the 1930s and, after the war, in a host of well-drawn comics like *Jack and Jill* and *Twinkle* ('specially for little girls'). Their 1980 annuals maintain the reassuring but mischievous quality of, say, the antics of Tiger Tilly and Co in the 1920s and 30s. These girl-animals were skirted versions of Tiger Tim and the Bruin Boys, and at Christmas in *Playbox* they romped their

way through pages of gently anarchic fun: '… no-one had missed Polly Parrot in the excitement and she had crept inside the huge cracker to surprise the others'.

Leaving aside the tales for tiny tots and returning to the mainstream of girls' fiction, we find a similar exhilaration in stories that star Barbara Redfern, Clara Trevlyn, Marjorie Hazeldene and the celebrated Bessie Bunter of Cliff House School.

After Dickens, no-one was more successful in conveying the old-world but eternally fresh spirit of Christmas than the writers and illustrators of these stories. High spirits rather than the high-mindedness of the Victorian magazines were the order of the day, as girl characters and readers relished all the trappings of rollicking, good-time celebrations. Chumminess as well as cheer overflowed during the festive season. The stories, with holly-decorated borders and snow-capped headings, also overflowed and filled several issues.

Parties of perfect chums assembled in stately homes whose lakes unfailingly froze solid for skating, and on Christmas Eve snow would obligingly blanket the surrounding countryside to make possible all those snowball fights and sledging races. Indoor jollification took place under the gaze of ancestral portraits and in the warmth of blazing logs that crackled in panelled halls hung with paper garlands and evergreens. In this kind of setting Bessie Bunter enjoyed orgies of roast turkey and munched her way through mountains of mince pies, while her more energetic mates participated in fancy dress dances or occasional ghost hunts. They were then almost certain to discover buried Cavalier treasure from clues hidden among the books in the ancient library.

Happily, however, the savouring of seasonal joys never prevented these schoolgirl heroines from lending a helping hand to people less fortunate than themselves. In the robust manner of Louisa Alcott's Jo, they would willingly trudge miles through slush-covered streets to enliven the Christmas of a sick child. And, more typically, they would face horrible hazards to rescue some teenage heiress who had been exploited by unscrupulous relatives and was incarcerated in a rambling, spook-ridden house or crumbling clock tower. Sometimes the Cliff House girls linked up with their boy chums for the festivities, which added a great deal of spice to the fun—though this determinedly remained at the 'good, clean and wholesome' level. Only bounders like Billy Bunter contributed slightly shady touches when they tried to grab unwilling kisses beneath the mistletoe.

In late twentieth century pop star- and boyfriend-orientated teenage papers, such chaste canoodling would have seemed fearfully tame. There is not, in fact, much emphasis on Christmas in these, although party gear is a common subject of discussion in December issues. A *Diana* annual promised 'Mystery, Romance, Fun, Thrills in pacey picture stories'—and there is nothing starry-eyed or sentimental about its heroines. In *My Guy*, too, romance had an earthy quality—'Blimey—he's gorgeous!'—and the *Blue Jeans* kind of loving was similarly practical: 'A boyfriend is all out to replace your old teddy as the cuddliest person of the year. 'Cept he's better … he cuddles you back.'

*Aunt Judy's Magazine* would, one feels sure, have preferred the teddy bear as a Christmas symbol.

*It may seem strange that I'm including two chapters about Christmas.*
*However, as I've always loved this season so much, I am indulging myself by*
*describing what, for me, was a very special Christmas.*

# CHRISTMAS IN INDIA

I can't remember any time in my life when I have not been intrigued by India. My grandfather was an Indian Army officer, and my mother spent much of her early life there. It is not therefore surprising that the far-removed-from-the-seething-subcontinent semi-detached house in Bromley, Kent, where I grew up contained Indian textiles, ornaments and photos of the family posing against exotic backgrounds. These became a vivid focus for my childhood imagination, stimulating long-standing dreams of travel to the colourful country of their origin which my mother so often described. Her anecdotes of British-Indian Army life were rounded out and enhanced by 1930s films about the Raj, which, I think, must have proved a potent inspiration not only for me but for many boys and girls of my generation.

Particularly memorable was the 1935 production of *The Lives of a Bengal Lancer*. I have since discovered that this bears little resemblance to the F Yeats-Brown novel of the same name which it was supposed to have dramatised. The book is more concerned with individual mystical enquiry than the military splendours and tribal adventures which make up the thrills and chills of the Paramount picture—but with Gary Cooper giving charismatic life to the hero, Lieutenant McGregor, ably supported by Franchot Tone, Sir Guy Standing and C Aubrey Smith, who could ask for more! Incidentally, in the film Cooper was 'Mac' to his friends; my then nine-year-old brother, also named Mac, loved the movie as much as I did and—I swear—spent the rest of his life (in common with many other small boys on both sides of the Atlantic) trying to look like Gary Cooper. To some extent he succeeded!

Yeats-Brown wrote an introduction to the programme for the London première, praising the men from the Punjab and the Pathan tribes and the British officers who served so gallantly in those cavalry regiments along the North-West frontier. He said:

> India may be changing, like the rest of the world, but the basic things remain: courage, faith, adventure. We hear too little about them. We know too little about our soldiers on the frontiers of India, keepers of the King's peace. It is good to travel in imagination … to that land of vivid contrasts, the Marches of the North-West, where there is blazing heat and bitter cold, feud and friendship, loyalty and treachery, and where men hold their lives lightly, but their honour high.

Another film which stirred me with the desire to see India was *The Drum*, based on the book by A E W Mason. This starred Roger Livesey and Valerie Hobson, who, cast as the wife of a British officer in a remote and constantly threatened garrison, looked extraordinarily fetching and quintessentially English in tailored blouses and jodhpurs. (My admiration for her as an actress began with *The Drum*. Since then I've admired her too for her off-screen dignity and loyalty to her husband throughout the widely publicised Profumo affair.)

Books, of course, also drew me to India, from Kipling to the stories in the children's papers. I don't recall the Cliff House girls going to India, but serials and 'shorts' in the girls' weeklies sometimes used the setting of the Raj. The stories in Frank Richards's 'India' series were published too early (1926) to have become part of my childhood reading. I've devoured it since and been impressed by the authenticity of its atmosphere. Something of this filtered through in the character of Hurree Jamset Ram Singh, the Indian schoolboy 'Nabob', who adorned the *Magnet* tales which I read during the 1930s. *The Times of India*—or at any rate its special Christmas numbers— occasionally arrived at our home, and I remember being fascinated by its photographs of Indian places and people— and particularly of its dancers and musicians. There were pictures of Bengal Lancers in full, uniformed splendour; of Rajas' palaces and gardens; of Delhi,

Mary in India in 1981

Bombay or Calcutta street scenes, and the architectural magnificence of Sir Edwin Lutyens' government buildings. A great deal of this was seen from the viewpoint of the British, but an extraordinarily languorous oriental charm came across, which to me, as a schoolgirl who had never gone further afield than Clacton, seemed both strangely remote and unbearably intriguing.

It was to be many years afterwards, in 1980, that I had the opportunity to visit India for the first time. For a large part of my working life, I have been involved with the Krishnamurti Foundation, an educational charitable trust which, as part of its work, maintains schools in several parts of India. Through this I have made many friends there, who pressed me to attend some special meetings scheduled to take place from mid-December 1980 to mid-January 1981. Although my long-held ambition was to be realised, I accepted the invitation with some reluctance—because I would be travelling without my family, and missing that warm and wonderful festival, the British Christmas.

I knew that my hosts in India came mainly from Brahmin families and made virtually no acknowledgement of Christmas, and I wondered how I would feel as December 25th approached and I found myself far removed from the Dickensian traditions which I so much appreciate. I love every Yuletide trapping and symbol, from the fripperies of tinsel and crackers to the magnificence of the Christmas music from Handel's *Messiah* and the Festival of Nine Lessons and Carols broadcast from King's College Chapel in Cambridge on Christmas Eve. The holly, the candles, the mistletoe, the paper chains, the tree, the ritual wrapping of parcels and the writing of cards, the food—nuts, dates and tangerines (and memories of these stuffed into our Christmas stockings), the scrumptiousness of chocolate Christmas-tree decorations, shortbread, mince pies, crystallised fruits, plum pudding, iced cake (decorated with tiny Father Christmases and reindeer and bounding 'Eskimo' children) and of course the traditional Christmas dinner with everything cooked succulently to a turn. Then there are those boisterous party games and the quieter pencil-and-paper ones such as Consequences, and board games (our family, despite changes in fashion, have remained remarkably faithful to Cluedo and Monopoly).

Rather forlornly wondering if there was any way in which I could carry some part of an English Christmas with me to India, I decided that I could do so through my reading matter. And, sure enough, in between astounding days of sight-seeing, of hearing India's music and watching its sacred dances, and, of course, of meeting its remarkably resilient people from many walks of life, I dipped long and lovingly into the books and papers which I had brought with me from England.

Before I outline some of the delights of these, I should mention one or two outstanding memories of my Indian trip. I had the privilege of meeting Mrs Gandhi—then, of course, the Prime Minister—and of having dinner with her, and her son Rajiv and his wife. Before dining *al fresco*, we watched a magical and floodlit performance of Indian dance against the background of a giant banyan tree. I responded warmly to the beauty of many of the ancient temples, especially those built on the sea-shores, and to India's animals and birds, particularly the so-strong and so-patient elephants. Over all there was a strangely clear and beautiful light that gave the countryside (which was far greener than I had expected) a translucent quality.

There were also the cultural shocks, about which I had been forewarned by friends but which nevertheless hit me hard. I don't think anyone can fully understand the poverty—and the amazing robustness—of the really poor in India unless they have seen these at first hand. Less dramatic and rather amusing cultural shocks also came my way when Indian friends told me that a department store in Madras was in every way as wonderful as Harrods, and that it was full of fine Christmas fare. I went there, prepared to enthuse—but was sadly disappointed. For me it bore absolutely no resemblance to the celebrated Knightsbridge establishment: it offered badly-recorded canned carols (mainly *Good King Wenceslas* repeated *ad nauseam*!), and crude decorations which were un-Christmassy hangovers from some Hindu festival, and whose livid cerise, orange and yellow-green colours made me yearn for the darker green-and-red of British holly and paper chains. The *pièce de résistance* offered by the Madras store was a real live Father Christmas. This engaging but horribly out-of-place character was a small, skinny Indian who pitifully lacked the plump, sturdy stature which we have come to expect of dear old Santa's embodiments. He wore the usual cotton wool whiskers and moustache, but sported something which we don't see on the faces of the Father Christmases who do their 'Ho, ho, ho-ing' in the toy departments of our British shops. This Madras Santa had covered his dark visage with a hideous pink plastic mask which to me was more suggestive of Guy Fawkes than Father Christmas. It's awful to seem ungrateful, but I was unimpressed, too, by the range and quality of all the objects offered for sale. In fact I came away with only two or three modest—but important—purchases: toilet rolls! (These, I understand, are not an essential part of Hindu culture, and I had been told by English friends who were hardened travellers to India never to miss an opportunity of buying them as they were often in short supply.)

Christmas Day dawned, horribly hot and humid, and I yearned intensely for the crisp, cold but often sunny brightness that so often occurs in England on December 25th. Of course, to have seen snow would have been like receiving a gift from the gods!

Our truly kind hosts informed our party of Brits, Canadians and Americans that we would celebrate a happy and unforgettable Christmas with them in Madras, and, indeed, they tried extremely hard to make us feel at home on that very special day. In the morning a recital of religious chanting was laid on (all in Sanskrit, by Hindu priests who—though admirable performers—could hardly be expected to create a Christmassy atmosphere). We were then told that lunch was to be really traditional—and we weren't allowed to enter the dining-room at the normal time because the food was taking longer than usual to prepare and the room was still being decorated.

When the doors were eventually flung open in triumph, the sight that greeted us was beautiful. The room was full of wonderful roses which had been flown in especially from Delhi for the occasion. We were touched by our hosts' consideration (even though we basely longed for holly and mistletoe and crepe-paper chains rather than roses). Then came the lunch which had been so exuberantly 'trailed'. The first course was good but, so far as we could make out, without seasonable connections. It was curry as usual, but particularly spicy and tasty.

Then came the great moment! We were told that we were to have Christmas Pudding, imported from England and cooked by the chef in our traditional British way. We had delightful visions of rich, brown, fruity pud, with custard or cream—or even flaming brandy. In came the smiling servant, bearing a large, covered dish. It was put on the table and the lid was taken off with a flourish to reveal lots of thin and very dry and rather tasteless slices of *cold* Christmas Pudding. To this day I can't imagine how the chef cooked it. We nobly munched and muttered appreciatively—after all, as we are so often told, it is the thought that counts.

And I, of course, was sustained by the thought of the feast of traditional Christmas reading that would be mine later on that day when I could retire to my room and immerse myself in those wonderful books and papers which I had brought with me.

I dipped first into *Peg's Paper* of December 15, 1928. Noticing that it was a Christmas number, I had grabbed it rather at the last minute before leaving home and didn't know quite what to expect. It had a promising cover—snow-tipped title, holly and mistletoe borders—but frankly, as a reminder of the British Christmas, it was very disappointing.

The only complete story, 'What a Girl Wants', turned out to be a tale 'of love, romance and adventure on a lonely islet on the coast of Italy, where skies and seas are always blue'. No trace of Yuletide atmosphere there. The other stories, 'Would Marriage Save Her?' and 'The Girl Who Feared Love', similarly had no Christmas flavour. Neither did the horoscope feature conducted by Miss Nell St John Montague under the heading 'When Will You Marry?' Even the agony-aunt page, 'My Christmas Post-Bag' (which had a picture of Father Christmas carrying a sack marked 'Peg's Letters'), made no mention of the festive season and contained only the usual cautious advice to the lovelorn.

A feature called 'Christmas Presents from Hollywood' looked hopeful, but the gossip about the stars (or starlets—in fact they never became famous) lacked lustre, being confined mainly to what they wore. Someone called Evelyn Brent had sent 'a pair of exquisite shoe buckles', another Hollywood denizen named Estelle Taylor had donated a 'gorgeous coolie coat', and, to win these, readers had to enter a curious competition. This was to make up a sentence or phrase (apparently about anything) 'using for the words composing this' only words which had appeared on the *Peg's Paper* page announcing the competition.

Christmas *was* marked in a holly-bordered snippety feature called 'Whispering'—but this was hardly redolent of good cheer and Christmas chumminess: 'Why is the Brixton Hill girl so terrified at the thought of her husband eating the Christmas pudding she made in November?'; 'What will happen if the Crewe girl's elderly aunt really

comes to spend Christmas with them, and is it true she will let down all her frocks?'

So—I moved on from *Peg's Paper* in my search for some Dickensian atmosphere. In complete and wonderful contrast to that romantic-story magazine was *The Christmas Happy Extra* for 1929, from Newnes, the publishers of the celebrated *Happy Mag*. I had brought this with me mainly because it had a wonderfully seasonable cover which featured Richmal Crompton's William having to endure being kissed beneath the mistletoe—Thomas Henry in full colour, at his iconoclastic best yet exhilaratingly conveying the mood of the season. This *Happy Extra* certainly didn't disappoint. It positively overflowed with Christmas cheer. There was the bonus of two William features, for a start: 'William's Christmas Truce' and 'William Writes a Play'. There was also a story by Evadne Price—not about her anti-heroine Jane but an adult tale, a light-hearted romance called 'First Prize—Cinderella', about confused identities and a masked ball. It was illustrated with lovely pictures by Arthur Ferrier.

There were lots of other Christmassy stories, poems, pictures and cartoons, as well as seven pages 'for the children' of fairy-stories, picture-strips, etc. This truly happy magazine did a great deal to make my Christmas in exile merry. I get it out now almost every December and browse through its goodies with love and gratitude.

Naturally, Christmas series featuring my favourite girl characters also accompanied me. Because of the limitation of luggage space, I had chosen examples of the compact *Schoolgirls' Own Library*, rather than the serials in the weeklies.

I read the Morcove School story, 'The Legend of Swanlake', with immense satisfaction. This brings Betty Barton and her chums to a Christmas house-party at Swanlake, the gracious and expansive Devonshire home of Pam Willoughby. The author, Marjorie Stanton (in reality Horace Phillips, of course), wastes no time in creating the seasonable mood. He hurls snow down from the skies as the girls make their way by car from Morcove to Swanlake: the car can no longer cope with the great drifts, and the girls gamely agree to walk the rest of the way (seven miles!) while the chauffeur struggles on foot to the nearest village to find someone who'll take their luggage on by horse and cart. The girls remain remarkably high-spirited—despite having to press on through a virtual blizzard:

> … for an hour and more it was a case of their simply tramping on through the foot-deep snow, with all too many breathless flounderings through shallow drifts. And on they forged once more, their cheeks as red as holly-berries, such strenuous work it was!

(All this, of course, was heady stuff to me, sweltering at the time in steamy Madras.)

However, after a few miles the girls' way is eased. Madcap Polly Linton's brother Jack (who, with his boy chums from Grangemoor School, is already installed at Swanlake for the hols) has organised a rescue party. He and his mates come to meet the Morcove juniors with sledges, thermos flasks of coffee and packages of eatables. (They are, of course, perfect role-model brothers!)

Pam has whiled away part of the journey by telling her friends the ghostly legend of Swanlake, which is summed up in a couplet that has been known to her family for generations:

> When 'tween the trees Grey Man is seen,
> Woe to Swanlake on Christmas E'en.

Pam assures them all that as far as she knows the Grey Man or ghost has never been seen within living memory, but almost as soon as the chums reach Swanlake and pour into the old house's warmly lighted and richly decorated interior, Pam—who lingers outside for a moment to have a word with her father—sees the greyish, phantom-like figure of a man running between the trees a short distance from the house …

Naturally the ghostly mystery informs the holiday, although there is also a great deal of high-spirited fun. Horace Phillips never missed a trick in his holiday adventures. The traditional English Christmas was celebrated *par excellence*, with indoor parties, dancing, charades and a lively, impromptu play called *The Haunted Inn*, while outside there was plenty of snowballing, skating and sledging. As Naomer Nakara, the adolescent African queen who was one of the Morcove chummery, would have said, it was all 'absolutely *gorjus*!'

'The Legend of Swanlake' is, to my mind, just about the perfect Christmas story, offering both good cheer and suspense, and intensity and idealism as well as fun and high-jinks.

The Cliff House *Schoolgirls' Own Library* which accompanied me was 'Babs and Co's Magic Christmas' by John Wheway, writing, of course, as Hilda Richards. Magic is indeed the operative word, but in the sense of wonder and imagination rather than anything airy-fairy. It was a good choice for Christmas in India, combining the traditional olde English trappings with touches of Oriental splendour. The chums are the guests of Andros Bey, a fabulously wealthy Egyptian prince, and his teenage daughter, Naida, at Luxor Hall. Although this mansion is buried in the heart of the home counties (which in turn are buried under several feet of snow) it is a place of Arabian Nights magnificence, with towering lotus pillars supporting a blue ceiling in which wink golden stars; with shining, glass-like parquet floors; walls carved and painted with scenes from ancient Egypt; and the icing on the cake of gold-inlaid furniture. There are also lots of 'soft-footed servants like the genie of Aladdin's lamp' constantly at the girls' elbows, ready to dispense food and drink whenever these are required. An ideal Christmas for Bessie Bunter, in fact. She makes more use of this amenity than of the indoor marbled and mosaic swimming pool which her more athletic chums, Clara Trevlyn and Janet Jordan, very much appreciate. There is also a ghost, not, as Jemima sagely comments, a common or garden spectre like 'the jolly old knight who clanks around at Christmas at Delma Castle' (her own Yorkshire home) but a young princess from ancient Egypt called Nut Hapi. (One wonders if the Wheway tongue was in his cheek with this strangely named phantom: inevitably it suggests the appellation of 'Not Happy', and the princess is one of a trio of mummies at Luxor Hall who are all of the Nut Hapi dynasty.)

As is their frequent custom, Babs and Co befriend a waif-type employee of their hosts; she is Nilos Rosetta, a young dancer who adds sparkle to the festivities. They also have to outwit a gang of Egyptian thieves and thugs who plan to kidnap the Princess Naida. I was transported by this splendid story into satisfyingly Christmassy reflections and memories because, despite the theme of exotic oriental intrigues, good old British traditions shine through. There is a carol-singing sequence (girlish voices ringing across the snows) that brings pure joy. There are loving descriptions of the girls' party dresses.

(Bessie, just like her brother Billy, borrows clothes from others in the party and—also like the Fat Owl—bursts seams frequently; Wheway cleverly uses this by making a switch of costume a quintessential part of the foiling of one of the kidnapping attempts.)

There are evocative descriptions of the Christmas tree, which is so high that Jemima's father, Colonel Carstairs, another of the guests, has to climb a ladder to remove and distribute the presents. And *such* presents! Clara receives a rowing machine, Marjorie Hazeldene an ebony and ivory, silver-initialled workbox, Barbara Redfern a beautiful cedarwood box of paints and finest camel-hair brushes, Jemima a slender malacca cane with a solid gold knob, Mabs a marvellous model theatre, Janet a silver teapot ('which would be the envy and admiration of every study at Cliff House') and Bessie 'nothing less than a moving picture camera with projector and films all complete'.

Yes, John Wheway as Hilda Richards, like Horace Phillips as Marjorie Stanton, never disappoints. And neither of course does that master of the Christmas mood, Frank Richards. With so many wonderful series to choose from, I had some difficulty in deciding which *Magnet*s to take to India. (By the way, I'd re-read the *Magnet*'s 'India' series a little earlier, to help prepare me for my trip.)

A Magnificent, Extra-Long, Complete Story of Harry Wharton & Co.'s Christmas Holidays. By FRANK RICHARDS.

Again, the limitations of luggage space had to be observed, so a short series was necessary. And—for me—it *had* to be one which took the chums to Harry Wharton's ancestral home. So I decided on the 1933 'Mystery of Wharton Lodge' series. I also took 'The Mystery of the Christmas Candles', complete in a single issue of the *Magnet*. I'd first read this story in the 1939 *Holiday Annual*. Although it features Hurree Jamset Ram Singh, its Christmas setting is a London mansion, and, as in the 'Cliff House' series at Luxor Hall, English and oriental atmospheres were successfully blended. It seemed a most appropriate single number for me to re-savour in India and, predictably, I much enjoyed reading it there.

In 'The Mystery of Wharton Lodge' every ingredient of the Frank Richards Christmas magic is included: Wharton and the Nabob established cosily at the Lodge awaiting the arrival of their chums to complete the party; the joyous anticipation and eventual celebration of the great festival; Billy Bunter's unwelcome-but-sticking-like-glue antics; the Cliff House girls arriving for a Boxing Day fancy-dress dance—and, as well as all the goodwill and seasonable cheer, the mystery of the unknown intruder who from time to time disrupts the household, throwing suspicion of theft on the servants and causing temporary misunderstandings between the chums. And, to top everything, lashings of snow and lots of great Christmas grub!

Bunter blots his copy-book even before he gets to Wharton Lodge: unluckily for him he mistakes Colonel Wharton for Harry on the telephone—and refers to the ex-military gentleman as an old fathead, a donkey, a wet blanket and a savage old bulldog. Not surprisingly, the Colonel is distinctly ruffled and forbids Harry to allow that 'young rapscallion' Bunter into the house.

How the Fat Owl gate-crashes the party, at first by hiding out in one of the attics and eventually by alerting the household to the presence of a criminal intruder, makes mirthful reading. There are so many wonderful moments in the Greyfriars Christmas stories that it is always easy to find atmospheric quotations. I particularly like those which set the scene just before the right merry and peaceful Christmas which the chums are expecting to enjoy:

> The Surrey hills gleamed white through the December dusk. Another fall of snow had come on rather suddenly, and caught the two juniors a mile from home. Flakes danced on a keen, searching wind, which seemed to the Indian junior to penetrate through his thick overcoat as if it had been paper. Wharton and the nabob had gone for a ramble that afternoon, and they were returning by a snowy and rather sticky lane … the old leafless trees, ridged with snow, rose like spectres in the dusk …
>
> 'Ripping weather for Christmas!' Wharton remarked.
>
> 'Eh? Oh, yes!' gasped the nabob. 'The ripfulness is terrific! Perhaps a little too terrific! Oooogh!'

Great, nostalgic reading for me in Madras in December 1980 on my first visit to India. When, long ago, Hurree Singh was temporarily exiled from Greyfriars, he said: 'My heart had the hungerfulness for my esteemed chums.' In my case the hunger was for a family Christmas with dollops of Dickensian trappings and good cheer. *The Christmas Happy Extra*, 'The Legend of Swanlake', 'Babs and Co's Magic Christmas', 'The Mystery of the Christmas Candles' and 'The Mystery of Wharton Lodge' provided me with gratifying touches of these, and helped in large measure to ward off any pangs of homesickness.

# CALAMITY JANE!

Between 1928 and 1947, Evadne Price produced ten books featuring her engaging and anarchic heroine Jane Turpin. The genre is drawing-room comedy spiced with a dash of music-hall rumbustiousness. The narrative tone fluctuates between the firmly down-to-earth and the mock-heroic; the setting (Little Duppery, a village in the stockbroker belt) is unshakeably middle-class, conservative and parochial, and this, of course, throws the stories' progressive outlook—and Jane's hoydenism—into sharp relief.

Jane is the natural leader of her contemporaries, a despiser of all things 'soppy', and the debunker of hypocritical adults. The inventive nature of her iconoclastic activities, and Evadne Price's flair for piling one farcical entanglement upon another and then deftly unravelling them, has prompted several critics to point out affinities between the 'Jane' stories and their forerunners, Richmal Crompton's 'William' books. Evadne Price, however, who died in 1985 in her eighty-ninth year, always repudiated suggestions that William was the Adam's rib from which Jane sprang.

Claiming to have been 'a hellish child', she declared that Jane's adventures were inspired by events in her own early life. Nevertheless there are undeniable similarities between Jane and William. Both are archetypal, unbookish, energetic children who wreak constant havoc on adult enterprises like fêtes and garden-parties, charity bazaars, political meetings and amateur theatricals. Both Jane and William come from affluent 'cook-and-housemaid' families; they live in surprisingly elastic villages which house a host of soured spinsters, peppery old gents, susceptible youths, flirtatious flappers, ineffectual clerics, batty artists, weedy aesthetes and daunting devotees of the weird and wonderful cults that flourished between the wars.

Both Jane and William are 1920s variants of the 'terrible children' who—in the context of popular culture—have trodden a somewhat teetering path from late-Victorian 'pickles' to little horrors like Dennis the Menace, Beryl the Peril and their derivatives in more recent comic papers. Both sagas, of course, take subversive side-swipes at several conventional 'adult' values, and are firmly on the side of the child.

Further affinities between the Price and Crompton books could be itemised, but it would be far from correct to suggest that Jane is merely following in the wake of William. Evadne Price's stories have their own singular interest and distinction. Jane is a robust character in her own right: active, assertive, outspoken and very much in advance of her time in being a democrat (who frequently demolishes her dreadful mother's social-climbing schemes), and an instinctive feminist. She is almost certainly the first girl leader of boys in English popular fiction. Her feminism is absolutely unselfconscious. She simply takes it for granted that she can and will live as exciting a life as any boy. Her idea of enjoyment is to 'roll about in the dirt … playing footer', Red Indians or detectives with her boy companions Pug and Chaw.

The obverse of Jane's straightforwardness is expressed in the bickering and bitchiness

that characterise the organised and the unofficial women's groups of Little Duppery. Mrs Turpin (Jane's mother), Mrs Tweeddale (the vicar's wife) and Miss Baldock (a vain and vinegary lady who is described as 'a sweet young thing of some fifty summers') vie for control through carefully modulated insults and one-upwomanship.

High-spirited, independent and ambitious, Jane was an unusually positive model for girl readers in the 1920s and 30s, and there is strong and sustained endorsement of her radicalism in the narrative view. Jane was never—like L M Alcott's Jo, Mrs de Horne Vaizey's Pixie and so many of the fictional tomboys who preceded her—forced by her author eventually to abandon the role of initiator and to become passive ('womanly'). Evadne Price cannily petrified Jane in pre-pubescence; had she allowed her to grow older during the course of the series, the disruptive nature of some of her activities might well have alienated the parents of Jane's potential readers. (It was just about acceptable for the eleven-year-old heroine, in one of her typical gestures of defiance, to be found 'stark naked … crawling along the drainpipe twenty-five feet above street level'—but, of course, no fourteen- or fifteen-year-old would have been permitted such extreme measures.)

As a comic counterbalance to Jane, Evadne Price created her arch-enemy, Amelia Tweeddale (dubbed Soppy 'Melia by Jane). Apparently polite (but actually smarmy), lady-like (prissy) and helpful (tale-telling), Amelia seems on the surface to conform to the period's adult image of the ideal little girl.

The author highlights the horrors of such conformity; under Jane's leadership the juvenile community of Little Duppery cold-shoulders Soppy 'Melia, but—an embryonic missionary and a fully fledged masochist—she smugly thrives on her ostracism!

Evadne Price was a professional actress before she became a writer, astrologer and television personality. She always retained, and expressed in her stories, a sharp eye for the theatrical and a keen ear for dialogue. She shares with Richmal Crompton a rare talent for conveying the rhythm and rhetoric of children's conversations, and for this purpose frequently uses phonetically inspired wrong spellings with aplomb.

Despite the period flavour of the stories and their sense of locality, Jane and many of the supporting cast seem to burst from their environment, and to embody broader views and values. Jane and her gang live in the country, but the games they play in ditches, fields and woods find echoes in the games of real-life children in city and suburban streets, parks and playgrounds. There is a strange timelessness about Jane's antics and aspirations, which retain their sparkle and freshness. Above all, of course, the stories are funny. There is knockabout humour for the unsophisticated, and plenty of irony for those who can spot it. (Evadne Price never wrote down to children, which perhaps is why the books are so often enjoyed and collected by adults.) There are merciless parodies of literary styles and stereotypes, of family sagas, romances, 'good sweet maids', and all those criminal-foiling and life-saving heroes and heroines who have abounded in juvenile fiction.

In the 1980s reprint of Evadne Price's *Jane and Co* there was no updating. The children of Little Duppery still wore the clothes of the 1930s and had not been time-shifted into tee-shirts and trainers. Frank Grey's zany and exactly appropriate illustrations were retained.

Unlike the stories of Just William, with whom Evadne Price's anti-heroine has such distinct affinities, the reprints did not herald a relaunch of the whole series. However, one suspects that Jane's saga is not entirely defunct. It may have to wait in the wings for some time, but surely some future perceptive historians and enterprising publishers will discern the literary and social significance of the quirky, punchy and feminist character, Jane Turpin, and put her back into print.

# GIRL GUIDE GRIT

'Great stuff, this Guiding! We've always been keen on it at Cliff House.'
(Clara Trevlyn)

As the Boy Scouts have recently been celebrating their centenary, let us also spare some thoughts for the Girl Guides who rapidly followed the boys' movement not only in fact but also in fiction. *Terry the Girl Guide* (1912) began a lively new sub-genre; and, even slightly earlier, the publishers of weekly papers could not wait to chronicle the exploits of this fresh, satisfying and very exciting activity for girls.

The Boy Scout movement, founded by General Sir Robert Baden-Powell (later Lord Baden-Powell) in 1907, was actually gate-crashed by the girls. BP originally made no provision for them. He feared that their participation might make Scouting unacceptable to boys, and encourage hoydenism in young girls. However, soon after his *Scouting for Boys* was published in 1908, some 6,000 girls up and down the country had formed themselves into unofficial patrols of 'Girl Scouts'. With relish and considerable pioneering vigour, they started to practise the tracking and tramping, drilling, First-Aiding and adventure-seeking that BP had so attractively gone into in his now classic manual. By the end of 1909, he realised that the girls, if ignored, would not simply go away, and he drew up a scheme formally to establish a feminine membership. BP had a strong sense of protectiveness towards the girls, and he named them Guides rather than Scouts to emphasise their separateness from the masculine mainstream of his quickly expanding organisation. He also stressed that training techniques used for his Boy Scouts would have to be 'administered with great discernment' for the Guides, and under the control of the 'right kind of ladies … You do not want to make tomboys of refined girls, yet you want to attract, and thus raise, the slum-girl from the gutter'.

In spite of BP's concern about not encouraging hoydenism, however, there seems to have been an extremely robust feeling amongst the early Girl Guides, and

TERRY THE GIRL GUIDE

DOROTHEA MOORE

With an Introduction by the Chief Commissioner, Lady Baden-Powell fiction echoed fact by producing a spate of vivid adventures that featured tomboyish heroines.

The favourable social effects of the Scout organisation on boys from different backgrounds have often been acknowledged, but it is likely that Guiding had an even more drastic effect on its adherents. Before the advent of the movement, for many girls social life outside the home had of course been pretty tame and restrictive. Agnes Baden-Powell (BP's sister, who became the first Girl Guide President), in her preface to Dorothea Moore's *Terry the Girl Guide*, commented that 'bright' and 'clever' girls were likely to find that 'prowess in the jungle, tracking Red Indians' had attractions that home routines of chat about 'hats or the new stitch in crochet' lacked.

The first Girl Guide story I have come across is in Northcliffe's *Girls' Reader*, where Evelyn Yates's serial 'The Girl Scouts' started in July 1909. It appeared before the original Girl Scouts had officially metamorphosed into Guides; and, as the *Girls' Reader* was a paper for the older girl rather than for schoolgirls, the story's heroines seem also to be fairly mature. They are Mollie and Virginia, nieces of the Bishop of Hawkesbury who agrees to provide a temporary home for the 'two sweet darling motherless little girls' whilst their father's regiment is in India. Of course the Bishop gets much more than he bargained for. His nieces turn out to be strapping damsels of fourteen and sixteen, who make their entrance into his life at a sedate garden party for colonial Church delegates. They advance towards him 'with long, steady strides—a couple of straight-backed, eager-looking young girls clad in khaki skirts and soft felt "cowboy" hats, and each carrying a pole …'

At this time, of course, uniforms were improvised, as the girls' movement was still unofficial. The early Girl Scouts seemed to compete with each other in wearing the broadest brimmed hats and carrying extraordinarily long staves (made from broom-handles). Mollie and Virginia further disrupt the garden party by an illustration of Scouting prowess, their 'long, lusty ear-splitting yell, the call of the Curlew patrol', which the Bishop likens to a steam siren. However, although he longs for his nieces to abandon belts, broom-handles and haversacks in favour of 'dainty' attire, the Bishop soon has to admit that Scouting gives them a high standard of consideration for others. As the story unfolds, Mollie and Virginia cheerfully put right several social wrongs, and make wholesale converts to BP's movement.

*Terry the Girl Guide*, the first full-length story of Guiding aspirations and activities, was written by Dorothea Moore, who was to become a Guide Commissioner. Terry's adventures, set in a girls' boarding-school, created the pattern for dozens—probably hundreds—of novels which were to follow. Terry is intrepid and independent. Her love for her country is expressed as 'Imperialism' (something that was not perhaps always in harmony with Guiding and Scouting's broader feeling for internationalism and equality).

Terry demonstrates the resourcefulness so characteristic of the early Guides by forming herself with some school friends into an unadopted patrol and improvising their uniforms. 'The Patrol were unanimous in favour of the "Dolly Dye" and Terry undertook to lock herself into a bathroom with the dye and six white blouses, and turn the Patrol out khaki-coloured at the cost of fourpence halfpenny.' (Early companies frequently favoured the khaki of their male counterparts rather than the dark blue which eventually became the recognised Guide uniform colour.) Having thus successfully launched Guiding at her school, Terry next heroically defends some small children from attack by a mad dog. She then has a series of exciting adventures, the climax of which comes when, scorched and almost suffocated, she removes a small box of gunpowder to prevent an explosion.

Her exploits were echoed in many stories by other authors, with heroines often receiving medals for spectacular bravery. In fact, the early Guides who were standing by with their staves and stretchers frequently had little opportunity of showing their mettle to a society which refused to take them seriously, and it was even sometimes difficult to find opportunities for the 'good deed a day'. Adventure was expressed 'in leaping over dykes, and crawling about in fields on hands and knees, or even on one's tummy' rather than in administering first-aid to the injured or courageously saving lives.

In its early years, the Girl Guide movement could not afford its own journal. (They were less fortunate than the Scouts in this respect.) Pearsons allocated two pages of its weekly women's paper, *Home Notes*, for reporting Guide matters. The fact that an adult paper rather than a juvenile one was used for this suggests again that the majority of recruits might then have been older girls. Looking back, *Home Notes* seems a strange platform for robust Guiding issues, which had to rub shoulders there with romantic stories and advice to the lovelorn. Rose Kerr, in her *Story of the Girl Guides* in 1932 (an excellent history), remarked that many upper class members objected to this accommodation: 'Miss Lawrence, for instance, said it was not at all the sort of paper for the Roedean girls and their like.'

Roedean remonstrances prevailed, and *Home Notes* was abandoned in favour of the *Golden Rule*, a monthly published by Martin Shaw, until, in 1914, the movement was able to start its own official magazine, the *Girl Guides' Gazette*.

From its early days, of course, the Guide Movement laid stress on self-reliance; and, of its many activities, camping most encouraged this. By the 1920s it was a commonplace but still much looked-forward-to activity for countless Girl Guides in fact, and of course in fiction: 'The Camping fever is in my blood. I shall go dotty when I see the lorry arrive,' remarks one young hopeful in May Wynne's *The Camping of the Marigolds* (1933). 'There were blackberries, raspberries, the promise of nuts, the jolliest brown rabbits, sunshine and shadows in these magic woods ...' Also, of course, songs round the campfire and pow-wows—and some less enjoyable camping incidents arising from bogs, bulls, tents collapsing and the challenges of primitive field kitchens. Enthusiasm and indefatigability are echoed in story after story in which Guide authors waxed lyrical on the adventures of camping.

Like many other Guide activities, camping had very special meaning for girls from squalid urban areas. Going away to camp was often their opportunity to visit the sea or the countryside for the first time in their lives:

'I'm longing to get to the sea … until today I'd never seen it.'

When at last the sea came into full view there was a long-drawn 'Oh—oh–oh!'

'Isn't it heavenly?' said Maude.

Nobody gives a better fictional account of a Guide camp than Mrs A C Osborn Hann in *Peg's Patrol* (1924), from which the above quotation was taken. Dorothy Hann was Captain of the 12th Southwark Guide Company during the 1920s and remained active in the organisation for many years. Her leading characters in *Peg's Patrol* and its sequels are girls from working-class families, for whom Guiding widened both physical and psychological horizons, and the stories have tremendous vigour and authenticity. Peg at first resists the apparently 'goody good' Girl Guides, who 'swanked about in uniforms and short skirts …' trying 'to boss the world and show their mothers how to do things'. But she is soon converted by the Guides' naturalness and sheer zest for life. Peg not only becomes a 'splendid' patrol leader, but a real champion of any awkward or graceless girls who, despite their handicaps, have ambitions to become efficient Guides.

This theme of the competent and attractive girl helping hopeless duffers or 'outsiders' soon became as popular in Guide fiction as it was in school stories (Barbara Redfern and Mabel Lynn always rallying round duffer Bessie Bunter; Betty Barton and Polly Linton teasing but always protecting Paula Creel, etc). Variations on the theme were used with great discernment and imagination by several well-established authors. Ethel Talbot, who set most of her Guide stories in boarding-school backgrounds, was one of these writers. In her *Peggy's Last Term* (1920), eleven-year-old Sylvia turns out to be the kind of cackhanded tenderfoot who 'doesn't know a Union Jack from a Stars and Stripes … or a granny from a reef-knot'. So, 'in a kind of frenzy', the other members of her patrol coach Sylvia intensively in every aspect of the Guide Law, the Salute, the Flag and woodcraft. Poor Sylvia, under all this pressure, not unnaturally overdoes things, scratching the Union Jack on her desk lid so that she can study it at any moment during class, drawing 'arrows and crosses with her fingers and toes at every odd hour of the day', and at night obsessively practising knots when she is supposed to be asleep.

Guiding stories began to crop up in an ever-widening range of weekly papers, and when the first issue of the *Schoolgirls' Own* came out in February 1921, it included a serial by Mildred Gordon called 'The Guides of the Poppy Patrol', as well as a whole page of tips and chat under the heading, 'The Girl Guides' Corner'. Even more indicative of the movement's appeal was the fact that the give-away photogravure picture in this first issue of the paper was of HRH Princess Mary, the then Girl Guides President, in full uniform. Mildred Gordon's serial starred Molly Marsh, the leader of the Poppy Patrol, and her understanding Guide Captain, Miss Robson. Molly's father is wrongly accused of embezzlement, and sent to prison, but she manages to hold her head high and remain at the head of the patrol in spite of the nasty jibes and innuendos of two snobbish girls, who are against her because of her humble origins. Miss Robson supports her through thick and thin, and so do most of the 'Poppies' and other Guides. Molly, using skills and preparedness in true BP style, of course eventually proves her father's innocence.

Though a commendable character, Molly wasn't, like the usual Amalgamated Press heroines, exactly charismatic. Her adventures continued only until *Schoolgirls' Own* No 10, and then Mildred Gordon's second Guide story started in the paper. This dealt with Stella Ray, the leader of the Robin patrol, in a town called Seaville, and it was much more colourful and dashing than the saga of Molly's activities. Stella had the great advantage of living by the sea, so she and her fellow Guides were called upon to respond to dramatic challenges like steep cliff-side rescues, being trapped in caves with the tide rapidly rising around them, and the threat of capture by smugglers. Stella's patrol also coped with farming adventures (wild bulls!), camping vicissitudes and even rescuing a baby from a burning building. During the course of her exploits, the *Schoolgirls' Own* announced that its sister paper, the *School Friend*, was bringing out a special Guide number of the Cliff House Weekly, including 'What the Guides Are Doing at Cliff House'. At this famous school, in fact, Guiding rarely played an integral part in the stories, although it was frequently mentioned over the years, and some of the girls were illustrated very fetchingly in Guide uniform.

It was obviously still a popular leisure-time activity there right into the 1930s. *Clara Trevlyn's Book For Girl Guides* was a pull-out supplement with *Schoolgirl* No 242, in March 1934. This was one of a series of attractive booklets, on different themes, ostensibly written by Cliff House pupils. (Others were *Barbara Redfern's Book of Etiquette*, *Marjorie Hazeldene's Book of Needlework*, *Stella Stone's Book for Pet Owners*, *Jemima Carstairs' Book of Party Magic*, etc.) The booklets were packed with helpful and interesting information, and were very probably the work of John Wheway, the then Hilda Richards, who was always having bright ideas for special features and supplements for the girls' weeklies and annuals. The booklet for Girl Guides adopts Clara's slightly slangy style: 'I hope you won't think it fearful cheek on my part writing these paragraphs about patrol-leaders as I'm only a Second … I need hardly say what a ripping patrol leader Babs is …' Clara kicks off with, 'Great stuff, this Guiding …' and ends the booklet by saying:

> 'Well, now you've read all about the Girl Guide Movement, why not give it a trial yourself, if you do not already belong? I and my fellow Guides at Cliff House can assure you that you'll never regret joining!'

Generally speaking, the Guiding stories in the AP papers were even livelier than those in the Movement's official periodicals, though these included some appealing fiction. There was also a *Girl Guide's Book* (an annual published by Pearson's and compiled by M C Carey, the Editor of the *Girl Guide Gazette*). The 1923 edition of this features a message from the Chief Guide, Lady Olave Baden-Powell—who was, of course, the wife of the Founder of the Scout and Guide Movement. This makes it clear

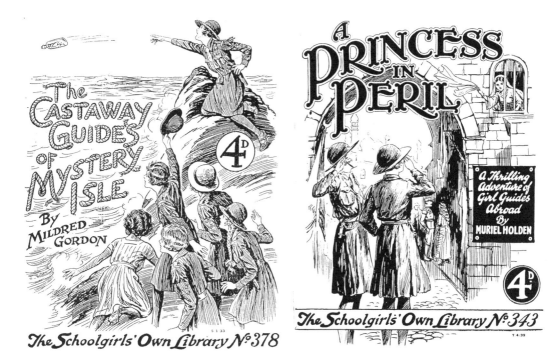

that the 1923 issue is the first edition of this annual, which is full of interesting articles, vivid pictures and good stories. It has two plays—one designed to be put on by Brownies and the other by Guides, and each has magical elements as well as the strongly practical ones that we always associate with Guiding. Guides and Brownies in those days had a wide range of resource, and many of the tips given in articles like 'Things All Guides Should Know' and 'Household Hints for Guides' are still useful. (The jobs to be tackled ranged from removing spots on carpets to driving nails into plastered walls.)

Lots of other weekly and monthly magazines for girls exploited the immense popularity of Guiding by including stories about the Movement, and some of the best of these were in the *Girl's Own Paper* and *Little Folks*, written by several celebrated authors. Amongst them were Elsie Oxenham, Dorothea Moore, May Wynne and Winifred Darch. Their stories caught the atmosphere of Guide camps and patrols during the 1920s and 30s. They were succeeded in the 1940s by writers who reflected the challenges that the Second World War had brought to the organisation, and its subsequent developments. Their tales, though extremely authentic, sometimes lack the colour and charm of earlier adventures, though Catherine Christian (who edited the official journal from 1939 to 1945) produced some exuberant books. In *The Kingfishers See It Through* (1942) she uses the tricky theme of the integration of evacuees from city slums into their new rural and affluent communities: '… stuck up, that's what you are. Guides! Yah! Yer never wanted us, ter begin wiv.' Happily, however, this uprooted Cockney patrol, who at first meet indifference and snobbery rather than the expected sisterly Guiding hand, soon become friends with their new associates in the 'posh' local company. The same author deals with another sensitive social issue in *The Seventh Magpie* (1946), in which an English Guide Patrol works for people who have suffered in Nazi-occupied countries. (They are, of course, reflecting the real-life activities of the Guide International Service Committee. The extraordinary capacity of Guides and even tiny Brownies to give a helping hand to others, individually, and on a vast, international scale, is something which should always be remembered, and it is good that quite a lot of Guide fiction owes its inspiration to this.)

In 2008, after its first (almost) one hundred years, the Girl Guide Movement has moved firmly forward to the modern world. This, of course, offers girls from most backgrounds a far greater range of activities than was available to the Edwardian Guide pioneers. However, the freedoms and challenges symbolised originally by their shorter skirts, camping and cowboy hats are still there for the taking in the Movement. And we can still relish the flowering of exciting fiction that Guiding inspired for so many years.

Eager the Rabbit
And swift is the Rook,
But lucky the Guide
Who owneth this Book.

# WORRALS AND FRECKS AS ROLE-MODELS

I sometimes ask myself why it is that Worrals speaks to me more firmly, loudly and persuasively than Biggles—who is, I know, the main hero in the Johns canon and, indeed, a household as well as an international name. I suppose it is partly that W E Johns created Worrals and Betty Lovell (Frecks), her attractive partner in derring-do and patriotic endeavour, at a stirring moment in our history. This was, of course, in October 1940, when France had fallen, when Britain stood absolutely alone against the Nazi might and when the RAF had so recently been slogging it out in the skies against the Luftwaffe for the survival of Britain and the way of life we so much cherished.

Worrals and Frecks took off from the launching-pad at exactly the right time for me personally. I was twelve: they were my introduction to Johns' work, and, believing implicitly in all their doings, I felt tremendous empathy with them in the thrills and chills with which they had to cope. No-one more convincingly than Worrals and Frecks conveyed the aspirations—and frustrations—of real-life young girls at that time who were *bursting* to do their bit for the war effort, even though they didn't quite know how and what they could contribute. In my view that delectable duo epitomised the determination and bloody-mindedness of the British with their backs to the wall.

The author's considerable skills were harnessed for their adventures, particularly in the early wartime stories. Johns had—after such a good run with Biggles and his associates—to create really new characters, and female ones at that, and he rose splendidly to the challenge. It is no wonder that, some time after the war, the distinguished writer Graham Greene was to say: 'Perhaps the spirit of all these wartime heroes is best exemplified by a woman, Worrals …'

Hurtling her aeroplanes through the skies as intrepidly as any long-experienced male pilot, Worrals uplifted my spirits and made me, although still a schoolgirl, feel that the world could truly be my oyster. Unlike Worrals and Frecks, I've never actually had to bolster my pluck with 'pre-war nut milk chocolate' after gruelling sessions with the Gestapo, nor had to cope with dope-peddlers, slave-traders or crazy would-be queens on remote Pacific islands. Neither have I had to grapple, as they did, with rats, sharks, wild buffalo, hyenas, rhinos, lions, bears and crocodiles. But I still feel that Worrals and Frecks have given me practical guidance on occasion as well as inspiration—and a lot of laughs! They were indeed role-models—as early and articulate teenage feminists, as courageous lovers of, and fighters for, England, and, most importantly, as friends who could absolutely trust and rely upon one another, if necessary to the death.

Let us look at their friendship. Worrals is Frecks' senior in age by two or three months, and also in rank. Johns tells us at the beginning of the saga that the two girls are very different. Worrals is dark-haired, 'attractive in a way not easy to define', with a thoughtful look often softened by a flash of humour. She has well-cut features, and eyes that can 'gleam aggressively' when things go wrong. Having been the Head Girl of her boarding-school, she is inclined to be studious but is also keen on games. Her skills are almost daunting: not only did she gain her pilot's licence at her own expense before she was eighteen, but having lived for periods abroad with her diplomat father, she can speak both French and German fluently enough to fox the natives—something which, of course, stands her in good stead on her secret service missions.

Frecks is blonde, never a Head Girl or a leader, from a less affluent family than Worrals and, were it not for the war, destined for a fairly mundane office job. Her addiction to Hollywood and the cinema was something that many of her readers— including myself—shared, especially in those sometimes dreary wartime days. Johns contrasts her untidiness with Worrals' crisply smart appearance—but I think that in some ways Frecks is the more endearing of the two girls. Worrals' courage and quick-wittedness often overshadow her friend's slower approach, but Frecks can be every bit as plucky as Worrals when she is forced to act on her own; also, as part of the intrepid twosome, Frecks advises caution and provides necessary curbs to Worrals' impulsiveness and overconfidence. Their friendship is so convincingly portrayed that it seems natural for them to decide to live together and run a civilian air-detection enterprise after their wartime adventures come to an end.

We are told that each girl 'was confident of the unshakeable loyalty of the other, a loyalty that had not yet been tested, although this was shortly to be weighed in the grim balance of active service'—and there are many examples of this in the books. Often, in moments of dire challenge and stress, Worrals has opportunities to save herself which she refuses to take, as this would mean leaving Frecks in jeopardy. And Frecks' devotion to her chum is touchingly illustrated on several occasions. For example, in *Worrals Goes East* (1944), she is prepared to face torture rather than betray the whereabouts of Worrals to a grisly German agent called Hylda:

> Hylda's smile broadened … They went a little way, entered a cave, and continued in the light of a torch which Hylda produced, to end up in a rock chamber lighted by an electric bulb. A printing machine stood on a bench. Hylda went to it and depressed a lever so that the iron presses opened a little way.
>
> 'Put her hands in there, Ali,' she commanded.
>
> Frecks made a sudden and desperate attempt to free herself, but she was powerless in the grip of the native who forced her hands between the metal plates. Hylda pressed gently on the lever. The plates closed, holding her hands fast.
>
> 'Now, dear English lady,' sneered Hylda. 'If you do not answer my questions truthfully, and politely, I am going to crush your hands flat. Where is your friend?'
>
> Frecks took a grip on herself. 'Find her, Nazi.' she spat through her teeth.
>
> Hylda's face paled with passion. 'Have it your own way.' she rasped …

And then there is that touching moment in *Worrals Flies Again* (1942) when Frecks thinks she has seen her chum burned to death in a plane crash:

> Frecks turned away and walked slowly down the steps towards her room. Her movements were those of a sleep-walker, slow and deliberate. She could not think, or even try to think. She was unconscious of her limbs. In some strange way she was detached from it all, a distant spectator of something so frightful that it could not be true. Thoughts, not her own, drummed through her brain in endless repetition. Worrals is dead … Worrals has gone … There is no Worrals …
>
> Reaching her room, she sank into a chair and buried her face in her hands. She felt that she ought to cry; she wanted to cry, but no tears came … Now that Worrals was gone, she cared not what became of herself. In fact, she pondered miserably, the sooner the Germans shot her and made an end of the whole business, the better.

So there we are: a great, devoted and long-lasting friendship.

In their different ways Frecks and Worrals equally express the meaning of loyalty. When it comes to feminism, however, Worrals is the prime exponent. Her conveyance of it may with adult hindsight seem trite and over the top, but we should remember that it is also meant to show Worrals' independence of thought—and that, in the psychological climate of the early 1940s, as a story-book heroine she was very much in advance of her time. Like most girls of my generation I was brought up to be generally conformist and, perhaps, over-respectful of the views of my elders, and of masculine aspirations and achievements compared with those of women and girls. You can therefore imagine that Worrals' early skirmishes with her male Commanding Officer were eye-openers to me:

> Squadron Leader McNavish actually smiled. 'You know all the answers, don't you?' he said softly. 'As one pilot to another I congratulate you on your skill and initiative … but officially, I must warn you that you simply must not do this sort of thing … Think what propaganda the enemy would make of the incident if it were learned that—er—ladies were now manning British aircraft.'
>
> 'It might give them ideas in the same direction,' suggested Worrals. 'The guns fired just as well for me as if a noble Wing Commander had pressed the button.'
>
> 'Yes—er—no doubt, no doubt. Guns are like that; they have no discrimination,' muttered the CO crisply.

This exchange, of course, occurs in the early pages of *Worrals of the W.A.A.F.* (1941) after our heroine has shot down a grey monoplane, in accordance with radio instructions

to all RAF fighter planes in the air at the time. Even though a desperate war was being fought, in Europe generally the idea of women as combatants seemed appalling. Although anxious to depict Worrals' determination and courage, Johns therefore felt obliged to justify her occasional and essential demolition of Germans or their sympathisers:

> Her face, although she did not know it, was like white marble: her lips a thin straight line; her eyes, expressionless. The hand that moved towards the gun control was stone cold. She jerked the handle up. Her thumb found the small round button which, when pressed, would spurt a hail of death. 'I've got to do it,' she told herself. Then again, 'I've got to do it. This is war.'

Worrals has qualms after her first killing; later on she is simply determined to do whatever is necessary in order to foil her country's enemies who, of course, are hardly celebrated for their chivalry or fair play. In *Worrals Carries On* (1942), the girls are working behind enemy lines. Worrals is sanctioning the killing of a German guard while Frecks harbours some doubts:

> 'This is getting positively shocking,' faltered Frecks.
> 'You'll think so if the Huns catch us,' replied Worrals sharply. 'We can't afford to be squeamish. Anyway, people who barge into a war must expect to see something of the seamy side. Frankly, I'm only concerned with getting home, and if a few Huns get hurt on the way I shan't saturate my pillow with tears on their account.'

And by the time, after the war, in *Worrals in the Wastelands* (1949) when they are asked to hunt down and arrest Anna Shultz, 'the she-devil of the Stenberg Internment Camp', neither Worrals nor Frecks has any doubts about their drastic mission:

> Worrals drew a deep breath. 'Never mind arresting her,' she said in a voice that was as brittle as ice. 'I'll hang her for you if you like—and so would any other woman who knows her ghastly record. I could hardly bear to read the details: there's a limit to what I can stand in the way of horrors. Don't call her a woman. She's a Gorgon. Her wretched victims used to call her the Devil's Sister. It gave me a physical pain when I heard that she'd got clean away.

I responded both to Worrals' necessary assertiveness and to her high principles. In *Worrals Carries On*, when she discovers that Joudrier, a so-called Free-Belgian pilot, is guilty of lying, she snorts: 'A man who lies in one matter will lie in another,' and, sure enough, Joudrier turns out to be a baddie and a Nazi spy. Even when, at one point in *Worrals Flies Again*, she is being cross-questioned by Wilhelm von Brundisch, 'the cleverest man in the German Secret Service' (who is at that moment fiendishly disguised as a nun), Worrals takes pride in the fact that—without giving herself away to him—she manages 'not actually to tell lies …' Both girls can be impulsive, but Frecks' caution generally holds Worrals' most impetuous schemes in check. Worrals' maxim is: when in doubt take the bold course, and, when danger threatens, to be ready 'to find the lion in his den'. Frecks, on the other hand, rather sensibly declares, 'Adventure, like chocolate, is best taken in small quantities, otherwise it is liable to lose its flavour.'

Worrals was not only a wonderfully loyal friend and an independent thinker of courage and initiative; she was also an optimist—holding on when circumstances seemed most bleak, with the odds stacked against her, and not giving up the fight even when Frecks and other allies advised her that this was the only realistic action to take. In *Worrals of the Islands* (1945), it seems that the girls cannot possibly proceed with their mission (to locate and rescue nine white nurses stranded on one of the ten thousand islands in the Japanese-dominated part of the Pacific Ocean—with only three weeks to achieve this before the monsoon sets in). A Japanese gun-boat has traced Worrals and Frecks and almost caught up with them. Frecks thinks that they must call off their search and try to escape—but not so the determined and ever-optimistic Worrals:

> 'If everyone in this war had packed up when it got sticky, we should have lost it long ago. Really, if we had had any sense we should have packed up after Dunkirk—only we didn't. The whole blessed country might well have packed up when the Luftwaffe came over all cock-a-hoop to toss bombs about. But it didn't. Not being entirely a fool, I realise as well as you do that we are in such a jam that the only sensible thing to do would be to go home. But we're not going.'

It seems extraordinary that two such appealing and nubile girls, constantly surrounded by vigorous servicemen, were not snapped up as wives, or, at any rate, as romantic partners. This is because Johns was writing as much for eleven- and twelve-year-old girls as for those who might be reaching the age when they would speculate about which of the services they might join. Frecks, in particular, remains singularly free of romantic involvement; men make passes at both of the girls (there is a marvellously bizarre moment in *Worrals Carries On* when, operating clandestinely in Nazi-occupied France, they are 'ogled' by some German officers!), but members of the male sex receive short shrift from the intrepid duo. Worrals has a long-standing admirer in Spitfire pilot Flying Officer Bill Ashton, who appears in the first chapter of the first book. He makes no secret of his strong feelings for Worrals, and it is implied from time to time that she has a soft spot for him, although she has no intention of letting this get out of hand. And Frecks is usually nearby to see that Worrals' resolution never wavers, and that what she calls 'sob-stuff' is stringently avoided.

Bill's passion is certainly articulated in a low-key manner; purple patches are no

part of the 'Worrals' tales, even when Bill has to fly Worrals and Frecks to France, where they are to parachute into unknown and possibly terrible hazards. Worrals simply can't understand why he is snappy and morose during the flight until he eventually blurts out:

'You know, kid, you mean an awful lot to me. If anything happened to you on this show I should never forgive myself.' Bill caught Worrals' hand, and held it. [He is permitted no greater intimacy during the course of the saga!]

For a moment Worrals stared in genuine surprise. Then, recovering herself, 'Bill,' she said, 'you're not by any chance making love to me, are you?'

When Bill says she can call it that if she likes, she admonishes him sternly: 'Be yourself. You'll laugh at this nonsense in the morning.'

Bill remains on friendly but frustrated terms with Worrals up to, and including, the seventh book, *Worrals in the Wilds* (1947), a post-war exploit set in Africa. After that he seems to have flown off into the sunset, perhaps accepting at last that Worrals is not for him. Other men who become her colleagues on various assignments are rather shadowy figures who offer no threat to her single state.

There is much to admire about Worrals. She does, however, have her weak spots, occasionally becoming over-bossy and belligerent, even trying Frecks'—and the devoted Bill Ashton's—patience. In *Worrals on the Warpath* (1943) tempers are fraying: the trio are in dire straits behind enemy lines, and Worrals questions Frecks' efficiency when she's actually been acting with perfect precision and competence. Worrals barks commands 'in a brittle voice' and so arrogantly *orders* Frecks to make her a pot of tea that even dear Bill feels obliged to address her (Worrals) as 'Boadicea'.

But these are only small and temporary blemishes. Generally Worrals and Frecks are made of stirring, inspirational and endearing stuff. Like Biggles, they embody the spirit of daring and high endeavour and a commitment to decency, loyalty and a concern for the underdog. In their exploits we find a love of everything good and positive that our country has to offer.

As a bonus, too, Johns manages to convey all this in a non-high-faluting, down-to-earth and immensely readable manner. No-one did a better job than he in creating compelling feminine role-models for my generation.

# MY FAVOURITE TOMBOYS

Almost without exception the characters I admired most in the girls' papers and books which I read as a child were those who could be classified as tomboys. Just after the middle of the nineteenth century, a few enterprising writers for girls had introduced boisterous heroines, realising that their readers were unlikely to find entertainment in the sedate and moralistic characters which most early Victorian authors had created in their girls' books. The vogue for lively tomboys—firmly established by Louisa M Alcott in 1867 with Jo in *Little Women*—continued into the twentieth century, when perhaps its most satisfying expression was found in the characterisation of Clara Trevlyn of Cliff House School. In my case it was, I suppose, a case of like appealing to like, for according to my long-suffering mother, I was every bit as tomboyish as the fictional schoolgirls whose exploits I so much enjoyed. Her assessment—coloured by the task of mending dresses and stockings which regularly disintegrated as a result of my participation in street games, tree climbing, etc—was not intended to be complimentary. However it never seemed to me that there was anything abnormal about the way in which I and my fictional heroines behaved. According to the dictionary, a tomboy is a wild romping girl; George Bernard Shaw in his preface to St Joan was perhaps more accurate when he spoke of the type of girl who refused to accept what society considered woman's specific lot to be. Jo March, Clara Trevlyn and all their kindred spirits in fact and fiction have actually demanded nothing more than the right to enjoy, as much as their brothers, a healthy and uninhibited childhood.

'Topsy Turvy' Jo, with her coltish figure, boyish slang, whistling and contempt for affectation, went so far as wanting to be a boy. In the beginning of the book, she is rebuked by elder sister Meg:

> 'You are old enough to leave off boyish tricks and behave better, Josephine. It didn't matter so much when you were a little girl; but now you are so tall, and turn up your hair, you should remember that you are a young lady.'
>
> 'I ain't! and if turning up my hair makes me one, I'll wear it in two tails till I'm twenty!' cried Jo, pulling off her net, shaking down a chestnut mane … 'I can't get over my disappointment in not being a boy, and it's worse than ever now for I'm dying to go and fight with papa, and I can only stay at home and knit like a poky old woman,' and Jo shook the blue army-sock till the needles rattled like castanets, and her ball bounded across the room …

One great consolation in Jo's life is the friendship of the boy next door, lively Theodore Laurence, 'Laurie', who—until he eventually falls in love with her—treats her like a 'boy chum': 'What a good fellow you are, Jo!' However in spite of the pride which she takes in her 'gentlemanly' behaviour, Jo is not above some feminine vanities. When her father is severely wounded in the American Civil War, she cuts off and sells her abundant chestnut hair to provide money for her mother's fare to the Army Hospital in Washington. In spite of her bravado—'A crop is so comfortable I don't think I'll ever have a mane again'—  Jo later disturbs her sister Meg when they are in bed by her stifled sobs:

> 'Jo, dear, what is it? Are you crying about father?'
> 'No, not now.'
> 'What, then?'
> 'My—my hair!' burst out poor Jo, trying vainly to smother her emotion
> in the pillow …

as she has her famous 'little private moan for my one beauty'. After Jo, more and more tomboys and madcaps were introduced into nineteenth-century girls' stories—although some of them were pretty uninspiring, created mainly to show how their wild spirits ought eventually to be forced into more passive and domesticated moulds by repressively large doses of religiosity, crippling accidents or bereavement.

At the time when Frank Richards was writing his first stories of Clara Trevlyn in the *Magnet*, Angela Brazil in the first decade of the twentieth century was pepping up girls' books with her 'harum-scarum schoolgirls', whose hockey and lacrosse sticks symbolised their liberation from out-dated Victorian primness. Her 'rosy, racy, healthy, hearty, well-grown set of twentieth-century schoolgirls, overflowing with vigorous young life and abounding spirits' matched the exuberance of their contemporaries— the Cliff House girls. Typical of Miss Brazil's heroines is *The Madcap of the School* (1917), Raymonde Armitage, whose 'irrepressible spirits were continually at effervescing point' and whose mission in life is to enliven her school: 'If you don't have a jinky term I'll consider myself a failure.' She expresses her intrepidness by starting secret societies to put down swanky and self-complacent new girls, and by outwitting prim teachers, as well as organising illicit botany rambles in which she climbs trees and wades through swamps in search of rare specimens. Botany rambles are the stuff of life for Miss Brazil—'… covering almost the entire surface of the water was a mass of the gorgeous pale-pink fringed blossoms of the bog bean …' She wrote to entertain, rather than to instruct her readers, and her stories are full of 'blossomy ideas', and characters who are voted 'absolute mascots'. The one I most responded to in Angela Brazil's books was Peggy Vaughan, heroine of *A Terrible Tomboy* (1904).

Madcap Polly Linton was always fiercely loyal to her brother and her chums.

Peggy endeared herself to me by fighting a big bully boy who had been terrorising her younger brother Bobby. One day, waiting for her brother after school, Peggy witnesses Jones minor tweaking Bobby's ears and pulling his hair. 'Peggy flew on to the scene like Diana on the war-path … she looked carefully round to see that no one was near, flung down her books with a bang on the pavement, and—simply went for Jones minor.'

Apparently she had 'the spirit of a Coeur de Lion and the courage of a Joan of Arc'. Readers must have been gratified to learn that though her method of boxing was unscientific, it was so punishing that she was able to roll Jones minor over like a ninepin, close both his eyes, punch his head, tweak his ears and hammer the soft portions of his body before he realised what had hit him: 'Like all bullies he was a coward at heart', soon roaring for mercy when Peggy 'with her foot on her foe's chest and her fist at his swollen nose' politely asks if he has had enough. The thrashing is witnessed by two senior boys from the Grammar school who are so full of admiration for 'the victorious Peggy … with split gloves, scarlet cheeks and wild-flying curls' that they swear to put down all forms of bullying at their school. This episode particularly appealed to me, because once I, too, fought a boy for bullying on my way home from school; my efforts were neither so successful nor so glorious as Peggy's, and in fact the fight was stopped by a passing teacher—to the great disappointment of participants and audience—but I *did* achieve a moral victory.

The Amalgamated Press papers' madcaps were of course not quite so boisterous as their tomboys, and Horace Phillips must have decided in the early days of his Morcove stories that Polly Linton, madcap, should be a rather more restrained character than tomboy Clara who was adding zest to the Cliff House saga in the *School Friend*. Polly is a bright star in the Morcove firmament, and Horace Phillips's stories often open vigorously with his madcap erupting happily on to the scene: 'Polly Linton came out of Morcove Schoolhouse like a shot out of a gun.' She is certainly boisterous in comparison with Betty Barton, her more sedate study mate. 'Polly Linton threw her hockey-stick into the corner, and Betty put hers on the table.' Polly is always teasing her languid chum, Paula Creel, who, like Frank Richards's Gussy, endeavours to be the 'glass of fashion and the mould of form'. Paula spends most of her time being 'pwostwate' after hockey practice and constant rumpling and dishevelling from Polly and Naomer's 'romps':

> 'Bai Jove: Pway don't look at me, deah geal! I'm tewwibly disweputable.'
> 'You never could be,' said Norah, 'You look a perfect picture in anything you wear. It doesn't matter how old your clothes are, you always look— well, a lady.'
> 'A muggins!' said Polly.
> 'Weally, Polly!'
> 'Don't take any notice of her!' laughed Norah. 'Polly never looks anything but a mud-heap, do you Polly? Still, I think I'd like your good spirits sometimes.'

In fact Polly—like every one of the Morcove girls—always looks impeccable in the *Schoolgirls' Own* illustrations, in which Leonard Shields made them the prettiest and trimmest of all fictional schoolgirls. Madcap Polly's light-heartedness is sometimes clouded by the problems which overtake brother Jack, at nearby Grangemoor School. Both Polly and Jack are lively adolescents, with a great deal of strength of character. They are loyal to each other through all the dramatic reversals of fortune which abound in the Morcove stories. 'The Madcap Remains Loyal' is the title of one story—and a recurring theme, best expressed in the 1927 series, 'Polly Linton's Brother Expelled'. The other strong male influence in Polly's life is Dave Cardew, Jack's 'quiet chum', whose modest and veiled declarations of affection Polly is always healthily deflecting:

> 'As for me ... But I am not going to say anything about that—'
> 'No, don't please!' laughed Polly.
> Nor did he—ever.

But in fact he *does*—often, in spite of Polly's unresponsiveness.

I liked Polly Linton, but she never impressed me half as much as Clara Trevlyn— who stands head and shoulders above all the other contenders for the title of My Favourite Tomboy. She was indeed the 'friend and companion of my youth'.

I loved Clara as much as any of my real-life friends, and at least until I was twelve I tried to model myself upon her. I first encountered Clara in the 1936 *Schoolgirl*, and, large-hearted, honest, but quick-tempered and stubborn, she seemed to me the most believable and rewarding fictional character I had ever known. Her creation was an inspired act on the part of Frank Richards, though reading his Cliff House stories in later life, I regret that he never fully developed Clara, who in the *Magnet* stories from 1909 to 1940 is delineated only superficially. Subsequent Cliff House writers (L E Ransome in the *School Friend* and John Wheway in the *Schoolgirl*) rounded her out while retaining the attractive attributes with which Hamilton had endowed her.

She is always 'boisterous Clara of the windswept bob'—which by the later 1920s had become an Eton crop—and there is a 'straying curl from her unruly hair which would persist in drooping over her forehead'. Actually, in T E Laidler's illustrations of the 1930s, Clara is easily recognisable by that wayward lock of hair, but it is represented as an upward-curling quiff rather than a drooping wave.

Clara is passionately loyal to her friends, particularly 'the gentle Marjorie Hazeldene' and Babs (Barbara Redfern). She protects 'duffer' Bessie from the results of her own stupidity, and from persecution by mean-minded members of Cliff House. However, Clara always comes down heavily on Bessie's boasting and conceited ways:

> Clara sighed.
> 'Girls, shall we bump her, just gag her, or throw her into the snow?'
> 'I refuse to be thrown into the snow!'
> 'Well be quiet, then!'
> Bessie glowered. But she knew that tone of voice. When Clara spoke
> like that, it behoved one to be very careful.

Clara also takes with a pinch of salt Bessie's celebrated postal order (which has been quite as long in the post as Billy's!).

> 'You don't mean to say that Sir Dustbin de Dishwater de Bunter has
> turned up trumps at last!'

Clara hero-worships her brother Jack, who is a few years older than herself. Towards the end of the Cliff House saga he is a handsome wartime RAF officer, trembling on the brink of a love affair with another of Clara's 'idols'—Dulcia Fairbrother, who is the Captain and Head Girl of the School (having replaced Stella Stone, an early Frank Richards character, who left Cliff House sometime during the 1930s). The other really strong influence in Clara's life is Pluto, her 'magnificent' Alsatian pet—who matches his mistress in courage, loyalty and intelligence. Stories which feature Clara and Pluto, in spite of their robustness, contain moments of unbearable poignancy: 'They Threatened to Take Away Her Pet', etc. Pluto endeared himself to thousands of readers, and was in fact inspired by an Alsatian dog owned at one time by Hilda Richards (John Wheway).

Clara is intrepid, if somewhat impetuous. In *School Friend* No 1 (1919) she is ready to give Billy Bunter the thrashing of his life because—according to Bessie—he has referred disparagingly to Clara's 'big feet'. She protects Marjorie when they are faced with death in darkest Africa. Trapped in a cave by the wild and hostile Intombi tribe,

the girls know there is a fire at one end, and the lair of several lions at the other. As the lions move towards them, growling and hungry, 'Fiercely Clara stood in front of Marjorie ...' We are often told that '... a dare of any description was never allowed to go unchallenged where tomboy Clara was concerned.' She does not allow herself—or other juniors—to be bullied by Cliff House's unpleasant prefects—Connie Jackson, Rona Fox and Sarah Harrigan. On one occasion in a 1933 *Schoolgirl* story, Clara is supposed to be fagging for Sarah Harrigan—under duress—and her response typifies her independence and integrity.

> Sarah went out, slamming the door. Clara, a grin on her face, got to work. She was nothing if not energetic. With Sarah's best duster, she picked up the coals, dusting each piece before carefully placing it between the sheets of Sarah's bed. Then she ... removed the pictures, placing those beneath the bed also. A few hairs from the broom furnished a giddy if reluctant moustache for the head of a plaster figure standing in the corner. In the cupboard she found a jug of milk, and thoughtfully transferred it to the lemonade bottle standing alongside it ...

Just as determinedly, Clara puts down any bossiness and arrogance which she comes across in boys, however exalted they might be in their school hierarchies. L E Ransome, who successfully developed Clara's tomboyish tendencies, gives an example of this in the 1927 *School Friend Annual*. Bell, a bullying fifth former at Lanchester College, has insulted the Cliff House girls: 'What—girls playing cricket! I say, make it easier you know. Pat-ball, isn't it? A bunch of flowers on the stumps, I suppose, and pretty little crocheted mats all down the middle of the pitch.' Readers are assured, however, that 'Clara wouldn't let a full pitch hit her in the eye. She'd lift it over the roof!' Bell deliberately splashes Clara when rowing past her, as she and her friends are picnicking beside the river:

> He then laughed aloud. 'Get wet?' he asked pleasantly.
> Clara did not reply. She was a young woman of action, not words. She picked up the large water jug they had brought with them, and oblivious of the fact that it was all they had for tea-making shot the contents straight at him. It smothered his head and shoulders and made him yell.
> 'Get wet?' asked Clara lightly.

Shortly afterwards she has the satisfaction of rescuing Bell when—unable to swim—he falls into the river. She had apparently 'gained medals for life-saving, and she knew that there were kind ways and unkind ways of rescue'. In this case Clara favours the latter: 'she just ... grasped George Bell's hair in a tight grip, then she struck out for the shore—' Humiliated before onlookers from Cliff House and his own school, 'his eyes smarting with the pain caused by Clara's energetic rescue', the arrogant Bell has to thank Clara, and apologise for previous insults. 'We'll call it quits,' said Clara, and held out her hand, 'only don't go about saying that girls are soft.'

Well, Clara certainly wasn't soft. She was perhaps occasionally too tough and uncompromising. I prefer to remember her as the fair-minded Junior Sports Captain, frequently declared 'a giddy heroine' by her schoolmates, who hoist her shoulder high after the repeated triumphs of her dazzling leadership on the hockey field:

> 'Whoops!'
> Up, laughing and protesting, Clara was hauled. Bubbling with excitement her victorious team-mates carried her to the touchline …

And, like us, they know that 'She's a jolly good fellow—and so say all of us!'

Clara Trevlyn

# MY PORTRAIT OF RICHMAL

The fairly recent republication of my book *Richmal Crompton, the Woman Behind Just William*, has stirred a few reflections which I should like to share with you. I suppose the average eight- to ten-year-old reader (of William and any other stories) doesn't on the whole think much about authors: children generally are just interested in the plots and characters of the stories which they enjoy. Even at Just William Society meetings with a wholly adult group, we concentrate almost entirely on our favourite characters. So now let's turn the spotlight on to someone even more important—William's only begetter, Richmal Crompton.

Although my book is often referred to by others as a biography, I have always described it as 'a portrait in depth' because it seemed to me, when I wrote it, that Richmal's life, like that of many prolific writers, was short on events and action, although rich in thought, imagination and insight. Fortunately, quite a lot of Richmal's personality comes through as we study and relish the texts of her William stories, and indeed some of her adult novels—especially when these two very different modes are seen in juxtaposition. They are surely at absolutely opposite ends of the family saga/drawing-room drama genre.

I have written seventeen books altogether, and from the Public Lending Rights cheques and statements which I receive, it is obvious that my portrait of Richmal is the most popular of all my titles, as a lot of pennies come my way through its being borrowed from libraries up and down the country. It is also the first of my books to go into a fifth edition. (I see this as a tribute to Richmal rather than to myself!)

Recently, two BBC researchers visited my home to interview me about school stories. Although the William saga falls well outside this sphere, at one point we found ourselves animatedly discussing William's exploits, and the genius of his author. One of these researchers asked whether I would want to add anything to my book, as of course further snippets of information always surface after a biography is published. I was able to reply, truthfully, that although I have added a little to it, I didn't want to extend it significantly. I feel it works well and has a completeness as it is.

However, I *do* think that a further book or booklet needs to be written about Richmal, and this would be one which looks more widely and deeply into her extremely rich inner life—her approaches to books and writing, to learning, language, religion, philosophy and mysticism. I'd love to tackle this sometime.

I very much enjoyed researching the original book, especially the time I spent at the home of Richmal Ashbee (Richmal Crompton's niece) and her husband, Paul. They were kind and generous in their hospitality, in sharing their memories and in making available to me anything and everything which they felt would help me to produce the book. And there were so many riches, some of which I'd very much like to look at again with Richmal Crompton's inner life in mind.

I found her endearing at several levels. I was, for example, particularly struck by

Richmal as a student in 1912

her way of recording her thoughts about plots, conversations, characters and their relationships. She often wrote notes for these on the backs of used envelopes, old letters (or torn-up parts of letters) and on other scraps of papers (perhaps also on the proverbial backs of bus- or train-tickets!). I tend to do the same. My husband and daughter buy me beautiful notebooks—which I find too good to spoil with my scrawl, so I generally use odd bits of paper for notes about proposed books and articles. Like Richmal, I use my nice notebooks as stuffed-out receptacles for these scribbled small pieces of paper.

The quality of the handwriting in Richmal's notes suggests that her thoughts were so fast-moving she could hardly keep up with them. Her scribbles might at first seem to indicate disorder and confusion, but in studying them one soon becomes aware of a mind that is not only sensitive and sharp, but also extremely well-ordered.

I think the key to this inner discipline was her openness, her capacity to view the world afresh, and, whatever her age and tribulations (I'm thinking of her having to suffer poliomyelitis and then breast cancer), to retain her capacity for discovery and humour. It is significant that once, when asked to produce an article about children's books, she said, 'Children enjoy assimilating new facts and ideas only if the author is willing to rediscover these with the children. You must be able to see the world as the child sees it. To "write down" is an insult that the child quickly perceives.'

One of the great joys of Richmal's writing, of course, is that what we appreciated in her stories as children is deepened and enhanced when we read her work with our adult sensibilities. As grownups we can see William as archetypal, as Everyman, and every boy. But as children we all had vivid, personal images of him and probably felt (I certainly did) that he lived just around the corner from ourselves. He was truly a part of our own individual worlds.

I was made conscious of this at a very early Just William Society meeting, when several enthusiasts were discussing the TV series which had featured Adrian Dannatt, Bonnie Langford and Diana Dors. Everyone seemed to feel that Bonnie (as Violet Elizabeth) and Diana (as Mrs Bott) had ably conveyed their characters, but opinions about Adrian Dannatt were less positive. One or two people felt he was too fat for William or too neat; and several warmly expressed the view that he didn't speak like William. This aspect of his performances hadn't worried me—but it suddenly occurred to me that this was because I am a southerner. Adrian Dannatt spoke rather as I do—and I'd always taken it for granted that William would have spoken like me (in my school-playground or playing-in-the-street mode). In fact, *everyone* attending that gathering, whether coming from Scotland, Wales, northern England, the Midlands, London or further south, felt this *local* affinity with William. Such is the power and universality of Richmal's writing. Interestingly, she was a northerner who settled in the south—a rich and potent amalgam.

I grew up thinking that William probably lived only a cycle-ride away from my home. In a way, he did—because I lived in Bromley and so did Richmal for the whole fifty-year period in which she wrote about him. As a child, it eventually penetrated my consciousness (how, I don't know, because Richmal avoided personal publicity) that William's creator, as well as NOT being a man, had at one time been a teacher at the Bromley High School for Girls, but I never had any contact with her in a local context.

It was only in the late 1940s, when I was nineteen, that I met her. At that time I had temporarily left the BBC because I was attracted to the idea of doing some direct social service. I became Secretary to the Welfare Committee of the Infantile Paralysis Fellowship, then situated in Tavistock Place in London. This charity was concerned with rehabilitating physically handicapped people. Richmal, herself disabled through polio, did a great deal to help us. She appealed for our organisation on BBC radio's *The Week's Good Cause*, raising the then considerable sum of over £4,000, and also personally donated generously to our funds and took a strong interest in our work.

She visited the office on two or three occasions while I was working there. At that time she would have been in her late 50s. I was surprised that she was so modestly and quietly dressed, and so unassuming, but deeply impressed that she brought into our terribly dark, poky and shabby two-roomed office a sense of warmth and sunlight. She was absolutely unpretentious and quickly able to put us all at ease in her company. Within minutes of her arrival she would have us all laughing, for example at some bureaucratic absurdity or other which she'd spotted, or simply about some incident that had occurred on her journey from Bromley to London. I was struck, after three years of working with professional comedians in the BBC Variety Department, by how warm and unmalicious her humour was.

I treasure the memory of meeting her, if only on those two or three occasions. I also curse my own incapacity, at that time, to communicate more fully with her. I was then shy and self-conscious, and inclined to be overawed when in the presence of a truly creative person whose work I admired, so I didn't manage to ask her anything about the William stories or any aspects of her writing. Neither, in fact, did anyone else who was working there, which is surprising as they were older and more confident than I was then. What a wasted opportunity!

I *wish* I had at least told her how much William had enriched my childhood. She might have liked that. Richmal Ashbee has told us that, after her aunt died, a friend had written to her:

> The first time I met Richmal Crompton I was raving about her work, and then said, 'Oh, you must get sick of all this praise.' She replied, 'My dear, you can't lay it on too thick.'

Richmal Crompton in 1929

Like any author, Richmal liked to know that her work was appreciated. But on the whole she kept a low profile about her achievements. An example of this, in her own words, is as follows:

> During the war, I shared a taxi from a bus stop to Victoria Station with a mother and small boy who were strangers to me. In the course of the journey the mother mentioned that the boy was anxious to reach home in time to hear the William broadcast. My vacant expression, as I debated with myself whether or not to tell them that I wrote the stories, and reflected that they probably wouldn't believe me if I did, convinced them that I had never heard of William before, and they hastened to enlighten me. They were still describing the stories and advising me to read them when we got to Victoria. (I didn't tell them.)

She *didn't* tell them, probably because she felt that in some way it might shatter that small boy's illusions about the reality of William, and of his own relationship with his hero.

Many years on from meeting her, I've had lots of opportunities to write about Richmal and to express my appreciation of her work. Writing a biography—or a portrait in depth—is a very peculiar business. However much one does research into the life of one's subject, however fully and conscientiously one studies her works, however carefully one listens to comments and remembrances from her friends and relatives, an *awful* question hovers over the whole process. Supposing—after all these endeavours— the final book 'just misses' all the way through—and does not convincingly convey the personality one is so concerned with. It could be possible, instead, to create a kind of out-of-focus portrait, a fuzzy, watery picture of someone like—but unlike—her; almost, in fact, the ghost or wraith of her. Worse still, an absolute travesty of her!

I must mention here how very grateful I was for Richmal Ashbee's comment, when I sent her a copy of my manuscript, that she felt I really had managed to convey an accurate picture of her aunt's life and work.

I had an intriguing and rather ghostly experience during the writing of the book. I was—as authors so often are—in danger of not meeting the deadline for the delivery of the manuscript. In those days I was fearfully conscientious about this, and the publishers, Allen and Unwin, were extremely pressing that I should complete the writing on time, as they were determined to get the book out in the October of 1986, to cash in on the Christmas market.

I was then still working as Company Secretary of an educational charity, in charge of its busy office, so, like much of my writing at the time, the Richmal Crompton book was mainly being written at night and in the small hours when I knew I would not be interrupted.

With the deadline imminent, and much still to be written, I went virtually without sleep for three nights. I nodded off occasionally sitting at the desk, to wake as soon as

my head hit the typewriter. When each night ended, I would bathe to revive myself, have breakfast and stagger to my nearby office. Amazingly, despite my eventual tiredness, the writing seemed to go well, and flowed easily. Nevertheless, by the third night mysterious things were beginning to happen. It seemed that my field of vision was growing smaller and smaller, and, disconcertingly, I felt that some presence was in the room with me, although Alex, my husband, was tucked up in bed and well and truly sleeping upstairs— so I had the room in which I was working entirely to myself! Yet, uncannily, it seemed that someone else was there. I didn't actually see anything—but there appeared to be an unusual movement and murmuring at the edge of my consciousness. Anyway, I finished the book!

I had decided, after that third through-the-night writing session, not to go to the office on the following day till much later than usual and, after a leisurely bath, I sat down to a late breakfast.

*I still had the feeling of not being alone.*

Then the telephone rang. I picked up the receiver, and a voice said, 'Hallo, Mary, it's Richmal here.'

'Good God!' I thought. 'I really have brought her back to life—and it is she who has been with me all night.'

It wasn't, of course! It was Richmal Ashbee. We didn't often telephone each other and it was truly weird that she should do so on that very morning.

I now know that sleep deprivation plays strange tricks with one's consciousness. No-one was in the room with me; no other presence was there, but tiredness and the intensity of my concentration on Richmal Crompton helped to create the illusion.

I didn't—and couldn't—bring her back to life, but I hope that, in some small way, all that I've written about her has helped to keep her image, and the knowledge of her books, as resilient and glowing as they deserve to be.

I receive a lot of letters from people who read my books—mostly appreciative (I suppose if people don't like them they won't waste time or a stamp in telling me so). One letter which particularly pleased me about four years ago was from a young woman who said that my books had introduced her to the works of both Richmal Crompton and Frank Richards, for which she was eternally grateful.

What more could I—or any biographer—want? I have not lived in vain!

# L'ENVOI

As an old Chinese saying suggests, 'There is an end to the fingers that feed the flames but the fire goes on for ever.' Perhaps 'for ever' in the context of commentaries on girls' fiction is a rather inflated concept. Nevertheless, I have no doubt that when readers and writers who are considerably younger than myself celebrate *their* eightieth birthdays, they will, with enthusiasm and affection, still be writing and talking about this endlessly fascinating genre.

# Girls Gone By Publishers

Girls Gone By Publishers republish some of the most popular children's fiction from the 20th century, concentrating on those titles which are most sought after and difficult to find on the second-hand market. We aim to make them available at affordable prices, thus making ownership possible for both existing collectors and new ones so that the books continue to survive. Authors on our list include Margaret Biggs, Elinor Brent-Dyer, Dorita Fairlie Bruce, Gwendoline Courtney, Monica Edwards, Antonia Forest, Lorna Hill, Clare Mallory, Violet Needham, Elsie Jeanette Oxenham, Malcolm Saville and Geoffrey Trease. We also publish some new titles which continue the traditions of this genre.

Our series '**Fun in the Fourth—Outstanding Girls' School Stories**' has enabled us to broaden our range of authors, allowing our readers to discover a fascinating range of books long unobtainable. It features authors who only wrote one or two such books, a few of the best examples from more prolific authors (such as Dorothea Moore), and some very rare titles by authors whose other books are generally easy to find secondhand (such as Josephine Elder).

We also have a growing range of non-fiction: more general works about the genre and books on particular authors. These include *Island to Abbey* by Stella Waring and Sheila Ray (about Elsie Oxenham), *The Marlows and their Maker* by Anne Heazlewood (about Antonia Forest) and *The Monica Edwards Romney Marsh Companion* by Brian Parks. These are in a larger format than the fiction, and are lavishly illustrated in colour and black and white.

For details of availability and ordering (please do not order until titles are actually listed) go to www.ggbp.co.uk or write for a catalogue to Clarissa Cridland or Ann Mackie-Hunter, GGBP, 4 Rock Terrace, Coleford, Bath, BA3 5NF, UK.